THE
LIFE
OF
GEORGE WASHINGTON

BY JOHN MARSHALL

VOL. IV

CHAPTER I.

Greene invests Camden.... Battle of Hobkirk's Hill.... Progress of Marion and Lee.... Lord Rawdon retires into the lower country.... Greene invests Ninety Six.... Is repulsed.... Retires from that place.... Active movements of the two armies.... After a short repose they resume active operations.... Battle of Eutaw.... The British army retires towards Charleston.

1781

IN South Carolina and Georgia, the campaign of 1781 was uncommonly active. The importance of the object, the perseverance with which it was pursued, the talents of the generals, the courage, activity, and sufferings of the armies, and the accumulated miseries of the inhabitants, gave to the contest for these states, a degree of interest seldom bestowed on military transactions, in which greater numbers have not been employed.

When Lord Cornwallis entered North Carolina, the military operations in the more southern states were committed to Lord Rawdon. For the preservation of his power, a line of posts slightly fortified had been continued from Charleston, by the way of Camden and Ninety Six, to Augusta, in Georgia. The spirit of resistance was still kept up in the north-western and north-eastern parts of the state, by Generals Sumpter and Marion, who respectively commanded a corps of militia. Their exertions, though great, seem not to have been successful; and they excited no alarm, because no addition to their strength was apprehended.

Such was the situation of the country when General Greene formed the bold resolution of endeavouring to reannex it to the American union. His army consisted of about eighteen hundred men. The prospect of procuring subsistence was unpromising, and the chance of reinforcements precarious. He was apprized of the dangers to be encountered, but believed it to be for the public interest to meet them. "I shall take every measure," said this gallant officer, in a letter communicating his plan of operations to General Washington, "to avoid a misfortune. But necessity obliges me to commit myself to chance, and if any accident should attend me, I trust my friends will do justice to my reputation."

The extensive line of posts maintained by Lord Rawdon, presented to Greene many objects, at which, it was probable he might strike with advantage. The day preceding his march from the camp on Deep river, he detached Lee to join General Marion, and communicated his intention of entering South Carolina to General Pickens with a request that he would assemble the western militia, and lay siege to Ninety Six, and Augusta.

April.
Green invests Camden.

Having made these arrangements, he moved from Deep river on the seventh of April, and encamped before Camden on the nineteenth of the same month, within half a mile of the British works. Lord Rawdon had received early notice of his approach, and was prepared for his reception.

April 24.

Camden stands on a gentle elevation, and is covered on the south and south-west by the Wateree,[1] and on the east by Pine-tree creek. A strong chain of redoubts, extending from the river to the creek, protected the north and west sides of the town. Being unable to storm the works or to invest them on all sides, Greene contented himself with lying before the place in the hope of being reinforced by militia, or some event which might bring on an action in the open field. With this view he retired a small distance, and encamped on Hobkirk's hill, about a mile and a half from the town. While in this situation, he received information that Colonel Watson was marching up the Santee with about four hundred men. A junction between these two divisions of the British army, could be prevented only by intercepting Watson while at a distance from Camden. For this purpose, he crossed Sand-hill creek and encamped east of Camden, on the road leading to Charleston. It being impracticable to transport the artillery and baggage over the deep marshes adjoining the creek, Colonel Carrington with the North Carolina militia was directed to convey them to a place of safety, and to guard them till farther orders. The army continued a few days in its new encampment, during which the troops subsisted on the scanty supplies furnished by the neighbourhood. Greene was compelled at length, by the want of provisions, to relinquish this position. About the same time he received intelligence which induced him to doubt the approach of Watson. On which he ordered Lieutenant Colonel Carrington to rejoin him; and on the 24th, returned to the north side of the town, and again encamped on Hobkirk's hill, a ridge covered with uninterrupted wood through which the great Waxhaw road passes. The army was encamped in order of battle, its left covered by the swamp of Pine-tree creek.

April 25.

A drummer, who deserted on the morning after Greene's return, and before he was rejoined by Lieutenant Colonel Carrington, gave information to Lord Rawdon that the artillery and militia had been detached. His lordship determined to seize this favourable occasion for fighting his enemy to advantage, and, at the head of nine hundred men, marched out of town on the morning of the twenty-fifth to attack the American army.

Lieutenant Colonel Carrington had arrived in camp that morning, and brought with him a supply of provisions which had been issued to the troops, some of whom were employed in cooking and others in washing their clothes. Notwithstanding those occupations, they were in reach of their arms, and were in readiness to take their ground and engage at a moment's warning.

Battle of Hobkirk's Hill.

By keeping close to the swamp, and making a circuit of some distance, Lord Rawdon gained the American left without being perceived; and about eleven, his approach was announced by the fire of the advanced piquets, who were half a mile in front of Greene's encampment. Orders were instantly given to form the American line of battle.

The Virginia brigade commanded by General Huger, consisting of two regiments under Campbell and Hawes, was drawn up on the right of the great road. The Maryland brigade commanded by Colonel Williams, consisting also of two regiments, under Gunby and Ford, was on the left, and the artillery was placed in the centre. The North Carolina militia under Colonel Read formed a second line; and Captain Kirkwood with the light infantry was placed in front for the purpose of supporting the piquets, and retarding the advance of the enemy. General Greene remained on the right, with Campbell's regiment.

Captain Morgan of Virginia, and Captain Benson of Maryland, who commanded the piquets, gave the enemy a warm reception; but were soon compelled to retire. Captain Kirkwood also was driven in, and the British troops appeared in view. Rawdon continued his march through the wood along the low ground in front of the Maryland brigade which was in the act of forming, until he reached the road, where he displayed his column.

Perceiving that the British advanced with a narrow front, Greene ordered Colonel Ford, whose regiment was on the extreme left, and Lieutenant Colonel Campbell, whose regiment was on the extreme right, severally to attack their flanks, while Gunby and Hawes should advance upon their front with charged bayonets. To complete their destruction by cutting off their retreat to the town, Lieutenant Colonel Washington was ordered to pass their left flank and charge them in the rear.

The regiments commanded by Ford and Campbell, being composed chiefly of new levies, did not change their ground, and perform the evolutions necessary for the duty assigned to them, with the requisite rapidity and precision; in consequence of which Rawdon, who instantly perceived the danger that threatened his flanks, had time to extend his front by bringing the volunteers of Ireland into his line.

This judicious movement disconcerted the design on his flanks, and brought the two armies into action fronting each other. But the regiments of Ford and Campbell were thrown into some confusion by the abortive attempt to gain the flanks of the British.

Colonel Washington too was compelled by the thick underwood and felled trees which obstructed his direct course, to make so extensive a circuit, that he came into the rear of the British at a greater distance from the scene of action than was intended, in consequence of which he fell in with their medical and other staff, and with a number of the followers of the army and idle spectators, who took no part in the action. Too humane to cut his way through this crowd, he employed so much time in taking their verbal parole, that he could not reach the rear of the British line until the battle was ended. These casualties disappointed this very interesting part of Greene's intended operations.[2]

The artillery, however, played on the enemy with considerable effect; and the regiments of Gunby and Hawes advanced on the British front with resolution. Some companies on the right of the Maryland regiment returned the fire of the enemy, and their example was followed by the others. Notwithstanding this departure from orders, they continued to advance with intrepidity, and Greene entertained sanguine hopes of victory. His prospects were blasted by one of those incidents against which military prudence can make no provision.

Captain Beaty, who commanded on the right of Gunby's regiment, was killed, upon which his company with that adjoining it got into confusion and dropped out of the line. Gunby ordered the other companies, which were still advancing, to fall back, and form, with the two companies, behind the hill which the British were ascending. This retrograde movement was mistaken for a retreat, and the regiment gave way. Encouraged by this circumstance, the British pressed forward with increased ardour, and all the efforts of Colonel Williams, and of Gunby and Howard, to rally the regiment were, for a time, ineffectual. This veteran regiment, distinguished alike for its discipline and courage, which with the cavalry of Washington, had won the battle of the Cowpens, and nearly won that at Guilford court house, was seized with an unaccountable panic which, for a time, resisted all the efforts of their officers.

The flight of the first Maryland regiment increased the confusion which the change of ground had produced in the second; and, in attempting to restore order, Colonel Ford was mortally wounded. Lord Rawdon improved these advantages to the utmost. His right gained the summit of the hill, forced the artillery to retire, and turned the flank of the second Virginia regiment, commanded by Lieutenant Colonel Hawes, which had advanced some distance down the hill. By this time the first Virginia regiment, which Greene had endeavoured to lead in person against the left flank of the British, being also in some disorder, began to give ground. Perceiving this reverse in his affairs, and knowing that he could not rely on his second line, Greene thought it most adviseable to secure himself from the hazard of a total defeat by withdrawing the second Virginia regiment from the action.

The Maryland brigade was in part rallied; but Lord Rawdon had gained the hill, and it was thought too late to retrieve the fortune of the day. Greene determined to reserve his troops for a more auspicious moment, and ordered a retreat.

Finding that the infantry had retreated, Colonel Washington also retired with the loss of only three men, bringing with him about fifty prisoners, among whom were all the surgeons belonging to the British army.

The Americans retreated in good order about four miles from the field of battle, and proceeded, next day, to Rugeley's mills. The pursuit was continued about three miles. In the course of it, some sharp skirmishing took place, which was terminated by a vigorous charge made by Colonel Washington on a corps of British horse who led their van. This corps being broken and closely pursued, the infantry in its rear retreated precipitately into Camden.

April 26.

The number of continental troops engaged in this action amounted to about twelve hundred[3] men, and the loss in killed, wounded, and missing, to two hundred and sixty-six. Among the killed was Captain Beaty, of Maryland, who was mentioned by General Greene as an ornament to his profession; and among the wounded was Colonel Ford, of Maryland, a gallant officer, whose wounds proved mortal. The militia attached to the army amounted to two hundred and sixty-six, of whom two were missing. The total loss sustained by the British army has been stated at two hundred and fifty-eight, of whom thirty-eight were killed in the field.

The plan which the strength of Camden and his own weakness had induced General Greene originally to adopt, was still substantially pursued. He remained in the vicinity of that place, and by the activity of his cavalry, straightened the communication of the garrison with the neighbouring country. Their distress for provisions had been considerably increased by the progress of Marion and Lee.

Several British posts taken.

Lieutenant Colonel Lee joined Marion a few days after he was detached from the camp on Deep river; and these two officers commenced their operations against the line of communication between Camden and Charleston, by laying siege to fort Watson, which capitulated in a few days. The acquisition of this fort afforded the means of interrupting the intercourse between Camden and Charleston, and opposed an obstacle to the retreat of Lord Rawdon which he would have found it difficult to surmount.

From the increasing perils of his situation, his lordship was relieved by the arrival of Colonel Watson.

In attempting to obey the orders, which were given by Lord Rawdon on the approach of Greene, to join him at Camden, that officer found himself opposed by Marion and Lee, who had seized the passes over the creeks in his route; and had thus completely arrested his march. To elude these vigilant adversaries, Watson returned down the Santee, and crossing that river near its mouth, marched up its southern side, and recrossing it above the American detachment, and, eluding all the measures taken to intercept him, accomplished his object with much toil and hazard.

This reinforcement gave the British general a decided superiority; and Greene entertained no doubt of its being immediately employed. On the day of its arrival, therefore, he withdrew from the neighbourhood of Camden, and took a strong position behind Sawney's creek.

May 7.

On the night of the seventh, as had been conjectured, Rawdon passed the Wateree at Camden ferry, intending to turn the flank of his enemy, and to attack his rear, where the ground was less difficult than in front. On being informed that the American army had changed its position, he followed it to its new encampment. This was so judiciously chosen that he despaired of being able to force it; and, after some ineffectual manoeuvres to draw Greene from it, returned to Camden.

Eighth.

Lord Rawdon had been induced to relinquish, thus hastily, his designs upon Greene, by the insecurity of his situation. The state of the British power in South Carolina was such as to require a temporary surrender of the upper country. Marion and Lee, after completely destroying his line of communication on the north side of the Santee, had crossed that river, and permitted no convoy from Charleston to escape their vigilance. On the eighth of May, after Watson had passed them, they laid siege to a post at Motte's house, on the south side of the Congaree, near its junction with the Wateree, which had been made the depot of all the supplies designed for Camden.

From the energy of this party as well as from the defection of the inhabitants, Lord Rawdon had reason to apprehend the loss of all his lower posts, unless he should take a position which would support them. He had therefore determined to evacuate Camden, unless the issue of a battle with Greene should be such as to remove all fears of future danger from that officer.

Lord Rawdon retires into the lower country.

May 12.

Having failed in his hope of bringing on a general engagement, he evacuated Camden, and marched down the river on its north side to Neilson's ferry. Among the objects to be obtained by this movement was the security of the garrison at Motte's house. But the siege of that place had been so vigorously prosecuted that, on crossing the river, his lordship received the unwelcome intelligence that it had surrendered on the twelfth, and that its garrison, consisting of one hundred and sixty-five men, had become prisoners. On the preceding day, the post at Orangeburg had surrendered to Sumpter.

On the evening of the fourteenth, Lord Rawdon moved from Neilson's ferry, and marched to Monk's Corner, a position which enabled him to cover those districts from which Charleston drew its supplies.

May.

While the British army was thus under the necessity of retiring, the American force was exerted with a degree of activity which could not be surpassed. After the post at Motte's house had fallen, Marion proceeded against Georgetown, on the Black river, which place he reduced; and Lee marched against fort Granby, a post on the south of the Congaree, which was garrisoned by three hundred and fifty-two men, principally militia. The place was invested on the evening of the fourteenth, and the garrison capitulated the next morning.

The late movement of the British army had left the garrison of Ninety Six and of Augusta exposed to the whole force of Greene, and he determined to direct his operations against them. Lee was ordered to proceed against the latter, while the general should march in person to the former.

The post at Ninety Six was fortified. The principal work, which, from its form, was called the Star, and which was on the right of the village, consisted of sixteen salient and reentering angles, and was surrounded by a dry ditch, fraize, and abattis. On the left was a valley, through which ran a rivulet that supplied the place with water. This valley was commanded on one side by the town prison, which had been converted into a block-house, and on the other by a stockade fort, in which a block-house had been erected. The garrison, commanded by Lieutenant Colonel Cruger, was ample for the extent of the place, but was furnished with only three pieces of artillery.

On evacuating Camden, Lord Rawdon had given directions that the garrison of Ninety Six should retire to Augusta; but his messengers were intercepted; and Cruger, remaining without orders, determined to put his post in the best possible state of defence.

Greene invests Ninety Six.

On the 22nd of May the American army, consisting of about one thousand continental troops, appeared before the town, and encamped in a wood, within cannon shot of the place. On the following night they broke ground, within seventy yards of the British works; but the besieged having mounted several guns in the star, made a vigorous sally under their protection, and drove the advanced party of the besiegers from their trenches, put several of them to the bayonet, and brought off their intrenching tools.

This sortie was made with such rapidity, that, though General Greene put his whole army in motion, the party making it had accomplished the object and retired into the fort, before he could support his troops in the trenches. After this check, the siege was conducted with more caution, but with indefatigable industry.

On the 8th of June, Lee rejoined the army with the troops under his command.

The day after the fall of fort Granby, that active officer proceeded with great celerity to join General Pickens, and lay siege to Augusta. On the march, he took possession of fort Golphin, on the northern bank of the Savannah, which surrendered on the 21st of May; immediately after which the operations against Augusta were commenced.

The place was bravely defended by Lieutenant Colonel Brown; but the approaches of the besiegers were so well conducted, that on the 5th of June he was reduced to the necessity of capitulating; and the prisoners, amounting to about three hundred, were conducted by Lee to the main army.

This reinforcement enabled General Greene, who had till then made his approaches solely against the star, to commence operations against the works on the left also. The direction of the advances to be made in that quarter was entrusted to Lieutenant Colonel Lee. While the besiegers urged their approaches in the confidence that the place must soon capitulate, Lord Rawdon received a reinforcement which enabled him once more to overrun the state of South Carolina.

June 7.

On the third of June three regiments arrived from Ireland; and, on the seventh of that month, Lord Rawdon marched at the head of two thousand men to the relief of Ninety Six. Greene received intelligence of his approach on the eleventh, and ordered Sumpter, to whose aid the cavalry was detached, to continue in his front, and to impede his march by turning to the best account every advantage afforded by the face of the country. But Lord Rawdon passed Sumpter below the junction of the Saluda and Broad rivers, after which that officer was probably unable to regain his front.

Greene had also intended to meet the British and fight them at some distance from Ninety Six, but found it impossible to draw together such aids of militia as would enable him to execute that intention with any prospect of success. The only remaining hope was to press the siege so vigorously as to compel a surrender before Lord Rawdon could arrive.

June 17.

In the execution of this plan, the garrison was reduced to extremities, when the near approach of his lordship was communicated to Cruger, by a loyalist who passed through the American lines, and extinguished every hope of carrying the place otherwise than by storm. Unwilling to relinquish a prize he was on the point of obtaining, Greene resolved to essay every thing which could promise success; but the works were so strong that it would be madness to assault them, unless a partial attempt to make a lodgement on one of the curtains of the star redoubt, and at the same time to carry the fort on the left, should the first succeed.

June 18.
Is repulsed and retires from before that place.

The proper dispositions for this partial assault being made, Lieutenant Colonel Lee, at the head of the legion infantry and Kirkwood's company, was ordered to assault the works on the left of the town; while Lieutenant Colonel Campbell was to lead the first regiment of Maryland, and the first of Virginia, against the star redoubt. The lines of the third parallel were manned, and all the artillery opened on the besieged. About noon the detachments on this service marched cheerfully to the assault. Lee's attack on the left was successful. He forced the works in that quarter and took possession of them. But the resistance on the right was more determined, and Campbell, though equally brave, was less fortunate. Lieutenants Duval of Maryland, and Selden of Virginia, led the forlorn hope, and entered the ditch with great intrepidity; but its depth, and the height of the parapet opposed obstructions which could not be surmounted. After a severe conflict of more than half an hour, during which Lieutenants Duval and Selden were both badly wounded, and nearly all the forlorn hope were either killed or wounded, the assault was relinquished, and the few who remained alive were recalled from the ditch. The next day, Greene raised the siege, and, crossing the Saluda, encamped on Little River. The loss of the besieging army, in killed and wounded, amounted to one hundred and fifty-five men, among the former of whom was Captain Armstrong of Maryland. That of the garrison has been stated at eighty-five.

On the morning of the 21st of June, Lord Rawdon arrived at Ninety Six; and, on the evening of the same day, marched in quest of the American army. In the preceding operations of the campaign, he had felt the want of cavalry so severely that, while at Monk's Corner, and in Charleston, he had formed a corps of one hundred and fifty horse.

Active movements of the two armies.

Greene, foreseeing that his active adversary would avail himself to the utmost of his superiority, had sent his sick and wounded northward; and, as soon as Rawdon had crossed the Saluda, he retreated towards Virginia. Lord Rawdon pursued him to the Eunora, whence he returned to Ninety Six.

The retreat ceased with the pursuit. General Greene halted near the cross roads, on the north of Broad River.

As Rawdon retired, he was followed close by the legion as far as Ninety Six, at which place he remained but two days. Still retaining the opinion that circumstances required him to contract his posts, he left the principal part of his army, under the command of Lieutenant Colonel Cruger, to protect the loyalists while removing within those limits which were to be maintained by the British forces; and, at the head of less than one thousand men, marched in person towards the Congaree.

Supposing that his adversary intended to preserve the post at Ninety Six, where the royalists were numerous, and to establish one or two on the Congaree, where provisions were more plentiful than in any other part of the state, Greene determined to interrupt the execution of the plan which he believed to have been formed. Leaving his sick and baggage at Wynnsborough, to be conducted to Camden, he marched with the utmost expedition for Friday's ferry on the Congaree, at which place Lord Rawdon had arrived two days before him. As Greene drew near to his enemy, a detachment from the legion under the command of Captain Eggleston, announced his approach by attacking a foraging party within a mile of the British camp, and bringing off a troop consisting of forty-five men, with their officers and horses. Rawdon retreated the next day to Orangeburg, where he formed a junction with a detachment from Charleston, commanded by Lieutenant Colonel Stuart.

July 11.

On the Congaree, Greene was reinforced by Sumpter and Marion with about one thousand men; and, on the 11th of July, marched towards Orangeburg with the intention of attacking the British army at that place. He arrived there the next day, but found it so strongly posted as to be unassailable. He offered battle, but prudence restrained him from attacking the enemy in his camp.

July 13.

At this place, intelligence was received of the evacuation of Ninety Six, and that Lieutenant Colonel Cruger was marching down to Orangeburg. The north branch of the Edisto, which, for thirty miles, was passable only at the place occupied by Rawdon, interposed an insuperable obstacle to any attempt on Cruger; and Greene thought it most adviseable to force the British out of the upper country by threatening their lower posts at Monk's corner and at Dorchester. Sumpter, Marion, and Lee, were detached on this service; and, on the same day, Greene moved towards the high hills of Santee, a healthy situation, where he purposed to give some refreshment and repose to his harassed army, and where he hoped to be joined by a few continental troops and militia from North Carolina.

The detachments ordered against the posts in the north-eastern parts of the state, under the command of Sumpter, were not so completely successful as their numbers, courage, and enterprise deserved. The several corps took distinct routes, intending to fall on the different posts between Ashley and Cooper rivers, at the same time. That at Dorchester was broken up, on the approach of Lee, who captured horses, military stores, and baggage to a considerable amount, and obtained some trivial successes over the flying enemy. Lieutenant Colonel Wade Hampton, of the state cavalry, fell in with a body of mounted refugees, dispersed the whole, and made forty or fifty prisoners.

Sumpter advanced against Monk's corner. This post was defended by Lieutenant Colonel Coates with the 19th British regiment, and a troop of horse. He had taken possession of a brick church at a bridge over Biggin creek, the most northern of the water courses which form the west branch of Cooper river. After passing Biggin, the road to Charleston crosses first Wattoo, and then Quinby creek; neither of which is passable except at the bridges over which the road leads, and at a ferry over Quinby.

On the sixteenth, Sumpter approached Monk's corner, but, not supposing himself strong enough to hazard an attack until all his detachments should be collected, sent a party to seize the bridge over Wattoo, and either to hold or to destroy it. This party being attacked by a superior force, retired from the bridge without completing its destruction, and without informing Sumpter that his orders had not been fully executed.

Marion had joined Sumpter. Lee arrived late in the evening, and the resolution was taken to attack Coates early next morning.

In the course of the night he set fire to the church, in order to destroy the stores which were collected in it, and commenced his march to Charleston, by the road east of Cooper. Having repaired the bridge over Wattoo, he met with no obstruction; and proceeded with his infantry on the road leading to Quinby bridge, directed his cavalry to take a road turning to the right, and crossing the creek at the ferry.

About three next morning, the flames bursting through the roof of the church announced the retreat of the British; and the pursuit was immediately commenced. Sumpter was preceded by the legion, supported by the state cavalry. A detachment from this regiment followed the British horse, in the vain hope of overtaking the troop at the ferry, while Lee pursued the infantry. Within a short distance of the bridge, which is eighteen miles from Monk's corner, he perceived the rear guard of the British, consisting of about one hundred men, commanded by Captain Campbell, which the cavalry charged, sword in hand. They threw down their arms, and begged for quarter; upon which they were placed under the care of a few militia horsemen, and the American cavalry resumed the pursuit.

They had not proceeded far, when Lee was called to the rear, by information that the prisoners had been ordered to resume their arms. At this critical moment, Armstrong, at the head of the leading section, came in sight of Coates, who having passed the bridge, and loosened the planks, lay, unapprehensive of danger, intending to destroy it as soon as his rear guard should cross the creek. Armstrong, in obedience to orders, given in the expectation that he would overtake Coates before passing the creek, dashed over the bridge on the guard stationed at the opposite end with a howitzer, which he seized. In this operation, his horses threw off some of the loosened planks, and made a chasm, over which the following section, led by Lieutenant Carrington, leaped with difficulty. In doing this some other planks were thrown off, and the horses of the third section refused to take the leap. At this time Lee came up, and every effort was made to replace the planks, but without success. The creek was too deep and miry to afford foot hold to those who attempted to raise them from the water.

This halt revived the courage of the British soldiers, who returned to the support of their commander, then engaged in an equal conflict with the cavalry who had passed the bridge. These gallant men[4] finding themselves overpowered by numbers, and that their comrades could not support them, pressed over the causeway, and wheeling into the woods, made their escape.

After finding the impracticability of replacing the planks on the bridge, in attempting which, Doctor Irvin, surgeon of the legion cavalry, and several of the troopers were wounded, Lee withdrew from the contest, and moved some distance up the creek, to a ford where he was soon joined by the infantry of the legion.

Coates then completed the demolition of the bridge, and retired to an adjoining plantation, where he took possession of the dwelling house and out buildings that surrounded it.

As the Americans were obliged to make a considerable circuit, Sumpter, who unfortunately left his artillery behind, did not arrive on the ground till three in the afternoon, and at four the house was attacked. The fire was kept up chiefly by Marion's division, from a fence near the house, till evening, when the ammunition was exhausted, and the troops were called off. In the course of the night, it was perceived that the loss had fallen almost entirely on Marion. Great discontent prevailed, and many of the men left him. The infection was communicated to Sumpter's troops, and there being reason to fear the approach of Lord Rawdon, the enterprise was abandoned. Sumpter crossed the Santee; and the legion rejoined the army, then encamped at the high hills of that river.

The intense heat of this sultry season demanded some relaxation from the unremitting toils which the southern army had encountered. From the month of January, it had been engaged in one course of incessant fatigue, and of hardy enterprise. All its powers had been strained, nor had any interval been allowed to refresh and recruit the almost exhausted strength and spirits of the troops.

The continued labours and exertions of all were highly meritorious; but the successful activity of one corps will attract particular attention. The legion, from its structure, was peculiarly adapted to the partisan war of the southern states; and, by being detached against the weaker posts of the enemy, had opportunities for displaying with advantage all the energies it possessed. In that extensive sweep which it made from the Santee to Augusta, which employed from the 15th of April to the 5th of June, this corps, acting in conjunction, first with Marion, afterwards with Pickens, and sometimes alone, had constituted an essential part of the force which carried five British posts, and made upwards of eleven hundred prisoners. Its leader, in the performance of these services, displayed a mind of so much fertility of invention and military resource, as to add greatly to his previous reputation as a partisan.

The whole army had exhibited a degree of activity, courage, and patient suffering, surpassing any expectation that could have been formed of troops composed chiefly of new levies; and its general had manifested great firmness, enterprise, prudence, and skill.

The suffering sustained in this ardent struggle for the southern states was not confined to the armies. The inhabitants of the country felt all the miseries which are inflicted by war in its most savage form. Being almost equally divided between the two contending parties, reciprocal injuries had gradually sharpened their resentments against each other, and had armed neighbour against neighbour, until it became a war of extermination. As the parties alternately triumphed, opportunities were alternately given for the exercise of their vindictive passions. They derived additional virulence from the examples occasionally afforded by the commanders of the British forces. After overrunning Georgia and South Carolina, they seem to have considered those states as completely reannexed to the British empire; and they manifested a disposition to treat those as rebels, who had once submitted and again taken up arms, although the temporary ascendency of the continental troops should have induced the measure. One of these executions, that of Colonel Hayne, took place on the third of August, while Lord Rawdon[5]was in Charleston, preparing to sail for Europe. The American army being at this time in possession of great part of the country, the punishment inflicted on this gentleman was taken up very seriously by General Greene, and was near producing a system of retaliation. The British officers, pursuing this policy, are stated to have executed several of the zealous partisans of the revolution who fell into their hands. These examples had unquestionably some influence in unbridling the revengeful passions of the royalists, and letting loose the spirit of slaughter which was brooding in their bosoms. The disposition to retaliate to the full extent of their power, if not to commit original injury, was equally strong in the opposite party. When fort Granby surrendered, the militia attached to the legion manifested so strong a disposition to break the capitulation, and to murder the most obnoxious among the prisoners who were inhabitants of the country, as to produce a solemn declaration from General Greene, that any man guilty of so atrocious an act should be executed. When fort Cornwallis surrendered, no exertions could have saved Colonel Brown, had he not been sent to Savannah protected by a guard of continental troops. Lieutenant Colonel Grierson, of the royal militia, was shot by unknown marksmen; and, although a reward of one hundred guineas was offered to any person who would inform against the perpetrator of the crime, he could never be discovered. "The whole country," said General Greene in one of his letters, "is one continued scene of blood and slaughter."

Greene was too humane, as well as too judicious, not to discourage this exterminating spirit. Perceiving in it the total destruction of the country, he sought to appease it by restraining the excesses of those who were attached to the American cause.

At the high hills of Santee the reinforcements expected from North Carolina were received. The American army, counting every person belonging to it, was augmented to two thousand six hundred men; but its effective force did not exceed sixteen hundred.

Active movements of the two armies.

After the retreat of General Greene from Orangeburg, Lord Rawdon was induced by ill health to avail himself of a permit to return to Great Britain, and the command of the British forces in South Carolina devolved on Lieutenant Colonel Stuart. He again advanced to the Congaree; and encamping near its junction with the Wateree, manifested a determination to establish a permanent post at that place. Though the two armies were within sixteen miles of each other on a right line, two rivers ran between them which could not be crossed without making a circuit of seventy miles; in consequence of which Lieutenant Colonel Stuart felt himself so secure, that his foraging parties were spread over the country. To restrain them, and to protect the inhabitants, General Greene detached Marion towards Combahee ferry, and Washington over the Wateree. Frequent skirmishes ensued, which, from the superior courage and activity of the American cavalry, uniformly terminated in their favour.

Finding that Lieutenant Colonel Stuart designed to maintain his important position on the Congaree, Greene prepared to recommence active operations. Breaking up his camp at the high hills of Santee, he crossed the Wateree near Camden, and marched towards Friday's ferry.

After a short repose, they resume active operations.

On being informed of his approach, the British army retired to Eutaw, where it was reinforced by a detachment from Charleston. Greene followed by slow and easy marches, for the double purpose of preserving his soldiers from the effects of fatigue under a hot sun, and of giving Marion, who was returning from a critical expedition to the Edisto, time to rejoin him. In the afternoon of the seventh that officer arrived; and it was determined to attack the British camp next day.

September 8.
Battle of Eutaw.

At four in the morning of the eighth, the American army moved from its ground, which was seven miles from Eutaw, in the following order: The legion of Lee and the state troops of South Carolina formed the advance. The militia moved next, and were followed by the regulars. The cavalry of Washington and the infantry of Kirkwood brought up the rear. The artillery moved between the columns.

At eight in the morning, about four miles from the British camp, the van fell in with a body of horse and foot, who were escorting an unarmed foraging party, and a brisk action ensued. The British were instantly routed. The cavalry made their escape at the sight of the legion dragoons, and the infantry were killed or taken. About forty, including their captain, were made prisoners. The foraging party which followed in the rear saved themselves by flight, on hearing the first musket. Supposing this party to be the van of the English, Greene arranged his army in order of battle.

The militia, commanded by Generals Marion and Pickens, composed the first line. The second was formed of the continental infantry. The North Carolina brigade, commanded by General Sumner, was placed on the right; the Virginians, commanded by Lieutenant Colonel Campbell, formed the centre; and the Marylanders, commanded by Colonel Williams, the left. The legion of Lee was to cover the right flank; the state troops of South Carolina, commanded by Colonel Henderson, the left; and the cavalry of Washington, with the infantry of Kirkwood, formed the reserve. Captain Lieutenant Gaines, with two three-pounders, was attached to the first line; and Captain Brown, with two sixes, to the second.

The British line also was immediately formed. It was drawn up across the road, in an oblique direction, in a wood, on the heights near the Eutaw springs, having its right flank on Eutaw creek. This flank was also covered by a battalion commanded by Major Majoribanks, which was posted in a thicket, in a line forming an obtuse angle with the main body. The left flank was protected by the cavalry commanded by Major Coffin, and by a body of infantry held in reserve. A detachment of infantry was pushed forward about a mile, with a field piece to employ the Americans until his arrangements should be completed.

The American van continuing to move forward, encountered the British advanced party; upon which Captain Lieutenant Gaines came up with his field pieces, which opened on the enemy with considerable effect. General Greene also ordered up his first line with directions to move on briskly, and to advance as they fired. As this line came into action, the legion formed on its right flank, and the state troops of South Carolina on its left.

The British advanced party was soon driven in; and the Americans, continuing to press forward, were engaged with the main body. Lieutenant Colonel Stuart, perceiving the materials of which this line was composed, and probably anticipating its speedy discomfiture, to avoid exposing his flanks to the American cavalry, had directed his troops not to change their position. His design was to meet the American regulars without any alteration of the arrangement originally made. But the militia, many of whom had frequently faced an enemy, being commanded by generals of experience and courage, exhibited a degree of firmness not common to that species of force, and maintained their ground with unexpected obstinacy. In the ardour of action, the order not to advance was disregarded, and the British pressed forward as the militia retired. The artillery which was placed in the road was well served on both sides, and did great execution till both the three-pounders commanded by Captain Lieutenant Gaines were dismounted. About the same time, one of the British shared the same fate.

When the militia gave way, Lee and Henderson still maintained the engagement on the flanks, General Sumner was ordered up to fill the place from which Marion and Pickens were receding; and his brigade, ranging itself with the legion infantry, and the state regiment of South Carolina, came into action with great intrepidity. The British, who had advanced upon the militia, fell back to their first ground, upon which Stuart ordered the corps of infantry posted in the rear of his left wing into the line, and directed Major Coffin with his cavalry to guard that flank. About this time Henderson received a wound which disabled him from keeping the field, and the command of his corps devolved on Lieutenant Colonel Hampton.

After sustaining the fire of the enemy with considerable resolution, Sumner's brigade began to give way, and the British rushed forward in some disorder. Greene then directed Williams and Campbell to charge with the bayonet, and at the same time ordered

Washington to bring up the reserve, and to act on his left. Williams charged without firing a musket; but the soldiers of Campbell's regiment, being chiefly new levies, returned the fire of the enemy as they advanced. In this critical moment, Lee, perceiving that the American right extended beyond the British left, ordered Captain Rudolph, of the legion infantry, to turn their flank and give them a raking fire. This order was instantly executed with precision and effect. Charged thus both in front and flank, 'the British broke successively on the left, till the example was followed by all that part of the line. The Marylanders under Williams, had already used the bayonet, and before the troops opposed to them gave way, several had fallen on both sides, transfixed with that weapon.

The British left, when driven off the field, retreated through their encampment towards Eutaw creek, near which stood a three story brick house, surrounded with offices, and connected with a strongly enclosed garden, into which Major Sheridan, in pursuance of orders previously given by Lieutenant Colonel Stuart, threw himself with the New York volunteers. The Americans pursued them closely, and took three hundred prisoners and two pieces of cannon. Unfortunately for their hopes of victory, the refreshments found in camp furnished a temptation too strong to be resisted; and many of the soldiers left their ranks, and, under cover of the tents, seized the spirits and food within their view. The legion infantry, however, pressed the rear so closely as to make a serious struggle to enter the house with the British. The door was forcibly shut in their faces, and several British officers and men were excluded. These were made prisoners, and mixed with the Americans, so as to save them from the fire of the house while retiring from it.

As the British left gave way, Washington was directed to charge their right. He advanced with his accustomed impetuosity, but found it impossible, with cavalry, to penetrate the thicket occupied by Majoribanks. Perceiving an interval between the British right and the creek, he determined to pass through it round their flank and to charge them in the rear. In making the attempt, he received a fire which did immense execution. The British occupied a thicket almost impervious to horse. In attempting to force it, Lieutenant Stuart who commanded the leading section was badly wounded, his horse killed under him, and every man in his section killed or wounded. Captain Watts, the second in command, fell pierced with two balls. Colonel Washington was wounded, and his horse was killed. They fell together; and, before he could extricate himself, he was made a prisoner.

After nearly all the officers, and a large portion of the men were killed or wounded, the residue of the corps was drawn off by Captain Parsons, assisted by Lieutenant Gordon. Soon after the repulse of Washington, Lieutenant Colonel Hampton and Captain Kirkwood with his infantry, came up and renewed the attack on Majoribanks. Great efforts were made to dislodge him, but they were ineffectual. Finding it impracticable to employ horse to advantage on that ground, Hampton drew off his troops and retired to the road.

The corps commanded by Sheridan kept up a continual and destructive fire from the house in which they had taken shelter; and Greene ordered up the artillery to batter it. The guns were too light to make a breach in the walls, and, having been brought within the range of the fire from the house, almost every artillerist was killed, and the pieces were abandoned.

The firm stand made by Majoribanks, and the disorder which had taken place among a part of the Americans, gave Stuart an opportunity of rallying his broken regiments, and bringing them again into action. They were formed between the thicket occupied by Majoribanks, and the house in possession of Sheridan.

Major Coffin, who had repulsed the legion cavalry about the time the British infantry was driven off the field, still maintained a formidable position on their left; and no exertions could dislodge Majoribanks or Sheridan from the cover under which they fought. Perceiving that the contest was maintained on ground, and under circumstances extremely disadvantageous to the Americans, Greene withdrew them a small distance, and formed them again in the wood in which the battle had been fought. Thinking it unadviseable to renew the desperate attempt which had just failed, he collected his wounded, and retired with his prisoners to the ground from which he had marched in the morning, determined again to fight the British army when it should retreat from the Eutaws.

Every corps engaged in this hard fought battle received the applause of the general. Almost every officer whose situation enabled him to attract notice was named with distinction. "Never," he said, "was artillery better served;" but, "he thought himself principally indebted for the victory he had gained, to the free use made of the bayonet by the Virginians and Marylanders, and by the infantry of the legion and of Kirkwood." To Colonel Williams he acknowledged himself to be particularly indebted. He gave that praise too to the valour of his enemy which it merited. "They really fought," he said, "with courage worthy a better cause."

The loss on both sides bore a great proportion to the numbers engaged. That of the Americans was five hundred and fifty-five, including sixty officers. One hundred and thirty were killed on the spot. Seventeen commissioned officers were killed, and four mortally wounded. "This loss of officers," said their general, "is still more heavy on account of their value than their numbers."

Among the slain was Lieutenant Colonel Campbell, who received a mortal wound while leading the Virginia brigade to that bold and decisive charge which broke the adverse line.

The loss of the British army was stated by themselves at six hundred and ninety-three men, of whom only eighty-five were killed in the field. If this statement be correct,[6] the American dead greatly exceeded that of the adversary, which was probably the fact, as the carnage of the former, during their unavailing efforts to dislodge the latter from the house and strong adjoining ground, was immense.

Each party had pretensions to the victory, and each claimed the merit of having gained it with inferior numbers. The truth probably is that their numbers were nearly equal.

Nor can the claim of either to the victory be pronounced unequivocal. Unconnected with its consequences, the fortune of the day was nearly balanced. But if the consequences be taken into the account, the victory unquestionably belonged to Greene. The result of this, as of the two preceding battles fought by him in the Carolinas, was the expulsion of the hostile army from the territory which was the immediate object of contest.

Four six-pounders, two of which had been taken in the early part of the day, were brought to play upon the house, and, being pushed so near as to be within the command of its fire, were unavoidably abandoned; but a three-pounder which had been also taken, was brought off by Captain Lieutenant Gaines, whose conduct was mentioned with distinction by General Greene. Thus the trophies of victory were divided.

The thanks of congress were voted to every corps in the army; and a resolution was passed for "presenting to Major General Greene, as an honourable testimony of his merit, a British standard, and a golden medal, emblematic of the battle and of his victory."

September 9.

On the day succeeding the action, Lieutenant Colonel Stuart marched from Eutaw to meet Major M'Arthur, who was conducting a body of troops from Charleston. The junction was effected about fourteen miles from Eutaw; and this movement saved M'Arthur from Marion and Lee, who had been detached on the morning of the same day to intercept any reinforcement which might be coming from below. Stuart continued his retreat to Monk's corner, to which place he was followed by Greene, who, on finding that the numbers and position of the British army were such as to render an attack unadviseable, returned to the high hills of Santee.

The ravages of disease were added to the loss sustained in battle, and the army remained for some time in too feeble a condition for active enterprise.

Nov. 18.

The capitulation at Yorktown was soon followed by the evacuation of Wilmington, in North Carolina, and the British seemed to limit their views in the south to the country adjacent to the sea coast. As the cool season approached, the diseases of the American army abated; and Greene, desirous of partaking in the abundance of the lower country, marched from the high hills of Santee towards the Four Holes, a branch of the Edisto. **Nov.**

28. Leaving the army to be conducted by Colonel Williams, he proceeded in person at the head of his cavalry, supported by about two hundred infantry, towards the British posts at

Dorchester, where six hundred and fifty regular troops and two hundred royal militia were understood to be stationed.

The British army retires towards Charleston.

Though his march was conducted with the utmost secrecy, the country through which he passed contained so many disaffected, that it was impossible to conceal this movement; and intelligence of his approach was communicated to the officer commanding in Dorchester, the night before he reached that place. The advance, commanded by Lieutenant Colonel Hampton, met a small party, which he instantly charged, and, after killing and taking several, drove the residue over the bridge under cover of their works. In the course of the following night, the stores at Dorchester were burnt, and the garrison retired to the Quarter House, where their principal force was encamped. Greene returned to the army at the Round O, at which place he purposed to await the arrival of the reinforcements marching from the north under the command of General St. Clair. In the mean time, General Marion and Lieutenant Colonel Lee were stationed on each side of Ashley, so as to cover the country between the Cooper and the Edisto; thus confining the influence of the British arms to Charleston neck, and the adjacent islands.[7]

While in his camp at the Round O, General Greene was informed that large reinforcements from Ireland and from New York were expected by the army in Charleston. This intelligence excited the more alarm, because the term of service for which the levies from Virginia were engaged was about expiring, and no adequate measures had been taken for supplying their places. It proved untrue; but such was its impression, that the general addressed a letter to the governors of South Carolina, in which, after taking a serious view of the state of his army, he recommended that it should be recruited from the slaves. The governor thought the proposition of sufficient importance to be laid before the legislature, which was soon afterwards convened; but the measure was not adopted.

On the fourth of January, General St. Clair, who conducted the reinforcement from the north, arrived in camp, and, five days afterward, General Wayne,[8] with his brigade, and the remnant of the third regiment of dragoons, commanded by Colonel White, was detached over the Savannah for the recovery of Georgia.

General Greene crossed the Edisto and took post six miles in advance of Jacksonborough, on the road leading to Charleston, for the purpose of covering the state legislature, which assembled at that place on the eighteenth. Thus was civil government re-established in South Carolina, and that state restored to the union.

It is impossible to review this active and interesting campaign without feeling that much is due to General Greene; and that he amply justified the favourable opinion of the Commander-in-chief. He found the country completely conquered, and defended by a regular army estimated at four thousand men. The inhabitants were so divided, as to leave it doubtful to which side the majority was attached. At no time did the effective continental force which he could bring into the field, amount to two thousand men; and of these a considerable part were raw troops. Yet he could keep the field without being forced into action; and by a course of judicious movement, and of hardy enterprise, in which invincible constancy was displayed, and in which courage was happily tempered with prudence, he recovered the southern states. It is a singular fact, well worthy of notice, which marks impressively the soundness of his judgment, that although he never gained a decisive victory, he obtained, to a considerable extent, even when defeated, the object for which he fought.

A just portion of the praise deserved by these achievements, is unquestionably due to the troops he commanded. These real patriots bore every hardship and privation[9] with a degree of patience and constancy which can not be sufficiently admired. And never was a general better supported by his inferior officers. Not shackled by men who, without merit, held stations of high rank obtained by political influence, he commanded young men of equal spirit and intelligence, formed under the eye of Washington, and trained in the school furnished in the severe service of the north, to all the hardships and dangers of war.

A peculiar importance was given to these successes in the south by the opinion that a pacific temper was finding its way into the cabinets of the belligerent powers of Europe. The communications from the court of Versailles rendered it probable that negotiations for peace would take place in the course of the ensuing winter; and dark hints had been given on the part of Great Britain to the minister of his most Christian Majesty, that all the American states could not reasonably expect to become independent, as several of them were subdued. Referring to the precedent of the low countries, it was observed that of the seventeen provinces originally united against the Spanish crown, only seven obtained their independence.

Additional motives for exertion were furnished by other communications from the French monarch. These were that, after the present campaign, no farther pecuniary or military aids were to be expected from France. The situation of affairs in Europe would, it was said, demand all the exertions which that nation was capable of making; and the forces of his most Christian Majesty might render as much real service to the common cause elsewhere as in America.[10]

CHAPTER II.

Preparations for another campaign.... Proceedings in the Parliament of Great Britain.... Conciliatory conduct of General Carleton.... Transactions in the south.... Negotiations for peace.... Preliminary and eventual articles agreed upon between the United States and Great Britain.... Discontents of the American army.... Peace.... Mutiny of a part of the Pennsylvania line.... Evacuation of New York.... General Washington resigns his commission and retires to Mount Vernon.

1782
Preparations for another campaign.

THE splendid success of the allied arms in Virginia, and the great advantages obtained still farther south, produced no disposition in General Washington to relax those exertions which might be necessary to secure the great object of the contest. "I shall attempt to stimulate congress," said he, in a letter to General Greene written at Mount Vernon, "to the best improvement of our late success, by taking the most vigorous and effectual measures to be ready for an early and decisive campaign the next year. My greatest fear is, that viewing this stroke in a point of light which may too much magnify its importance, they may think our work too nearly closed, and fall into a state of languor and relaxation. To prevent this error, I shall employ every means in my power, and, if unhappily we sink into this fatal mistake, no part of the blame shall be mine."

On the 27th of November he reached Philadelphia, and congress passed a resolution granting him an audience on the succeeding day. On his appearance the President addressed him in a short speech, informing him that a committee was appointed to state the requisitions to be made for the proper establishment of the army, and expressing the expectation that he would remain in Philadelphia, in order to aid the consultations on that important subject.

The secretary of war, the financier, and the secretary of foreign affairs, assisted at these deliberations; and the business was concluded with unusual celerity.

A revenue was scarcely less necessary than an army; and it was obvious that the means for carrying on the war must be obtained, either by impressment, or by a vigorous course of taxation. But both these alternatives depended on the states; and the government of the union resorted to the influence of the Commander-in-chief in aid of its requisitions.

But no exertions on the part of America alone could expel the invading army. A superiority at sea was indispensable to the success of offensive operations against the posts which the British still held within the United States. To obtain this superiority, General Washington pressed its importance on the minister of France and commanding officers of the French troops, as well as on the Marquis de Lafayette, who was about to return to his native country.

Proceedings in the British parliament.

The first intelligence from Europe was far from being calculated to diminish the anxieties still felt in America by the enlightened friends of the revolution. The parliament of Great Britain reassembled in November. The speech from the throne breathed a settled purpose to continue the war; and the addresses from both houses, which were carried by large majorities, echoed the sentiment.

In the course of the animated debates which these addresses occasioned, an intention was indeed avowed by some members of the administration to change their system. The plan indicated for the future was to direct the whole force of the nation against France and Spain; and to suspend offensive operations in the interior of the United States, until the strength of those powers should be broken. In the mean time, the posts then occupied by their troops were to be maintained.

This development of the views of administration furnished additional motives to the American government for exerting all the faculties of the nation, to expel the British garrisons from New York and Charleston. The efforts of the Commander-in-chief to produce these exertions were earnest and unremitting, but not successful. The state legislatures declared the inability of their constituents to pay taxes. Instead of filling the continental treasury, some were devising means to draw money from it; and some of those who passed bills imposing heavy taxes, directed that the demands of the state should be first satisfied, and that the residue only should be paid to the continental receiver. By the unwearied attention and judicious arrangements of the minister of finance, the expenses of the nation had been greatly reduced. The bank established in Philadelphia, and his own high character, had enabled him to support in some degree a system of credit, the advantages of which were incalculably great.

He had through the Chevalier de la Luzerne obtained permission from his most Christian Majesty to draw for half a million of livres monthly, until six millions should be received. To prevent the diversion of any part of this sum from the most essential objects, he had concealed the negotiation even from congress, and had communicated it only to the Commander-in-chief; yet, after receiving the first instalment, it was discovered that Doctor Franklin had anticipated the residue of the loan, and had appropriated it to the purposes of the United States. At the commencement of the year 1782, not a dollar remained in the treasury; and, although congress had required the payment of two millions on the 1st of April, not a cent had been received on the twenty-third of that month; and, so late as the 1st of June, not more than twenty thousand dollars had reached the treasury. Yet to the financier every eye was turned; to him the empty hand of every public creditor was stretched forth; and against him, instead of the state governments, the complaints and imprecations of every unsatisfied claimant were directed. In July, when the second quarter annual payment of taxes ought to have been received, the minister of finance was informed by some of his agents, that the collection of the revenue had been postponed in some of the states, in consequence of which the month of December would arrive before any money could come into the hands of the continental receivers. In a letter communicating this unpleasant intelligence to the Commander-in-chief, he added, "with such gloomy prospects as this letter affords, I am tied here to be baited by continual clamorous demands; and for the forfeiture of all that is valuable in life, and which I hoped at this moment to enjoy, I am to be paid by invective. Scarce a day passes in which I am not tempted to give back into the hands of congress the power they have delegated, and to lay down a burden which presses me to the earth. Nothing prevents me but a knowledge of the difficulties I am obliged to struggle under. What may be the success of my efforts God only knows; but to leave my post at present, would, I know, be ruinous. This candid state of my situation and feelings I give to your bosom, because you who have already felt and suffered so much, will be able to sympathize with me."

Livingston Manor, Dobbs Ferry, New York

A monument erected by the Sons of the Revolution on the lawn of this historic mansion, overlooking the Hudson River, states that here, on July 6, 1781, the French allies under Rochambeau joined the American Army. Here also, on August 14, 1781, Washington planned the Yorktown campaign which brought to a triumphant end the War for American Independence; and here, on May 6, 1783, Washington and Sir Guy Carleton arranged for the evacuation of American soil by the British. A concluding paragraph reads: "And opposite this point, May 8, 1783, a British sloop of war fired 17 guns in honor of the American Commander-in-Chief, the first salute by Great Britain to the United States of America."

Fortunately for the United States, the temper of the British nation on the subject of continuing the war did not accord with that of its sovereign. That war, into which the people had entered with at least as much eagerness as the minister, had become almost universally unpopular.

February 27.

Motions against the measures of administration respecting America were repeated by the opposition; and, on every experiment, the strength of the minority increased. At length, on the 27th of February, General Conway moved in the house of commons, "that it is the opinion of this house that a farther prosecution of offensive war against America would, under present circumstances, be the means of weakening the efforts of this country against her European enemies, and tend to increase the mutual enmity so fatal to the interests both of Great Britain and America." The whole force of administration was exerted to get rid of this resolution, but was exerted in vain; and it was carried. An address to the king, in the words of the resolution, was immediately voted, and was presented by the whole house. **March 4.** The answer of the crown being deemed inexplicit, it was on the 4th of March resolved, "that the house will consider as enemies to his majesty and the country, all those who should advise, or attempt a farther prosecution of offensive war on the continent of North America."

These votes were soon followed by a change of ministers, and by instructions to the officers commanding the forces in America, which conformed to them.

While General Washington was employed in addressing circular letters to the state governments, suggesting all those motives which might stimulate them to exertions better proportioned to the exigency, English papers containing the debates in parliament on the various propositions respecting America, reached the United States. Alarmed at the impression these debates might make, he introduced the opinions it was deemed prudent to inculcate respecting them, into the letters he was then about to transmit to the governors of the several states. "I have perused these debates," he said, "with great attention and care, with a view, if possible, to penetrate their real design; and upon the most mature deliberation I can bestow, I am obliged to declare it as my candid opinion, that the measure, in all its views, so far as it respects America, is merely delusory, having no serious intention to admit our independence upon its true principles, but is calculated to produce a change of ministers to quiet the minds of their own people, and reconcile them to a continuance of the war, while it is meant to amuse this country with a false idea of peace, to draw us from our connexion with France, and to lull us into a state of security and inactivity, which taking place, the ministry will be left to prosecute the war in other parts of the world with greater vigour and effect. Your excellency will permit me on this occasion to observe, that, even if the nation and parliament are really in earnest to obtain peace with America, it will undoubtedly be wisdom in us to meet them with great caution and circumspection, and by all means to keep our arms firm in our hands, and instead of relaxing one iota in our exertions, rather to spring forward with redoubled vigour, that we may take the advantage of every favourable opportunity, until our wishes are fully obtained. No nation yet suffered in treaty by preparing (even in the moment of negotiation) most vigorously for the field.

"The industry which the enemy is using to propagate their pacific reports, appears to me a circumstance very suspicious; and the eagerness with which the people, as I am informed, are catching at them, is, in my opinion, equally dangerous."

May.

Conciliatory conduct of General Carleton.

Early in May, Sir Guy Carleton, who had succeeded Sir Henry Clinton in the command of all the British forces in the United States, arrived at New York. Having been also appointed in conjunction with Admiral Digby, a commissioner to negotiate a peace, he lost no time in conveying to General Washington copies of the votes of the British Parliament, and of a bill which had been introduced on the part of administration, authorizing his Majesty to conclude a peace or truce with those who were still denominated "the revolted colonies of North America." These papers, he said, would manifest the dispositions prevailing with the government and people of England towards those of

America; and, if the like pacific temper should prevail in this country, both inclination and duty would lead him to meet it with the most zealous concurrence. He had addressed to congress, he said, a letter containing the same communications, and he solicited a passport for the person who should convey it.

At this time, the bill enabling the British monarch to conclude a peace or truce with America had not become a law; nor was any assurance given that the present commissioners were empowered to offer other terms than those which had been formerly rejected. General Carleton therefore could not hope that negotiations would commence on such a basis; nor be disappointed at the refusal of the passports he requested by congress, to whom the application was, of course, referred. The letter may have been written for the general purpose of conciliation, and of producing a disposition in the United States on the subject of hostilities, corresponding with that which had been expressed in the House of Commons. But the situation of the United States justified a suspicion of different motives; and prudence required that their conduct should be influenced by that suspicion. The repugnance of the king to a dismemberment of the empire was understood; and it was thought probable that the sentiments expressed in the House of Commons might be attributable rather to a desire of changing ministers, than to any fixed determination to relinquish the design of reannexing America to the crown.

Under these impressions, the overtures now made were considered as opiates, administered to lull the spirit of vigilance which the guardians of the public safety laboured to keep up, into a state of fatal repose; and to prevent those measures of security which it might yet be necessary to adopt.

This jealousy was nourished by all the intelligence received from Europe. The utmost address of the British cabinet had been employed to detach the belligerents from each other. The mediation of Russia had been accepted to procure a separate peace with Holland; propositions had been submitted both to France and Spain, tending to an accommodation of differences with each of those powers singly; and inquiries had been made of Mr. Adams, the American minister at the Hague, which seemed to contemplate the same object with regard to the United States. These political manoeuvres furnished additional motives for doubting the sincerity of the English cabinet. Whatever views might actuate the court of St. James on this subject, the resolution of the American government to make no separate treaty was unalterable.[11]

But the public votes which have been stated, and probably his private instructions, restrained Sir Guy Carleton from offensive war; and the state of the American army disabled General Washington from making any attempt on the posts in possession of the British. The campaign of 1782 consequently passed away without furnishing any military operations of moment between the armies under the immediate direction of the respective commanders-in-chief.

August.

Negotiations for peace.

Early in August a letter was received by General Washington from Sir Guy Carleton and Admiral Digby, which, among other communications manifesting a pacific disposition on the part of England, contained the information that Mr. Grenville was at Paris, invested with full powers to treat with all the parties at war, that negotiations for a general peace were already commenced, and that his Majesty had commanded his minister to direct Mr. Grenville, that the independence of the thirteen provinces should be proposed by him in the first instance, instead of being made a condition of a general treaty. But that this proposition would be made in the confidence that the loyalists would be restored to their possessions, or a full compensation made them for whatever confiscations might have taken place.

This letter was, not long afterwards, followed by one from Sir Guy Carleton, declaring that he could discern no further object of contest, and that he disapproved of all farther hostilities by sea or land, which could only multiply the miseries of individuals, without a possible advantage to either nation. In pursuance of this opinion, he had, soon after his arrival in New York, restrained the practice of detaching parties of Indians against the frontiers of the United States, and had recalled those which were previously engaged in those bloody incursions.

These communications appear to have alarmed the jealousy of the minister of France. To quiet his fears, congress renewed the resolution "to enter into no discussion of any overtures for pacification, but in confidence and in concert with his most Christian Majesty;"[12] and again recommend to the several states to adopt such measures as would most effectually guard against all intercourse with any subjects of the British crown during the war.

The same causes which produced this inactivity in the north, operated to a considerable extent with the armies of the south.

When General Wayne entered Georgia, the British troops in that state retired to the town of Savannah; and the Americans advanced to Ebenezer. Though inferior to their enemy in numbers, they interrupted his communications with the country, and even burned some magazines which had been collected and deposited under the protection of his guns.

Not receiving the aids from the militia which he had expected, Wayne pressed Greene for reinforcements, which that officer was unable to furnish, until Lieutenant Colonel Posey arrived from Virginia with about two hundred men. He proceeded immediately to Georgia, and reached the camp at Ebenezer on the 1st of April.

These troops, though new levies, were veteran soldiers, who, having served the times for which they enlisted, had become the substitutes of men who were designated, by lot, for tours of duty they were unwilling to perform. Being commanded by old officers of approved courage and experience, the utmost confidence was to be placed in them; and Wayne, though still inferior to his enemy in numbers, sought for opportunities to employ them.

The Indians, who occupied the southern and western parts of Georgia, were in the habit of assembling annually at Augusta, for the purpose of receiving those presents which were indispensable to the preservation of British influence over them. The usual time for holding these meetings was arrived; but the Americans being in possession of Augusta, it was necessary to transfer them to a British post, and the Indians were invited to keep down the south side of the Altamaha to its mouth, whence they were to be conveyed through the inland passage to Savannah. Arrangements had been made for bringing a strong party of Creeks and Choctaws, assembled on the south side of Altamaha, to Harris's bridge, on the Ogechee, about seven miles from that town, and Colonel Brown marched at the head of a strong detachment to convoy them into it. The Indians having quarrelled, instead of proceeding to Ogechee, returned home, and Brown marched back his detachment.

Wayne received intelligence of this movement; and, determining to avail himself of the opportunity given by this division of his enemy to fight him in detail, immediately put his army in motion. He was soon informed that Brown was on his return, and would reach Savannah that night. Disregarding the danger of throwing himself with inferior numbers between the two divisions of the British army, he determined on hazarding an action, and his advance, consisting of a troop of Virginia cavalry, commanded by Captain Hughes and Lieutenant Boyer, and a light company of Virginia infantry, commanded by Captain Parker, entered the road along which Brown was marching about twelve at night, just as his front appeared in view. A vigorous charge was instantly made, which, being entirely unexpected, was completely successful. The British, struck with a panic, dispersed among the thickets and fled in all directions. Colonel Douglass and about forty men were killed, wounded, or taken. The American loss was five men killed and two wounded. The next day, after parading in view of Savannah, Wayne resumed his position at Ebenezer.

The resolution of Parliament against the farther prosecution of active war in America was followed by instructions to the officers commanding the armies of Britain, in consequence of which propositions for the suspension of hostilities were made in the southern department, about the time that they were rejected in the north. The same motives continuing to influence congress, they were rejected in the south also, and the armies still continued to watch each other with vigilance. To avoid surprise, Wayne frequently changed his ground, and was continually on the alert. While his whole attention was directed towards Savannah, an enemy entirely unlooked for came upon his rear, entered his camp in the night, and, had not his army been composed of the best materials, must have dispersed it.

A strong party of Creeks, led by a gallant warrior, Emistasigo, or Guristersego, instead of moving down on the south side of the Altamaha, passed through the centre of Georgia with the determination of engaging the American posts. Marching entirely in the night, through unfrequented ways, subsisting on meal made of parched corn, and guided by white men, they reached the neighbourhood of the American army then encamped at Gibbon's plantation, near Savannah, without being perceived, and made arrangements to attack it. In the night they emerged from the deep swamp in which they had been concealed, and, approaching the rear of the American camp with the utmost secrecy, reached it about three in the morning. The sentinel was killed before he could sound the alarm, and the first notice was given by the fire and the yell of the enemy. The Indians rushed into the camp, and, killing the few men they fell in with, seized the artillery. Fortunately some time was wasted in the attempt to turn the pieces on the Americans. Captain Parker, who commanded the light company, had been employed on a very fatiguing tour of duty near Savannah, and had returned that evening to camp. To allow his harassed soldiers some repose, he was placed in the rear near the artillery, and was asleep when the Indians entered the camp. Roused by the fire, and perceiving that the enemy was amidst them, he judiciously drew off his men in silence, and formed them with the quarter guard behind the house in which the general was quartered. Wayne was instantly on horseback, and, believing the whole garrison from Savannah to be upon him, determined to repulse the enemy or die in the attempt. Parker was directed to charge immediately with the bayonet, and orders were despatched to Posey, the commanding officer in camp, to bring up the troops without delay. The orders to Parker were so promptly executed, that Posey, although he moved with the utmost celerity, could not reach the scene of action in time to join in it. The light troops and quarter guard under Parker drove every thing before them at the point of the bayonet. The Indians, unable to resist the bayonet, soon fled, leaving their chief, his white guides, and seventeen of his warriors dead upon the spot. Wayne, who accompanied his light troops, now first discovered the character of his enemy, and adapted his pursuit to it. Yet only twelve prisoners were made. The general's horse was shot under him, and twelve privates were killed and wounded.[13]

This sharp conflict terminated the war in Georgia. Information was soon given of the determination to withdraw the British troops from Savannah; and arrangements being made, with the sanction of the civil government, for the security of such individuals as might remain in town, the place was evacuated. The regular troops retired to Charleston, and Colonel Brown conducted his loyalists through the islands into Florida. Wayne was directed to rejoin General Greene.

In South Carolina the American army maintained its position in front of Jacksonborough, and that of the British was confined to Charleston and its immediate vicinity. The situation of the ground as well as the condition of his army, was unfavourable to offensive operations on the part of General Greene; and General Leslie, who commanded in Charleston, was not strong enough to attempt the recovery of the lower country. While the two armies continued to watch each other, occasional enterprises were undertaken by detachments, in some of which a considerable degree of merit was displayed. In one of them, the corps of Marion, its general being attending in the legislature, was surprised and dispersed by the British Colonel Thompson; and in another, an English guard galley, mounting twelve guns, and manned with forty-three seamen, was captured by Captain Rudolph, of the legion.

From the possession of the lower country of South Carolina, which was known to contain considerable quantities of rice and beef cattle, the army had anticipated more regular and more abundant supplies of food than it had been accustomed to receive. This hope was disappointed by the measures of the government.

The generals, and other agents acting under the authority of congress, had been accustomed in extreme cases, which too frequently occurred, to seize provisions for the use of the armies. This questionable power had been exercised with forbearance, most commonly in concert with the government of the state, and under the pressure of such obvious necessity as carried its justification with it.

The war being transferred to the south at a time when the depreciation of paper money had deprived congress of its only fund, it became indispensably necessary to resort more generally to coercive means in order to procure subsistence for the troops. Popular discontent was the natural consequence of this odious measure, and the feelings of the people were communicated to their representatives. After the termination of the very active campaign of 1781 in Virginia, the legislature of that state passed a law prohibiting all impressment, "unless it be by warrant from the executive in time of actual invasion;" and the assembly of South Carolina, during the session at Jacksonborough, also passed a law forbidding impressment, and enacting, "that no other persons than those who shall be appointed by the governor for that purpose, shall be allowed or permitted to procure supplies for the army."

The effect of this measure was soon felt. The exertions of the agent appointed by the governor failed to procure subsistence for the troops, and General Greene, after a long course of suffering, was compelled to relieve his urgent wants by an occasional recurrence to means forbidden by the law.

Privations, which had been borne without a murmur under the excitement of active military operations, produced great irritation during the leisure which prevailed after the enemy had abandoned the open field; and, in the Pennsylvania line, which was composed chiefly of foreigners, the discontent was aggravated to such a point as to produce a treasonable intercourse with the enemy, in which a plot is understood to have been laid for seizing General Greene and delivering him to a detachment of British troops, which would move out of Charleston for the purpose of favouring the execution of the design. It was discovered when it is supposed to have been on the point of execution; and a sergeant Gornell, believed to be the chief of the conspiracy, was condemned to death by a court martial, and executed on the 22nd of April. Some others, among whom were two domestics in the general's family, were brought before the court on suspicion of being concerned in the plot, but the testimony was not sufficient to convict them; and twelve deserted the night after it was discovered. There is no reason to believe that the actual guilt of this transaction extended farther.

July 11.

Charleston was held until the 14th of December. Previous to its evacuation, General Leslie had proposed a cessation of hostilities, and that his troops might be supplied with fresh provisions, in exchange for articles of the last necessity in the American camp. The policy of government being adverse to this proposition, General Greene was under the necessity of refusing his assent to it, and the British general continued to supply his wants by force. This produced several skirmishes with foraging parties, to one of which importance was given by the death of Lieutenant Colonel Laurens, whose loss was universally lamented.

This gallant and accomplished young gentleman had entered into the family of the Commander-in-chief at an early period of the war, and had always shared a large portion of his esteem. Brave to excess, he sought every occasion to render service to his country, and to acquire that military fame which he pursued with the ardour of a young soldier, whose courage seems to have partaken largely of that romantic spirit which youth and enthusiasm produce in a fearless mind. No small addition to the regrets occasioned by his loss was derived from the reflection that he fell unnecessarily, in an unimportant skirmish, in the last moments of the war, when his rash exposure to the danger which proved fatal to him could no longer be useful to his country.

From the arrival of Sir Guy Carleton at New York, the conduct of the British armies on the American continent was regulated by the spirit then recently displayed in the house of commons; and all the sentiments expressed by their general were pacific and conciliatory. But to these nattering appearances it was dangerous to yield implicit confidence. With a change of men, a change of measures might also take place; and, in addition to the ordinary suggestions of prudence, the military events in the West Indies were calculated to keep alive the attention, and to continue the anxieties of the United States.

After the surrender of Lord Cornwallis, the arms of France and Spain in the American seas had been attended with such signal success, that the hope of annihilating the power of Great Britain in the West Indies was not too extravagant to be indulged. Immense preparations had been made for the invasion of Jamaica; and, early in April, Admiral Count de Grasse sailed from Martinique with a powerful fleet, having on board the land forces and artillery which were to be employed in the operations against that island. His intention was to form a junction with the Spanish Admiral Don Solano, who lay at Hispaniola; after which the combined fleet, whose superiority promised to render it irresistible, was to proceed on the important enterprise which had been concerted. On his way to Hispaniola, De Grasse was overtaken by Rodney, and brought to an engagement, in which he was totally defeated, and made a prisoner. This decisive victory disconcerted the plans of the combined powers, and gave security to the British islands. In the United States, it was feared that this alteration in the aspect of affairs might influence the councils of the English cabinet on the question of peace; and these apprehensions increased the uneasiness with which all intelligent men contemplated the state of the American finances.

It was then in contemplation to reduce the army, by which many of the officers would be discharged. While the general declared, in a confidential letter to the secretary of war, his conviction of the alacrity with which they would retire into private life, could they be placed in a situation as eligible as they had left to enter into the service, he added—"Yet I cannot help fearing the result of the measure, when I see such a number of men goaded by a thousand stings of reflection on the past, and of anticipation on the future, about to be turned on the world, soured by penury, and what they call the ingratitude of the public; involved in debts, without one farthing of money to carry them home, after having spent the flower of their days, and, many of them, their patrimonies, in establishing the freedom and independence of their country; and having suffered every thing which human nature is capable of enduring on this side of death. I repeat it, when I reflect on these irritating circumstances, unattended by one thing to soothe their feelings, or brighten the gloomy prospect, I cannot avoid apprehending that a train of evils will follow of a very serious and distressing nature.

"I wish not to heighten the shades of the picture so far as the real life would justify me in doing, or I would give anecdotes of patriotism and distress which have scarcely ever been paralleled, never surpassed, in the history of mankind. But you may rely upon it, the patience and long sufferance of this army are almost exhausted, and there never was so great a spirit of discontent as at this instant. While in the field, I think it may be kept from breaking out into acts of outrage; but when we retire into winter quarters (unless the storm be previously dissipated) I can not be at ease respecting the consequences. It is high time for a peace."

To judge rightly of the motives which produced this uneasy temper in the army, it will be necessary to recollect that the resolution of October, 1780, granting half pay for life to the officers, stood on the mere faith of a government possessing no funds enabling it to perform its engagements. From requisitions alone, to be made on sovereign states, the supplies were to be drawn which should satisfy these meritorious public creditors; and the ill success attending these requisitions while the dangers of war were still impending, furnished melancholy presages of their unproductiveness in time of peace. In addition to this reflection, of itself sufficient to disturb the tranquillity which the passage of the resolution had produced, were other considerations of decisive influence. The dispositions manifested by congress itself were so unfriendly to the half pay establishment as to extinguish the hope that any funds the government might acquire, would be applied to that object. Since the passage of the resolution, the articles of confederation, which required the concurrence of nine states to any act appropriating public money, had been adopted; and nine states had never been in favour of the measure. Should the requisitions of congress therefore be respected, or should permanent funds be granted by the states, the prevailing sentiment of the nation was too hostile to the compensation which had been stipulated, to leave a probability that it would be substantially made. This was not merely the sentiment of the individuals then administering the government, which might change with a change of men. It was known to be the sense of the states they represented; and consequently the hope could not be indulged that, on this subject, a future congress would be more just, or would think more liberally. As therefore the establishment of that independence for which they had fought and suffered appeared to become more certain,—as the end of their toils approached—the officers became more attentive to their own situation; and the inquietude of the army increased with the progress of the negotiation.

In October, the French troops marched to Boston, in order to embark for the West Indies; and the Americans retired into winter quarters. The apparent indisposition of the British general to act offensively, the pacific temper avowed by the cabinet of London, and the strength of the country in which the American troops were cantoned, gave ample assurance that no military operations would be undertaken during the winter, which could require the continuance of General Washington in camp. But the irritable temper of the army furnished cause for serious apprehension; and he determined to forego every gratification to be derived from a suspension of his toils, in order to watch its discontents.

While the situation of the United States thus loudly called for peace, the negotiations in Europe were protracted by causes which, in America, were almost unknown, and which it would have been dangerous to declare. Although, so far as respected the dismemberment of the British empire, the war had been carried on with one common design, the ulterior views of the belligerent powers were not only different, but, in some respects, incompatible with each other. To depress a proud and hated rival was so eagerly desired by the house of Bourbon, that France and Spain might be disposed to continue hostilities for the attainment of objects in which America could feel no common interest. This circumstance, of itself, furnished motives for prolonging the war, after the causes in which it originated were removed; and additional delays were produced by the discordant views which were entertained in regard to those claims which were the subject of negotiation. These were, the boundaries which should be assigned to the United States, and the participation which should be allowed them in the fisheries. On both these points, the wishes of France and Spain were opposed to those of America; and the cabinets both of Versailles and Madrid, seemed disposed to intrigue with that of London, to prevent such ample concessions respecting them, as the British minister might be inclined to make.

Preliminary and eventual articles agreed upon between the United States and Great Britain.

Nov. 30.

After an intricate negotiation, in which the penetration, judgment, and firmness, of the American commissioners were eminently displayed, eventual and preliminary articles were signed on the 30th of November. By this treaty every reasonable wish of America, especially on the questions of boundary and of the fisheries, was gratified.

The liberality of the articles on these points attests the success which attended the endeavours of the plenipotentiaries of the United States, to prove that the real interests of England required that America should become independent in fact, as well as name; and that every cause of future discord between the two nations should be removed.

1783

The effect of this treaty was suspended until peace should be concluded between France and Great Britain. The connexions between their most Christian and Catholic Majesties not admitting of a separate peace on the part of either, the negotiations between the belligerent powers of Europe had been protracted by the persevering endeavours of Spain to obtain the cession of Gibraltar. At length, the formidable armament which had invested that fortress was repulsed with immense slaughter; after which the place was relieved by Lord Howe, and the besiegers abandoned the enterprise in despair. Negotiations were then taken up with sincerity; and preliminary articles of peace between Great Britain, France, and Spain, were signed on the 20th of January, 1783.

Discontents of the American Army.

In America, the approach of peace, combined with other causes, produced a state of things alike interesting and critical. The officers who had wasted their fortunes and their prime of life in unrewarded service, fearing, with reason, that congress possessed neither the power nor the inclination to comply with its engagements to the army, could not look with unconcern at the prospect which was opening to them. In December, soon after going into winter quarters, they presented a petition to congress, respecting the money actually due to them, and proposing a commutation of the half pay stipulated by the resolutions of October, 1780, for a sum in gross, which they flattered themselves, would encounter fewer prejudices than the half pay establishment. Some security that the engagements of the government would be complied with was also requested. A committee of officers was deputed to solicit the attention of congress to this memorial, and to attend its progress through the house.

Among the most distinguished members of the federal government, were persons sincerely disposed to do ample justice to the public creditors generally, and to that class of them particularly whose claims were founded in military service. But many viewed the army with jealous eyes, acknowledged its merit with unwillingness, and betrayed, involuntarily, their repugnance to a faithful observance of the public engagements. With this question, another of equal importance was connected, on which congress was divided almost in the same manner. One party was attached to a state, the other to a continental system. The latter laboured to fund the public debts on solid continental security, while the former opposed their whole weight to measures calculated to effect that object.

In consequence of these divisions on points of the deepest interest, the business of the army advanced slowly, and the important question respecting the commutation of their half pay remained undecided, when intelligence was received of the signature of the preliminary and eventual articles of peace between the United States and Great Britain.

Anonymous letters and the proceedings in consequence thereof.

The officers, soured by their past sufferings, their present wants, and their gloomy prospects—exasperated by the neglect which they experienced, and the injustice which they apprehended, manifested an irritable and uneasy temper, which required only a slight impulse to give it activity. To render this temper the more dangerous, an opinion had been insinuated that the Commander-in-chief was restrained, by extreme delicacy, from supporting their interests with that zeal which his feelings and knowledge of their situation had inspired. Early in March, a letter was received from their committee in Philadelphia, showing that the objects they solicited had not been obtained. On the 10th of that month, an anonymous paper was circulated, requiring a meeting of the general and field officers at the public building on the succeeding day at eleven in the morning; and announcing the expectation that an officer from each company, and a delegate from the medical staff would attend. The object of the meeting was avowed to be, "to consider the late letter from their representatives in Philadelphia, and what measures (if any) should be adopted to obtain that redress of grievances which they seemed to have solicited in vain."

On the same day an address to the army was privately circulated, which was admirably well calculated to work on the passions of the moment, and to lead to the most desperate resolutions. Full justice can not be done to this eloquent paper without inserting it entire.

"To the officers of the army.

"Gentlemen,

"A fellow soldier, whose interests and affections bend him strongly to you, whose past sufferings have been as great, and whose future fortune may be as desperate as yours, would beg leave to address you.

"Age has its claims, and rank is not without its pretensions, to advise; but though unsupported by both, he flatters himself that the plain language of sincerity and experience will neither be unheard nor unregarded.

"Like many of you, he loved private life, and left it with regret. He left it, determined to retire from the field with the necessity that called him to it, and not until then—not until the enemies of his country, the slaves of power, and the hirelings of injustice, were compelled to abandon their schemes, and acknowledge America as terrible in arms as she had been humble in remonstrance. With this object in view, he has long shared in your toils, and mingled in your dangers. He has felt the cold hand of poverty without a murmur, and has seen the insolence of wealth without a sigh. But too much under the direction of his wishes, and sometimes weak enough to mistake desire for opinion, he has until lately—very lately—believed in the justice of his country. He hoped that, as the clouds of adversity scattered, and as the sunshine of peace and better fortune broke in upon us, the coldness and severity of government would relax, and that more than justice, that gratitude would blaze forth upon those hands which had upheld her in the darkest stages of her passage from impending servitude to acknowledged independence. But faith has its limits, as well as temper, and there are points beyond which neither can be stretched without sinking into cowardice, or plunging into credulity. This, my friends, I conceive to be your situation.

Hurried to the very verge of both, another step would ruin you for ever. To be tame and unprovoked when injuries press hard upon you, is more than weakness; but to look up for kinder usage without one manly effort of your own, would fix your character, and show the world how richly you deserve those chains you broke. To guard against this evil, let us take a review of the ground upon which we now stand, and from thence carry our thoughts forward for a moment into the unexplored field of expedient.

"After a pursuit of seven long years, the object for which we set out is at length brought within our reach.—Yes, my friends, that suffering courage of yours was active once.—It has conducted the United States of America through a doubtful and a bloody war.—It has placed her in the chair of independency; and peace returns again to bless—whom?—A country willing to redress your wrongs, cherish your worth, and reward your services? A country courting your return to private life with tears of gratitude and smiles of admiration—longing to divide with you that independency which your gallantry has given, and those riches which your wounds have preserved? Is this the case? Or is it rather a country that tramples upon your rights, disdains your cries, and insults your distresses? Have you not more than once suggested your wishes and made known your wants to congress? Wants and wishes which gratitude and policy would have anticipated rather than evaded; and have you not lately, in the meek language of entreating memorials, begged from their justice what you could no longer expect from their favour? How have you been answered? Let the letter which you are called to consider to-morrow reply.

"If this then be your treatment while the swords you wear are necessary for the defence of America, what have you to expect from peace, when your voice shall sink, and your strength dissipate by division? When those very swords, the instruments and companions of your glory, shall be taken from your sides, and no remaining mark of military distinction left but your wants, infirmities, and scars? Can you then consent to be the only sufferers by this revolution, and, retiring from the field, grow old in poverty, wretchedness, and contempt? Can you consent to wade through the vile mire of dependency, and owe the miserable remnant of that life to charity which has hitherto been spent in honour? If you can—go—and carry with you the jest of tories, and the scorn of whigs;—the ridicule, and, what is worse, the pity of the world. Go,—starve and be forgotten. But if your spirit should revolt at this; if you have sense enough to discover, and spirit enough to oppose, tyranny under whatever garb it may assume; whether it be the plain coat of republicanism, or the splendid robe of royalty; if you have yet learned to discriminate between a people and a cause, between men and principles,—awake; attend to your situation, and redress yourselves. If the present moment be lost, every future effort is in vain; and your threats then will be as empty as your entreaties now.

"I would advise you therefore to come to some final opinion upon what you can bear, and what you will suffer. If your determination be in any proportion to your wrongs, carry your appeal from the justice to the fears of the government. Change the milk-and-water style of your last memorial. Assume a bolder tone,—decent, but lively, spirited, and determined; and suspect the man who would advise to more moderation and longer forbearance. Let two or three men who can feel as well as write, be appointed to draw up your *last remonstrance*; for I would no longer give it the sueing, soft, unsuccessful epithet of memorial. Let it be represented in language that will neither dishonour you by its rudeness, nor betray you by its fears, what has been promised by congress, and what has been performed;—how long and how patiently you have suffered;—how little you have asked, and how much of that little has been denied. Tell them that, though you were the first, and would wish to be the last to encounter danger; though despair itself can never drive you into dishonour, it may drive you from the field;—that the wound often irritated and never healed, may at length become incurable; and that the slightest mark of indignity from congress now must operate like the grave, and part you forever; that in any political event, the army has its alternative. If peace, that nothing shall separate you from your arms but death; if war, that courting the auspices, and inviting the directions of your illustrious leader, you will retire to some unsettled country, smile in your turn, and 'mock when their fear cometh on.' But let it represent also that, should they comply with the request of your late memorial, it would make you more happy and them more respectable. That while war should continue you would follow their

24

standard into the field; and when it came to an end, you would withdraw into the shade of private life, and give the world another subject of wonder and applause;—an army victorious over its enemies, victorious over itself."

Persuaded as the officers in general were of the indisposition of government to remunerate their services, this eloquent and impassioned address, dictated by genius and by feeling, found in almost every bosom a kindred though latent sentiment prepared to receive its impression. Quick as the train to which a torch is applied, the passions caught its flame, and nothing seemed to be required but the assemblage proposed for the succeeding day, to communicate the conflagration to the combustible mass, and to produce an explosion ruinous to the army and to the nation.

Fortunately, the Commander-in-chief was in camp. His characteristic firmness and decision did not forsake him in this crisis. The occasion required that his measures should be firm, but prudent and conciliatory,—evincive of his fixed determination to oppose any rash proceedings, but calculated to assuage the irritation which was excited, and to restore confidence in government.

Knowing well that it was much easier to avoid intemperate measures than to correct them, he thought it of essential importance to prevent the immediate meeting of the officers; but, knowing also that a sense of injury and a fear of injustice had made a deep impression on them, and that their sensibilities were all alive to the proceedings of congress on their memorial, he thought it more adviseable to guide their deliberations on that interesting subject, than to discountenance them.

With these views, he noticed in his orders, the anonymous paper proposing a meeting of the officers, and expressed his conviction that their good sense would secure them from paying any "attention to such an irregular invitation; but his own duty, he conceived, as well as the reputation and true interest of the army, required his disapprobation of such disorderly proceedings. At the same time, he requested the general and field officers, with one officer from each company, and a proper representation from the staff of the army, to assemble at twelve on Saturday, the 15th, at the new building, to hear the report of the committee deputed by the army to congress. After mature deliberation they will devise what farther measures ought to be adopted as most rational and best calculated to obtain the just and important object in view." The senior officer in rank present was directed to preside, and report the result of the deliberations to the Commander-in-chief.

The day succeeding that on which these orders were published, a second anonymous address appeared, from the same pen which had written the first. Its author, acquainted with the discontents of the army, did not seem to despair of impelling the officers to the desired point. He affected to consider the orders in a light favourable to his views:—"as giving system to their proceedings, and stability to their resolves."

But Washington would not permit himself to be misunderstood. The interval between his orders and the general meeting they invited, was employed in impressing on those officers individually who possessed the greatest share of the general confidence, a just sense of the true interests of the army; and the whole weight of his influence was exerted to calm the agitations of the moment, and conduct them to a happy termination. This was a work of no inconsiderable difficulty. So convinced were many that government designed to deal unfairly by them, that only the reliance they placed on their general, and their attachment to his person and character, could have moderated their resentments so far as to induce them to adopt the measures he recommended.

On the 15th, the convention of officers assembled, and General Gates[14] took the chair. The Commander-in-chief then addressed them in the following terms.

"Gentlemen,—

"By an anonymous summons, an attempt has been made to convene you together. How inconsistent with the rules of propriety, how unmilitary, and how subversive of all order and discipline, let the good sense of the army decide.

"In the moment of this summons, another anonymous production was sent into circulation, addressed more to the feelings and passions than to the judgment of the army. The author of the piece is entitled to much credit for the goodness of his pen; and I could wish he had as much credit for the rectitude of his heart; for as men see through different optics, and are induced by the reflecting faculties of the mind, to use different means to attain the same end, the author of the address should have had more charity, than to mark for suspicion the man who should recommend moderation and longer forbearance; or, in other words, who should not think as he thinks, and act as he advises. But he had another plan in view, in which candour and liberality of sentiment, regard to justice, and love of country, have no part; and he was right to insinuate the darkest suspicion to effect the blackest design. That the address was drawn with great art, and is designed to answer the most insidious purposes; that it is calculated to impress the mind with an idea of premeditated injustice, in the sovereign power of the United States, and rouse all those resentments which must unavoidably flow from such a belief; that the secret mover of this scheme, whoever he may be, intended to take advantage of the passions, while they were warmed by the recollection of past distresses, without giving time for cool deliberate thinking, and that composure of mind which is so necessary to give dignity and stability to measures, is rendered too obvious by the mode of conducting the business to need other proof than a reference to the proceedings.

"Thus much, gentlemen, I have thought it incumbent on me to observe to you, to show upon what principles I opposed the irregular and hasty meeting which was proposed to have been held on Tuesday last, and not because I wanted a disposition to give you every opportunity consistent with your own honour, and the dignity of the army, to make known your grievances. If my conduct heretofore has not evinced to you, that I have been a faithful friend to the army, my declaration of it at this time would be equally unavailing and improper. But as I was among the first who embarked in the cause of our common country; as I have never left your side one moment but when called from you on public duty; as I have been the constant companion and witness of your distresses, and not among the last to feel and acknowledge your merits; as I have ever considered my own military reputation as inseparably connected with that of the army; as my heart has ever expanded with joy when I have heard its praises, and my indignation has arisen when the mouth of detraction has been opened against it; it can scarcely be supposed, at this last stage of the war, that I am indifferent to its interests. But how are they to be promoted? The way is plain, says the anonymous addresser.—If war continues, remove into the unsettled country; there establish yourselves, and leave an ungrateful country to defend itself! But who are they to defend? Our wives, our children, our farms and other property which we leave behind us? Or, in this state of hostile separation, are we to take the two first (the latter can not be removed) to perish in a wilderness with hunger, cold, and nakedness?

"'If peace takes place, never sheath your swords,' says he, 'until you have obtained full and ample justice.' This dreadful alternative of either deserting our country in the extremest hour of her distress, or turning our arms against it, which is the apparent object, unless Congress can be compelled into instant compliance, has something so shocking in it, that humanity revolts at the idea. My God! what can this writer have in view by recommending such measures. Can he be a friend to the army? Can he be a friend to this country? Rather is he not an insidious foe: some emissary, perhaps, from New York, plotting the ruin of both, by sowing the seeds of discord and separation between the civil and military powers of the continent? And what a compliment does he pay to our understandings, when he recommends measures, in either alternative, impracticable in their nature? But here, gentlemen, I will drop the curtain, because it would be as imprudent in me to assign my reasons for this opinion, as it would be insulting to your conception to suppose you stood in need of them. A moment's reflection will convince every dispassionate mind of the physical impossibility of carrying either proposal into execution. There might, gentlemen, be an impropriety in my taking notice, in this address to you, of an anonymous production,—but the manner in which that performance has been introduced to the army, together with some other circumstances, will amply justify my observations on the tendency of that writing.

"With respect to the advice given by the author, to suspect the man who shall recommend moderate measures and longer forbearance, I spurn it, as every man who regards that liberty, and reveres that justice for which we contend, undoubtedly must; for if men are to be precluded from offering their sentiments on a matter which may involve the most serious and alarming consequences that can invite the consideration of mankind, reason is of no use to us. The freedom of speech may be taken away, and dumb and silent, we may be led like sheep to the slaughter. I can not in justice to my own belief, and what I have great reason to conceive is the intention of congress, conclude this address, without giving it as my decided opinion, that that honourable body entertain exalted sentiments of the services of the army, and, from a full conviction of its merits and sufferings, will do it complete justice. That their endeavours to discover and establish funds for this purpose have been unwearied, and will not cease until they have succeeded, I have not a doubt.

"But, like all other large bodies, where there is a variety of different interests to reconcile, their determinations are slow. Why then should we distrust them? And, in consequence of that distrust, adopt measures which may cast a shade over that glory which has been so justly acquired, and tarnish the reputation of an army which is celebrated through all Europe for its fortitude and patriotism? And for what is this done? To bring the object we seek nearer? No: most certainly, in my opinion, it will cast it at a greater distance. For myself, (and I take no merit in giving the assurance, being induced to it from principles of gratitude, veracity, and justice, and a grateful sense of the confidence you have ever placed in me,) a recollection of the cheerful assistance, and prompt obedience I have experienced from you, under every vicissitude of fortune, and the sincere affection I feel for an army I have so long had the honour to command, will oblige me to declare in this public and solemn manner, that in the attainment of complete justice for all your toils and dangers, and in the gratification of every wish, so far as may be done consistently with the great duty I owe my country, and those powers we are bound to respect, you may freely command my services to the utmost extent of my abilities.

"While I give these assurances, and pledge myself in the most unequivocal manner to exert whatever abilities I am possessed of in your favour, let me entreat you, gentlemen, on your part, not to take any measures which, viewed in the calm light of reason, will lessen the dignity, and sully the glory you have hitherto maintained. Let me request you to rely on the plighted faith of your country, and place a full confidence in the purity of the intentions of congress;—that, previous to your dissolution as an army, they will cause all your accounts to be fairly liquidated, as directed in the resolutions which were published to you two days ago; and that they will adopt the most effectual measures in their power to render ample justice to you for your faithful and meritorious services. And let me conjure you, in the name of our common country, as you value your own honour, as you respect the rights of humanity, and as you regard the military and national character of America, to express your utmost horror and detestation of the man who wishes, under any specious pretences, to overturn the liberties of our country, and who wickedly attempts to open the flood gates of civil discord, and deluge our rising empire in blood.

"By thus determining, and thus acting, you will pursue the plain and direct road to the attainment of your wishes; you will defeat the insidious designs of our enemies, who are compelled to resort from open force to secret artifice. You will give one more distinguished proof of unexampled patriotism and patient virtue, rising superior to the pressure of the most complicated sufferings; and you will by the dignity of your conduct, afford occasion for posterity to say, when speaking of the glorious example you have exhibited to mankind, had this day been wanting, the world had never seen the last stage of perfection to which human nature is capable of attaining."

These sentiments from a person whom the army had been accustomed to love, to revere, and to obey; the solidity of whose judgment, and the sincerity of whose zeal for their interests, were alike unquestioned, could not fail to be irresistible. No person was hardy enough to oppose the advice he had given; and the general impression was apparent. A resolution moved by General Knox, and seconded by Brigadier General Putnam, "assuring him that the officers reciprocated his affectionate expressions with the greatest sincerity of which the human heart is capable," was unanimously voted. On the motion of General Putnam, a committee consisting of General Knox, Colonel Brooks, and Captain Howard was then appointed, to prepare resolutions on the business before them, and to report in half an hour. The report of the committee being brought in and considered, the following resolutions were passed.

"Resolved unanimously, that at the commencement of the present war, the officers of the American army engaged in the service of their country from the purest love and attachment to the rights and privileges of human nature; which motives still exist in the highest degree; and that no circumstances of distress or danger shall induce a conduct that may tend to sully the reputation and glory which they have acquired at the price of their blood, and eight years faithful services.

"Resolved unanimously, that the army continue to have an unshaken confidence in the justice of congress and their country, and are fully convinced that the representatives of America will not disband or disperse the army until their accounts are liquidated, the balances accurately ascertained, and adequate funds established for payment; and in this arrangement, the officers expect that the half pay, or a commutation for it, shall be efficaciously comprehended.

"Resolved unanimously, that his excellency the Commander-in-chief, be requested to write to his excellency the president of congress, earnestly entreating the most speedy decision of that honourable body upon the subject of our late address, which was forwarded by a committee of the army, some of whom are waiting upon congress for the result. In the alternative of peace or war, this event would be highly satisfactory, and would produce immediate tranquillity in the minds of the army, and prevent any farther machinations of designing men, to sow discord between the civil and military powers of the United States.

"On motion, resolved unanimously, that the officers of the American army view with abhorrence and reject with disdain, the infamous propositions contained in a late anonymous address to the officers of the army, and resent with indignation the secret attempts of some unknown person to collect the officers together in a manner totally subversive of all discipline and good order.

"Resolved unanimously, that the thanks of the officers of the army be given to the committee who presented to congress the late address of the army; for the wisdom and prudence with which they have conducted that business; and that a copy of the proceedings of this day be transmitted by the president to Major General M'Dougal; and that he be requested to continue his solicitations at congress until the objects of his mission are accomplished."

The storm which had been raised so suddenly and unexpectedly being thus happily dissipated, the Commander-in-chief exerted all his influence in support of the application the officers had made to congress. The following letter, written by him on the occasion, will show that he was not impelled to this measure by the engagements he had entered into more strongly than by his feelings.

"The result of the proceedings of the grand convention of the officers, which I have the honour of enclosing to your excellency for the inspection of congress, will, I flatter myself, be considered as the last glorious proof of patriotism which could have been given by men who aspired to the distinction of a patriot army; and will not only confirm their claim to the justice, but will increase their title to the gratitude of their country.

"Having seen the proceedings on the part of the army terminate with perfect unanimity, and in a manner entirely consonant to my wishes, being impressed with the liveliest sentiments of affection for those who have so long, so patiently, and so cheerfully, suffered and fought under my direction; having from motives of justice, duty, and gratitude, spontaneously offered myself as an advocate for their rights; and having been requested to write to your excellency, earnestly entreating the most speedy decision of congress upon the subjects of the late address from the army to that honourable body; it now only remains for me to perform the task I have assumed, and to intercede in their behalf, as I now do, that the sovereign power will be pleased to verify the predictions I have pronounced of, and the confidence the army have reposed in, the justice of their country.

"And here I humbly conceive it is altogether unnecessary (while I am pleading the cause of an army which have done and suffered more than any other army ever did in the defence of the rights and liberties of human nature) to expatiate on their claims to the most ample compensation for their meritorious services, because they are perfectly known to the whole world, and because (although the topics are inexhaustible) enough has already been said on the subject. To prove these assertions, to evince that my sentiments have ever been uniform, and to show what my ideas of the rewards in question have always been, I appeal to the archives of congress, and call on those sacred deposites to witness for me. And in order that my observations and arguments in favour of a future adequate provision for the officers of the army may be brought to remembrance again, and considered in a single point of view, without giving congress the trouble of having recourse to their files, I will beg leave to transmit herewith an extract from a representation made by me to a committee of congress, so long ago as the 20th of January, 1778, and also the transcript of a letter to the president of congress, dated near Passaic falls, October the 11th, 1780.

"That in the critical and perilous moment when the last mentioned communication was made, there was the utmost danger a dissolution of the army would have taken place unless measures similar to those recommended had been adopted, will not admit a doubt. That the adoption of the resolution granting half pay for life has been attended with all the happy consequences I foretold, so far as respected the good of the service, let the astonishing contrast between the state of the army at this instant and at the former period, determine. And that the establishment of funds, and security of the payment of all the just demands of the army, will be the most certain means of preserving the national faith, and future tranquillity of this extensive continent, is my decided opinion.

"By the preceding remarks, it will readily be imagined that, instead of retracting and reprehending (from farther experience and reflection) the mode of compensation so strenuously urged in the enclosures, I am more and more confirmed in the sentiment; and if in the wrong, suffer me to please myself in the grateful delusion. For if, besides the simple payment of their wages, a farther compensation is not due to the sufferings and sacrifices of the officers, then have I been mistaken indeed. If the whole army have not merited whatever a grateful people can bestow, then have I been beguiled by prejudice, and built opinion on the basis of error. If this country should not in the event perform every thing which has been requested in the late memorial to congress, then will my belief become vain, and the hope that has been excited void of foundation. 'And if (as has been suggested for the purpose of inflaming their passions) the officers of the army are to be the only sufferers by this revolution; if, retiring from the field, they are to grow old in poverty, wretchedness, and contempt; if they are to wade through the vile mire of dependency, and owe the miserable remnant of that life to charity which has hitherto been spent in honour,' then shall I have learned what ingratitude is; then shall I have realized a tale which will embitter every moment of my future life.

"But I am under no such apprehensions. A country rescued by their arms from impending ruin, will never leave unpaid the debt of gratitude.

"Should any intemperate and improper warmth have mingled itself among the foregoing observations, I must entreat your excellency and congress that it may be attributed to the effusions of an honest zeal in the best of causes, and that my peculiar situation may be my apology; and I hope I need not, on this momentous occasion, make any new protestations of disinterestedness, having ever renounced for myself the idea of pecuniary reward. The consciousness of having attempted faithfully to discharge my duty, and the approbation of my country, will be a sufficient recompense for my services."

March 24.
Peace concluded.

These proceedings of the army produced a concurrence of nine states in favour of a resolution commuting the half pay into a sum in gross equal to five years full pay; immediately after the passage of which, the fears still entertained in America that the war might continue, were dissipated by a letter from the Marquis de Lafayette, announcing a general peace. This intelligence, though not official, was certain; and orders were immediately issued, recalling all armed vessels cruising under the authority of the United States. **April 19.** Early in April, the copy of a declaration published in Paris, and signed by the American commissioners, announcing the exchange of ratifications of the preliminary articles between Great Britain and France, was received; and on the 19th of that month, the cessation[15] of hostilities was proclaimed.

Measures for disbanding the army.

The attention of congress might now be safely turned to the reduction of the army. This, in the empty state of the treasury, was a critical operation. In addition to the anxieties which the officers would naturally feel respecting their provision for the future, which of necessity remained unsecured, large arrears of pay were due to them, the immediate receipt of part of which was required by the most urgent wants. To disband an army to which the government was greatly indebted, without furnishing the individuals who composed it with the means of conveyance to their respective homes, was a perilous measure; and congress was unable to advance the pay of a single month.

Although eight millions had been required for the year 1782, the payments into the public treasury had amounted to only four hundred and twenty thousand and thirty-one dollars, and twenty-nine ninetieths; and the foreign loans had not been sufficient to defray expenses it was impossible to avoid, at the close of that year, the expenditures of the superintendent of the finances had exceeded his receipts four hundred and four thousand seven hundred and thirteen dollars and nine ninetieths; and the excess continued to increase rapidly.

Congress urged the states to comply so far with the requisitions as to enable the superintendent of the finances to advance a part of the arrears due to the soldiers; but, as the foreign danger diminished, they became still less attentive to these demands; and the financier was under the necessity of making farther anticipations of the revenue. Measures were taken to advance three months pay in his notes; but, before they could be prepared, orders were issued for complying with a resolution of Congress for granting unlimited furloughs to the non-commissioned officers and privates who were engaged to serve during the war. These orders produced a serious alarm. The generals, and officers commanding regiments and corps cantoned on the Hudson, assembled, and presented an address to the Commander-in-chief, in which the most ardent affection to his person, and confidence in his attachment to the interests of the army, were mingled with expressions of profound duty and respect for the government. But they declared that, after the late explanation on their claims, they had confidently expected that their accounts would be liquidated, the balances ascertained, and adequate funds for the payment of those balances provided, before they should be dispersed or disbanded.

Bound to the army by the strongest ties of affection and gratitude, intimately convinced of the justice of their claims, and of the patriotic principles by which they were influenced, the General was induced by sentiment not less than by prudence, to regard this application. He returned an answer, on the succeeding day, in which, after declaring "that as no man could possibly be better acquainted than himself with the past merits and services of the army, so no one could possibly be more strongly impressed with their present ineligible situation; feel a keener sensibility at their distresses; or more ardently desire to alleviate or remove them." He added, "although the officers of the army very well know my official situation, that I am only a servant of the public, and that it is not for me to dispense with orders which it is my duty to carry into execution, yet as furloughs in all services are considered as a matter of indulgence, and not of compulsion; as congress, I am persuaded, entertain the best disposition towards the army; and as I apprehend in a very short time, the two principal articles of complaint will be removed; until the farther pleasure of congress can be known, I shall not hesitate to comply with the wishes of the army, under these reservations only, that officers sufficient to conduct the men who choose to receive furloughs, will attend them, either on furlough or by detachment."

This answer satisfied the officers. The utmost good temper was manifested; and the arrangements for retiring on furlough were made without a murmur. In the course of the summer, a considerable proportion of the troops enlisted for three years were also permitted to return to their homes; and, in October, a proclamation was issued by congress, declaring all those who had engaged for the war to be discharged on the third of December.

The Long Room in Fraunces' Tavern, New York City

It was here that Washington took formal leave of his officers, preparatory to resigning his commission as Commander-in-Chief of the Continental Army. Controlling his emotion with difficulty, the General arose,

Mutiny of a part of the Pennsylvania line.

While these excellent dispositions were manifested by the veterans serving under the immediate eye of their patriot chief, the government was exposed to insult and outrage from the mutinous spirit of a small party of new levies. About eighty men of this description belonging to Pennsylvania, were stationed at Lancaster. Revolting against the authority of their officers, they marched in a body to Philadelphia, with the avowed purpose of obtaining redress of their grievances from the executive council of the state. The march of these insolent mutineers was not obstructed; and, after arriving in Philadelphia, their numbers were augmented by the junction of some troops quartered in the barracks. They then marched in military parade, with fixed bayonets, to the state-house, in which congress and the executive council of the state were sitting; and, after placing sentinels at the doors, sent in a written message, threatening the executive of the state with the vengeance of an enraged soldiery, if their demands were not gratified in twenty minutes. Although these threats were not directed particularly against congress, the government of the union was grossly insulted, and those who administered it were blockaded for several hours by licentious soldiers. After remaining in this situation about three hours, the members separated, having agreed to reassemble at Princeton.

On receiving information of this outrage, the Commander-in-chief detached fifteen hundred men under the command of Major General Howe, to suppress the mutiny. His indignation at this insult to the civil authority, and his mortification at this misconduct of any portion of the American troops, were strongly marked in his letter to the president of congress.

"While," said he, "I suffer the most poignant distress in observing that a handful of men, contemptible in numbers, and equally so in point of service, (if the veteran troops from the southward have not been seduced by their example,) and who are not worthy to be called soldiers, should disgrace themselves and their country as the Pennsylvania mutineers have done by insulting the sovereign authority of the United States, and that of their own, I feel an inexpressible satisfaction, that even this behaviour can not stain the name of the American soldiery. It can not be imputed to, or reflect dishonour on, the army at large; but, on the contrary, it will, by the striking contrast it exhibits, hold up to public view the other troops in the most advantageous point of light. Upon taking all the circumstances into consideration, I can not sufficiently express my surprise and indignation at the arrogance, the folly, and the wickedness of the mutineers; nor can I sufficiently admire the fidelity, the bravery, and patriotism, which must forever signalize the unsullied character of the other corps of our army. For when we consider that these Pennsylvania levies, who have now mutinied, are recruits, and soldiers of a day, who have not borne the heat and burden of the war, and who can have in reality very few hardships to complain of; and when we at the same time recollect that those soldiers, who have lately been furloughed from this army, are the veterans who have patiently endured hunger, nakedness, and cold; who have suffered and bled without a murmur, and who, with perfect good order, have retired to their homes, without a settlement of their accounts, or a farthing of money in their pockets; we shall be as much astonished at the virtues of the latter, as we are struck with horror and detestation at the proceedings of the former, and every candid mind, without indulging ill-grounded prejudices, will undoubtedly make the proper discrimination."

Before the detachment from the army could reach Philadelphia, the disturbances were, in a great degree, quieted without bloodshed; but General Howe was ordered by congress to continue his march into Pennsylvania, "in order that immediate measures might be taken to confine and bring to trial all such persons belonging to the army as have been principally active in the late mutiny; to disarm the remainder; and to examine fully into all the circumstances relating thereto."

The interval between the treaty with Great Britain and his retiring into private life, was devoted by the Commander-in-chief to objects of permanent utility.

The independence of his country being established, he looked forward with anxiety to its future destinies. These might greatly depend on the systems to be adopted on the return of peace, and to those systems much of his attention was directed. The future peace establishment of the United States was one of the many interesting subjects which claimed the consideration of congress. As the experience of General Washington would certainly enable him to suggest many useful ideas on this important point, his opinions respecting it were requested by the committee to whom it was referred. His letter on this occasion, which was deposited, it is presumed, in the archives of state, will long deserve the attention of those to whom the interests of the United States may be confided. His strongest hopes of securing the future tranquillity, dignity and respectability of his country were placed on a well regulated and well disciplined militia, and his sentiments on this subject are entitled to the more regard, as a long course of severe experience had enabled him to mark the total incompetency of the existing system to the great purposes of national defence.

Evacuation of New York.

At length the British troops evacuated New York, and a detachment from the American army took possession of that town.

Guards being posted for the security of the citizens, General Washington, accompanied by Governor Clinton, and attended by many civil and military officers, and a large number of respectable inhabitants on horseback, made his public entry into the city; where he was received with every mark of respect and attention. His military course was now on the point of terminating; and he was about to bid adieu to his comrades in arms. This affecting interview took place on the 4th of December. At noon, the principal officers of the army assembled at Frances' tavern, soon after which, their beloved commander entered the room. His emotions were too strong to be concealed. Filling a glass, he turned to them and said, "With a heart full of love and gratitude, I now take leave of you; I most devoutly wish that your latter days may be as prosperous and happy, as your former ones have been glorious and honourable." Having drunk, he added, "I can not come to each of you to take my leave, but shall be obliged if each of you will come and take me by the hand." General Knox, being nearest, turned to him. Washington, incapable of utterance, grasped his hand, and embraced him. In the same affectionate manner he took leave of each succeeding officer. The tear of manly sensibility was in every eye; and not a word was articulated to interrupt the dignified silence, and the tenderness of the scene. Leaving the room, he passed through the corps of light infantry, and walked to White Hall, where a barge waited to convey him to Powles Hook. The whole company followed in mute and solemn procession, with dejected countenances, testifying feelings of delicious melancholy, which no language can describe. Having entered the barge, he turned to the company, and, waving his hat, bid them a silent adieu. They paid him the same affectionate compliment; and, after the barge had left them, returned in the same solemn manner to the place where they had assembled.[16]

Congress was then in session at Annapolis, in Maryland, to which place General Washington repaired, for the purpose of resigning into their hands the authority with which they had invested him.[17]He arrived on the 19th of December. The next day he informed that body of his intention to ask leave to resign the commission he had the honour of holding in their service; and requested to know whether it would be their pleasure that he should offer his resignation in writing, or at an audience.

To give the more dignity to the act, they determined that it should be offered at a public audience on the following Tuesday, at twelve.

General Washington resigns his commission and retires to Mount Vernon.

When the hour arrived for performing a ceremony so well calculated to recall the various interesting scenes which had passed since the commission now to be returned was granted, the gallery was crowded with spectators, and several persons of distinction were admitted on the floor of congress. The members remained seated and covered. The spectators were standing, and uncovered. The general was introduced by the secretary, and conducted to a chair. After a short pause, the president[18] informed him that "The United

States in congress assembled were prepared to receive his communications." With native dignity improved by the solemnity of the occasion, the general rose and delivered the following address.

"Mr. President,

"The great events on which my resignation depended, having at length taken place, I have now the honour of offering my sincere congratulations to congress, and of presenting myself before them, to surrender into their hands the trust committed to me, and to claim the indulgence of retiring from the service of my country.

"Happy in the confirmation of our independence and sovereignty, and pleased with the opportunity afforded the United States of becoming a respectable nation, I resign with satisfaction the appointment I accepted with diffidence; a diffidence in my abilities to accomplish so arduous a task, which however was superseded by a confidence in the rectitude of our cause, the support of the supreme power of the union, and the patronage of heaven.

"The successful termination of the war has verified the most sanguine expectations; and my gratitude for the interposition of Providence, and the assistance I have received from my countrymen, increases with every review of the momentous contest.

"While I repeat my obligations to the army in general, I should do injustice to my own feelings not to acknowledge in this place, the peculiar services and distinguished merits of the gentlemen who have been attached to my person during the war. It was impossible the choice of confidential officers to compose my family should have been more fortunate. Permit me, sir, to recommend in particular, those who have continued in the service to the present moment, as worthy of the favourable notice and patronage of congress.

"I consider it as an indispensable duty to close this last act of my official life, by commending the interests of our dearest country to the protection of Almighty God, and those who have the superintendence of them to his holy keeping.

"Having now finished the work assigned me, I retire from the great theatre of action, and, bidding an affectionate farewell to this august body, under whose orders I have so long acted, I here offer my commission, and take my leave of all the employments of public life."

After advancing to the chair and delivering his commission to the president, he returned to his place, and received standing the following answer of congress, which was delivered by the president.

"Sir,

"The United States in congress assembled, receive with emotions too affecting for utterance, the solemn resignation of the authorities under which you have led their troops with success through a perilous and a doubtful war. Called upon by your country to defend its invaded rights, you accepted the sacred charge, before it had formed alliances, and whilst it was without funds or a government to support you. You have conducted the great military contest with wisdom and fortitude, invariably regarding the rights of the civil power, through all disasters and changes. You have by the love and confidence of your fellow citizens, enabled them to display their martial genius, and transmit their fame to posterity. You have persevered until these United States, aided by a magnanimous king and nation, have been enabled under a just Providence, to close the war in freedom, safety, and independence; on which happy event we sincerely join you in congratulations.

"Having defended the standard of liberty in this new world, having taught a lesson useful to those who inflict and to those who feel oppression, you retire from the great theatre of action with the blessings of your fellow citizens. But the glory of your virtues will not terminate with your military command; it will continue to animate remotest ages.

"We feel with you our obligations to the army in general, and will particularly charge ourselves with the interests of those confidential officers who have attended your person to this affecting moment.

"We join you in commending the interests of our dearest country to the protection of Almighty God, beseeching him to dispose the hearts and minds of its citizens, to improve the opportunity afforded them of becoming a happy and respectable nation. And for you, we address to him our earnest prayers that a life so beloved, may be fostered with all his care; that your days may be as happy as they have been illustrious; and that he will finally give you that reward which this world can not give."

This scene being closed, a scene rendered peculiarly interesting by the personages who appeared in it, by the great events it recalled to the memory, and by the singularity of the circumstances under which it was displayed, the American chief withdrew from the hall of congress, leaving the silent and admiring spectators deeply impressed with those sentiments which its solemnity and dignity were calculated to inspire.

Divested of his military character, General Washington retired to Mount Vernon, followed by the enthusiastic love, esteem, and admiration of his countrymen. Relieved from the agitations of a doubtful contest, and from the toils of an exalted station, he returned with increased delight to the duties and the enjoyments of a private citizen. He indulged the hope that, in the shade of retirement, under the protection of a free government, and the benignant influence of mild and equal laws, he might taste that felicity which is the reward of a mind at peace with itself, and conscious of its own purity.

CHAPTER III.

General Washington devotes his time to rural pursuits.... to the duties of friendship.... and to institutions of public utility.... Resolves of Congress and of the Legislature of Virginia for erecting statues to his honour.... Recommends improvement in inland navigation.... Declines accepting a donation made to him by his native state.... The society of the Cincinnati.... He is elected President.... The causes which led to a change of the government of the United States.... Circular letter of General Washington to the governors of the several states.

1783 to 1787

After retiring to private life, General Washington devotes his time to rural pursuits, to the duties of friendship, and to institutions of public utility.

WHEN an individual, long in possession of great power, and almost unlimited influence, retires from office with alacrity, and resumes the character of a private citizen with pleasure, the mind is gratified in contemplating the example of virtuous moderation, and dwells upon it with approving satisfaction. We look at man in his most estimable character; and this view of him exalts our opinion of human nature. Such was the example exhibited by General Washington to his country and to the world. His deportment, and his language, equally attest that he returned with these feelings to the employments of private life. In a letter to Governor Clinton, written only three days after his arrival at Mount Vernon, he says, "The scene is at length closed. I feel myself eased of a load of public care, and hope to spend the remainder of my days in cultivating the affections of good men, and in the practice of the domestic virtues." "At length, my dear marquis," said he to his noble and highly valued friend, Lafayette, "I have become a private citizen on the banks of the Potomac; and under the shadow of my own vine, and my own fig tree, free from the bustle of a camp, and the busy scenes of public life, I am solacing myself with those tranquil enjoyments, of which the soldier who is ever in pursuit of fame—the statesman whose watchful days and sleepless nights are spent in devising schemes to promote the welfare of his own—perhaps the ruin of other countries, as if this globe was insufficient for us all—and the courtier who is always watching the countenance of his prince in the hope of catching a gracious smile—can have very little conception. I have not only retired from all public employments, but am retiring within myself, and shall be able to view the solitary walk, and tread the paths of private life, with heartfelt satisfaction. Envious of none, I am determined to be pleased with all; and this, my dear friend, being the order of my march, I will move gently down the stream of life, until I sleep with my fathers."

But a mind accustomed to labour for a nation's welfare, does not immediately divest itself of ancient habits. That custom of thinking on public affairs, and that solicitude respecting them, which belong to the patriot in office, follow him into his retreat. In a letter to General Knox, written soon after his resignation, General Washington thus expressed the feelings attendant upon this sudden transition from public to private pursuits. "I am just beginning to experience the ease and freedom from public cares, which, however desirable, takes some time to realize; for strange as it may seem, it is nevertheless true, that it was not until lately, I could get the better of my usual custom of ruminating, as soon as I awoke in the morning, on the business of the ensuing day; and of my surprise at finding, after revolving many things in my mind, that I was no longer a public man, or had any thing to do with public transactions. I feel now, however, as I conceive a wearied traveller must do, who, after treading many a painful step with a heavy burden on his shoulders, is eased of the latter, having reached the haven to which all the former were directed; and from his house-top is looking back, and tracing with an eager eye, the meanders by which he escaped the quick-sands and mires which lay in his way, and into which none but the all powerful Guide and Dispenser of human events could have prevented his falling."

For several months after arriving at Mount Vernon, almost every day brought him the addresses of an affectionate and grateful people. The glow of expression in which the high sense universally entertained of his services was conveyed, manifested the warmth of feeling which animated the American bosom. This unexampled tribute of voluntary applause, paid by a whole people, to an individual no longer in power, made no impression on the unassuming modesty of his character and deportment. The same firmness of mind, the same steady and well tempered judgment, which had guided him through the most perilous seasons of the war, still regulated his conduct; and the enthusiastic applauses of an admiring nation served only to cherish sentiments of gratitude, and to give greater activity to the desire still further to contribute to the general prosperity.

Resolves of Congress and of the legislature of Virginia for erecting statues in honour of him.

It was not by addresses alone that his country manifested its attachment to him. Soon after peace was proclaimed, congress unanimously passed a resolution for the erection of an equestrian statue of their general,[19] at the place which should be established for the residence of the government.

The legislature of Virginia too, at its first session after his resignation, passed the following resolution.[20]

"Resolved, that the executive be requested to take measures for procuring a statue of General Washington, to be of the finest marble and best workmanship, with the following inscription on its pedestal:

"The general assembly of the commonwealth of Virginia have caused this statue to be erected as a monument of affection and gratitude to GEORGE WASHINGTON, who, uniting to the endowments of the HERO, the virtues of the PATRIOT, and exerting both in establishing the liberties of his country, has rendered his name dear to his fellow citizens, and given the world an immortal example of true glory."

Although the toils of General Washington were no longer exhibited to the public eye, his time continued to be usefully employed. The judicious cultivation of the earth is justly placed among the most valuable sources of national prosperity, and nothing could be more wretched than the general state of agriculture in America. To its melioration by examples which might be followed, and by the introduction of systems adapted to the soil, the climate, and to the situation of the people, the energies of his active and intelligent mind were now in a great degree directed. No improvement of the implements to be used on a farm, no valuable experiments in husbandry, escaped his attention. His inquiries, which were equally minute and comprehensive, extended beyond the limits of his own country; and he entered into a correspondence on this interesting subject with those foreigners who had been most distinguished for their additions to the stock of agricultural science.

The Old Senate Chamber at Annapolis, Maryland, Where Washington Resigned His Commission

The fate of the Republic was in the hands of Washington when he resigned his commission to Congress, then sitting at Annapolis, December 23, 1783, and retired to private life. Had he so desired, it is probable that he could have founded a monarchy, sustained by his army. Instead, as he wrote to Lafayette, shortly after his return to Mount Vernon: "I have not only retired from all public employments but am retiring within myself, and shall be able to view the solitary walk, and tread the paths of private life, with heartfelt satisfaction. Envious of none, I am determined to be pleased with all; and this, my dear friend, being the order of my march, I will move gently down the stream of life, until I sleep with my fathers."

Mingled with this favourite pursuit, were the multiplied avocations resulting from the high office he had lately filled. He was engaged in an extensive correspondence with the friends most dear to his heart—the foreign and American officers who had served under him during the late war—and with almost every conspicuous political personage of his own, and with many of other countries. Literary men also were desirous of obtaining his approbation of their works, and his attention was solicited to every production of American genius. His countrymen who were about to travel, were anxious to receive from the first citizen of this rising republic, some testimonial of their worth; and all those strangers of distinction who visited this newly created empire, were ambitious of being presented to its founder. Among those who were drawn across the Atlantic by curiosity, and perhaps by a desire to observe the progress of the popular governments which were instituted in this new world, was Mrs. Macauley Graham. By the principles contained in her History of the Stuarts, this lady had acquired much reputation in republican America, and by all was received with marked attention. For the sole purpose of paying her respects to a person whose fame had spread over Europe, she paid a visit to Mount Vernon; and, if her letters may be credited, the exalted opinion she had formed of its proprietor, was "not diminished by a personal acquaintance with him."

To these occupations, which were calculated to gratify an intelligent mind, or which derived a value from the indulgence they afforded to the feelings of the heart, others were unavoidably added, in the composition of which, no palatable ingredient was intermixed. Of these unwelcome intrusions upon his time, General Washington thus complained to an intimate military friend. "It is not, my dear sir, the letters of my friends which give me trouble, or add aught to my perplexity. I receive them with pleasure, and pay as much attention to them as my avocations will permit. It is references to old matters with which I have nothing to do—applications which oftentimes can not be complied with—inquiries, to satisfy which would employ the pen of a historian—letters of compliment, as unmeaning perhaps as they are troublesome, but which must be attended to; and the common-place business—which employ my pen and my time often disagreeably. Indeed, these, with company, deprive me of exercise; and, unless I can obtain relief, must be productive of disagreeable consequences. Already I begin to feel their effects. Heavy and painful oppressions of the head, and other disagreeable sensations often trouble me. I am determined therefore to employ some person who shall ease me of the *drudgery* of this business. At any rate, if the whole of it is thereby suspended, I am determined to use exercise. My private affairs also require infinitely more attention than I have given, or can give them, under present circumstances. They can no longer be neglected without involving my ruin."

It was some time after the date of this letter before he could introduce into his family a young gentleman, whose education and manners enabled him to fill the station of a private secretary and of a friend.

This multiplicity of private avocations could not entirely withdraw the mind of Washington from objects tending to promote and secure the public happiness. His resolution never again to appear in the busy scenes of political life, though believed by himself, and by his bosom friends, to be unalterable, could not render him indifferent to those measures on which the prosperity of his country essentially depended.

To a person looking beyond the present moment, it was only necessary to glance over the map of the United States, to be impressed with the importance of connecting the western with the eastern territory, by facilitating the means of intercourse between them. To this subject, the attention of General Washington had been directed in the early part of his life. While the American states were yet British colonies, he had obtained the passage of a bill for opening the Potomac so as to render it navigable from tide water to Wills creek.[21] The river James had also been comprehended in this plan; and he had triumphed so far over the opposition produced by local interests and prejudices, that the business was in a train which promised success, when the revolutionary war diverted the attention of its patrons, and of all America, from internal improvements to the still greater objects of liberty and independence. As that war approached its termination, subjects which for a time had yielded their pretensions to consideration, reclaimed that place to which their real magnitude entitled them; and internal navigation again attracted the attention of the wise and thinking part of society. Accustomed to contemplate America as his country, and to consider with solicitude the interests of the whole, Washington now took a more enlarged view of the advantages to be derived from opening both the eastern and the western waters; and for this, as well as for other purposes, after peace had been proclaimed, he traversed the western parts of New England and New York. "I have lately," said he in a letter to the Marquis of Chastellux, a nobleman in pursuit of literary as well as of military fame, "made a tour through the lakes George and Champlain as far as Crown Point;—then returning to Schenectady, I proceeded up the Mohawk river to fort Schuyler, crossed over to Wood creek which empties into the Oneida lake, and affords the water communication with Ontario. I then traversed the country to the head of the eastern branch of the Susquehanna, and viewed the lake Otswego, and the portage between that lake and the Mohawk river at Cotnajohario. Prompted by these actual observations, I could not help taking a more contemplative and extensive view of the vast inland navigation of these United States, and could not but be struck with the immense diffusion and importance of it; and with the goodness of that Providence which has dealt his favours to us with so profuse a hand. Would to God we may have wisdom enough to improve them. I shall not rest contented until I have explored the western country, and traversed those lines (or great part of them) which have given bounds to a new empire."

Scarcely had he answered those spontaneous offerings of the heart, which flowed in upon him from every part of a grateful nation, when his views were once more seriously turned to this truly interesting subject. Its magnitude was also impressed on others; and the value of obtaining the aid which his influence and active interference would afford to any exertions for giving this direction to the public mind, and for securing the happy execution of the plan which might be devised, was perceived by all those who attached to the great work its real importance. A gentleman[22] who had taken an expanded view of it, concluded a letter to General Washington, containing a detailed statement of his ideas on the subject in these terms:

"But a most powerful objection always arises to propositions of this kind. It is, that public undertakings are carelessly managed, and much money spent to little purpose. To obviate this objection is the purpose of my giving you the trouble of this discussion. You have retired from public life. You have weighed this determination, and it would be impertinence in me to touch it. But would the superintendence of this work break in too much on the sweets of retirement and repose? If they would, I stop here. Your future time and wishes are sacred in my eye. If it would be only a dignified amusement to you, what a monument of your retirement would it be! It is one which would follow that of your public life, and bespeak it the work of the same great hand. I am confident, that would you either alone, or jointly with any persons you think proper, be willing to direct this business, it would remove the only objection, the weight of which I apprehend."

Recommends the opening and improving the inland navigation of the great rivers in Virginia.

In the autumn of 1784, General Washington made a tour as far west as Pittsburgh; after returning from which, his first moments of leisure were devoted to the task of engaging his countrymen in a work which appeared to him to merit still more attention from its political, than from its commercial influence on the union. In a long and interesting letter to Mr. Harrison, then governor of Virginia, he detailed the advantages which might be derived from opening the great rivers, the Potomac and the James, as high as should be practicable. After stating with his accustomed exactness the distances, and the difficulties to be surmounted in bringing the trade of the west to different points on the Atlantic, he expressed unequivocally the opinion, that the rivers of Virginia afforded a more convenient, and a more direct course than could be found elsewhere, for that rich and increasing commerce. This was strongly urged as a motive for immediately commencing the work. But the rivers of the Atlantic constituted only a part of the great plan he contemplated. He suggested the appointment of commissioners of integrity and abilities, exempt from the suspicion of prejudice, whose duty it should be, after an accurate examination of the James and the Potomac, to search out the nearest and best portages between those waters and the streams capable of improvement, which run into the Ohio. Those streams were to be accurately surveyed, the impediments to their navigation ascertained, and their relative advantages examined. The navigable waters west of the Ohio, towards the great lakes, were also to be traced to their sources, and those which empty into the lakes to be followed to their mouths. "These things being done, and an accurate map of the whole presented to the public, he was persuaded that reason would dictate what was right and proper." For the execution of this latter part of his plan he had also much reliance on congress; and in addition to the general advantages to be drawn from the measure, he laboured, in his letters to the members of that body, to establish the opinion, that the surveys he recommended would add to the revenue, by enhancing the value of the lands offered for sale. "Nature," he said, "had made such an ample display of her bounties in those regions, that the more the country was explored, the more it would rise in estimation."

The assent and co-operation of Maryland being indispensable to the improvement of the Potomac, he was equally earnest in his endeavours to impress a conviction of its superior advantages on those individuals who possessed most influence in that state. In doing so, he detailed the measures which would unquestionably be adopted by New York and Pennsylvania, for acquiring the monopoly of the western commerce, and the difficulty which would be found in diverting it from the channel it had once taken. "I am not," he added, "for discouraging the exertions of any state to draw the commerce of the western country to its sea-ports. The more communications we open to it, the closer we bind that rising world (for indeed it may be so called) to our interests, and the greater strength shall we acquire by it. Those to whom nature affords the best communication, will, if they are wise, enjoy the greatest share of the trade. All I would be understood to mean, therefore, is, that the gifts of Providence may not be neglected."

But the light in which this subject would be viewed with most interest, and which gave to it most importance, was its political influence on the union. "I need not remark to you, sir," said he in his letter to the governor of Virginia, "that the flanks and rear of the United States are possessed by other powers,—and formidable ones too: need I press the necessity of applying the cement of interest to bind all parts of the union together by indissoluble bonds,—especially of binding that part of it which lies immediately west of us, to the middle states. For what ties, let me ask, should we have upon those people, how entirely unconnected with them shall we be, and what troubles may we not apprehend, if the Spaniards on their right, and Great Britain on their left, instead of throwing impediments in their way as they now do, should hold out lures for their trade and alliance? when they get strength, which will be sooner than most people conceive, what will be the consequence of their having formed close commercial connexions with both, or either of those powers? it needs not, in my opinion, the gift of prophecy to foretell."

This idea was enlarged and pressed with much earnestness, in his letters to several members of congress.

The letter to the governor was communicated to the assembly of Virginia, and the internal improvements it recommended were zealously supported by the wisest members of that body. While the subject remained undecided, General Washington, accompanied by the Marquis de Lafayette, who had crossed the Atlantic, and had devoted a part of his time to the delights of an enthusiastic friendship, paid a visit to the capital of the state. Never was reception more cordial, or more demonstrative of respect and affection, than was given to these beloved personages. But amidst the display of addresses and of entertainments which were produced by the occasion, the great business of internal improvements was not forgotten; and the ardour of the moment was seized to conquer those objections to the plan, which yet lingered in the bosoms of members who could perceive in it no future advantages to compensate for the present expense.

An exact conformity between the acts of Virginia and of Maryland, being indispensable to the improvement of the Potomac, the friends of the measure deemed it adviseable to avail themselves of the same influence with the latter state, which had been successfully employed with the former; and a resolution was passed, soon after the return of General Washington to Mount Vernon, requesting him[23] to attend the legislature of Maryland, in order to agree on a bill which might receive the sanction of both states. This agreement being happily completed, the bills were enacted which form the first essay towards connecting the navigation of the eastern with the western waters of the United States.

These acts were succeeded by one, which conveys the liberal wishes of the legislature, with a delicacy scarcely less honourable to its framers, than to him who was its object. The treasurer had been instructed to subscribe, in behalf of the state, for a specified number of shares in each company. Just at the close of the session, when no refusal of their offer could be communicated to them, a bill was suddenly brought in, which received the unanimous assent of both houses, authorizing the treasurer to subscribe for the benefit of General Washington, the same number of shares in each company as were to be taken for the state. A preamble was prefixed to the enacting clause of this bill[24] in which its greatest value consisted. With simple elegance, it conveyed the sentiment, that in seizing this occasion, to make a donation which would in some degree testify their sense of the merits of their most favoured and most illustrious citizen, the donors would themselves be the obliged.

However delightful might be the sensations produced by this delicate and flattering testimony of the affection of his fellow citizens, it was not without its embarrassments. From his early resolution to receive no pecuniary compensation for his services, he could not permit himself to depart; and yet this mark of the gratitude and attachment of his country, could not easily be rejected without furnishing occasion for sentiments he was unwilling to excite. To the friend[25] who conveyed to him the first intelligence of this bill, his difficulties were thus expressed.

He declines accepting a donation made to him by his native state.

"It is not easy for me to decide by which my mind was most affected upon the receipt of your letter of the sixth instant—surprise or gratitude. Both were greater than I had words to express. The attention and good wishes which the assembly has evidenced by their act for vesting in me one hundred and fifty shares in the navigation of the rivers Potomac and James, is more than mere compliment,—there is an unequivocal and substantial meaning annexed. But, believe me, sir, no circumstance has happened since I left the walks of public life which has so much embarrassed me. On the one hand, I consider this act, as I have already observed, as a noble and unequivocal proof of the good opinion, the affection, and disposition of my country to serve me; and I should be hurt, if by declining the acceptance of it, my refusal should be construed into disrespect, or the smallest slight upon the generous intention of the legislature; or that an ostentatious display of disinterestedness, or public virtue, was the source of refusal.

"On the other hand, it is really my wish to have my mind and my actions, which are the result of reflection, as free and independent as the air, that I may be more at liberty (in things which my opportunities and experience have brought me to the knowledge of) to express my sentiments, and if necessary, to suggest what may occur to me, under the fullest conviction that, although my judgment may be arraigned, there will be no suspicion that sinister motives had the smallest influence in the suggestion. Not content then with the bare consciousness of my having in all this navigation business, acted upon the clearest conviction of the political importance of the measure, I would wish that every individual who may hear that it was a favourite plan of mine, may know also, that I had no other motive for promoting it, than the advantage of which I conceived it would be productive to the union at large, and to this state in particular, by cementing the eastern and western territory together, at the same time that it will give vigour and increase to our commerce, and be a convenience to our citizens."

At length he determined, in the same letter which should convey his resolution not to retain the shares for his private emolument, to signify his willingness to hold them in trust for such public institution as the legislature should approve. The following letter conveyed this resolution to the general assembly, through the governor of the state.

(October, 1785.)

"Sir,

"Your excellency having been pleased to transmit me a copy of the act appropriating to my benefit certain shares in the companies for opening the navigation of James and Potomac rivers, I take the liberty of returning to the general assembly through your hands, the profound and grateful acknowledgments inspired by so signal a mark of their beneficent intentions towards me. I beg you, sir, to assure them, that I am filled on this occasion with every sentiment which can flow from a heart warm with love for my country, sensible to every token of its approbation and affection, and solicitous to testify in every instance a respectful submission to its wishes.

"With these sentiments in my bosom, I need not dwell on the anxiety I feel in being obliged, in this instance, to decline a favour which is rendered no less flattering by the manner in which it is conveyed, than it is affectionate in itself. In explaining this, I pass over a comparison of my endeavours in the public service, with the many honourable testimonies of approbation which have already so far overrated, and overpaid them—reciting one consideration only which supersedes the necessity of recurring to every other.

"When I was first called to the station with which I was honoured during the late conflict for our liberties, to the diffidence which I had so many reasons to feel in accepting it, I thought it my duty to join a firm resolution to shut my hand against every pecuniary recompense. To this resolution I have invariably adhered, and from it (if I had the inclination) I do not consider myself at liberty now to depart.

"Whilst I repeat therefore my fervent acknowledgments to the legislature, for their very kind sentiments and intentions in my favour, and at the same time beg them to be persuaded that a remembrance of this singular proof of their goodness towards me, will never cease to cherish returns of the warmest affection and gratitude, I must pray that their act, so far as it has for its object my personal emolument, may not have its effect; but if it should please the general assembly to permit me to turn the destination of the fund vested in me, from my private emolument, to objects of a public nature, it will be my study, in selecting these, to prove the sincerity of my gratitude for the honour conferred upon me, by preferring such as may appear most subservient to the enlightened and patriotic views of the legislature."

The wish suggested in this letter, immediately received the sanction of the legislature; and at a subsequent time, the trust was executed by conveying the shares respectively to the use of a seminary of learning established in the vicinity of each river.

General Washington felt too strong an interest in the success of these works, to refuse the presidency of the companies instituted for their completion. In conducting the affairs of the Potomac company, he took an active part: to that formed for opening the navigation of the James, he could only give his counsel.

These were not the only institutions which occasionally drew the farmer of Mount Vernon from his retreat, and continued him in the public view.

The sentiments with which the officers of the American army contemplated a final separation from each other, will be comprehended by all who are conversant with the finest feelings of the human heart. Companions in virtuous suffering, in danger, and in glory— attached to each other by common exertions made in a severe struggle for the attainment of a common object—they felt that to part for ever was a calamity too afflicting to be supported. The means of perpetuating those friendships which had been formed, and of renewing that endearing social intercourse which had taken place in camp, were universally desired. Perhaps, too, that *esprit de corps* which, identifying the individual with the community, transfers to the aggregate of the society a portion of that self-love which is felt by every private person, and which inspires in the members with a repugnance to the dissolution of the political, not unlike in effect to that which is excited at the dissolution of the natural body, was not without its influence in suggesting some expedient which might preserve the memory of the army, while it cheered the officers who were on the point of separating, with the hope that the separation would not be eternal: that at distant intervals, they might still communicate with each other: that the bonds by which they were connected would not be totally dissolved: and that, for many beneficial purposes, the patriots of the American army would still form one great society.

Establishment of the society of the Cincinnati of which he is elected president.

This idea was suggested by General Knox, and was matured in a meeting composed of the generals, and of deputies from the regiments, at which Major General the Baron Steuben presided. An agreement was then entered into, by which the officers were to constitute themselves into one society of friends, to endure as long as they should endure, or any of their eldest male posterity; and, in failure thereof, any collateral branches who might be judged worthy of becoming its supporters and members, were to be admitted into it. To mark their veneration for that celebrated Roman between whose situation and their own they found some similitude, they were to be denominated, "The Society of the Cincinnati." Individuals of the respective states, distinguished for their patriotism and abilities, might be admitted as honorary members for life, provided their numbers should at no time exceed a ratio of one to four.

The society was to be designated by a medal of gold representing the American eagle bearing on its breast the devices of the order, which was to be suspended by a ribbon of deep blue edged with white, descriptive of the union of America and France. To the ministers who had represented his Most Christian Majesty at Philadelphia, to the admirals who had commanded in the American seas, to the Count de Rochambeau, and the generals and colonels of the French troops who had served in the United States, the insignia of the order were to be presented, and they were to be invited to consider themselves as members of the society; at the head of which the Commander-in-chief was respectfully solicited to place his name. An incessant attention, on the part of the members, to the preservation of the exalted rights and liberties of human nature for which they had fought and bled, and an unalterable determination to promote and cherish between the respective states, union and national honour, were declared to be the immutable principles of the society. Its objects were, to perpetuate the remembrance of the American revolution, as well as cordial affection and the spirit of brotherly kindness among the officers; and to extend acts of beneficence to those officers and their families, whose situation might require assistance. To give effect to the charitable object of the institution, a common fund was to be created by the deposite of one month's pay on the part of every officer becoming a member; the product of which fund, after defraying certain necessary charges, was to be sacredly appropriated to this humane purpose.

The military gentlemen of each state were to constitute a distinct society, deputies from which were to assemble triennially, in order to form a general meeting for the regulation of general concerns.

Without encountering any open opposition, this institution was carried into complete effect; and its honours were sought, especially by the foreign officers, with great avidity. But soon after it was organized, those jealousies which in its first moments had been concealed, burst forth into open view. In October, 1783, a pamphlet was published by Mr. Burk of South Carolina, for the purpose of rousing the apprehensions of the public, and of directing its resentments against the society. Perceiving or believing that he perceived, in the Cincinnati, the foundation of an hereditary order, whose base, from associating with the military the chiefs of the powerful families in each state, would acquire a degree of solidity and strength admitting of any superstructure, he portrayed, in the fervid and infectious language of passion, the dangers to result from the fabric which would be erected on it. The ministers of the United States too in Europe, and the political theorists who cast their eyes towards the west for support to favourite systems, having the privileged orders constantly in view, were loud in their condemnations of an institution from which a race of nobles was expected to spring. The alarm was spread throughout every state, and a high degree of jealousy pervaded the mass of the people. In Massachusetts, the subject was even taken up by the legislature; and it was well understood that, in congress, the society was viewed with secret disapprobation.

"It was impossible for General Washington to view with indifference this state of the public feeling. Bound to the officers of his army by the strictest ties of esteem and affection, conscious of their merits, and assured of their attachment to his person, he was alive to every thing which might affect their reputation, or their interests. However innocent the institution might be in itself, or however laudable its real objects, if the impression it made on the public mind was such as to draw a line of distinction between the military men of

41

America and their fellow citizens, he was earnest in his wishes to adopt such measures as would efface that impression. However ill founded the public prejudices might be, he thought this a case in which they ought to be respected; and, if it should be found impracticable to convince the people that their fears were misplaced, he was disposed to yield to them in a degree, and not to suffer that which was intended for the best of purposes, to produce a bad one."

A general meeting was to be held in Philadelphia in May, 1784; and, in the mean time, he had been appointed the temporary president.

To prepare the officers for those fundamental changes in the principles of the society, which he contemplated as a necessary sacrifice to the public apprehensions, his ideas were suggested to his military correspondents; and to give weight to the measures which might be recommended, his utmost influence was exerted to obtain a full assemblage of deputies, which should be respectable for its numbers, and for its wisdom.

Officers of high respectability entertained different opinions on surrendering those parts of the institution which were deemed objectionable. By some, the public clamour was attributed to a spirit of persecution, which only attached them more closely to the order. Many, it was said, were in quest of a cause of quarrel with their late protectors; and the removal of one ground of accusation against them, would only induce the substitution of some other. The source of the uneasiness which had been manifested was to be found in the temper of the people, not in the matters of which they complained; and if the present cause of irritation was removed, their ill humour would be openly and avowedly directed against the commutation.

General Washington was too much in the habit of considering subjects of difficulty in various points of view, and of deciding on them with coolness and deliberation, to permit his affections to influence his judgment. The most exact inquiries, assiduously made into the true state of the public mind, resulted in a conviction that opinions unfriendly to the institution, in its actual form, were extensively entertained; and that those opinions were founded, not in hostility to the late army, but in real apprehensions for equal liberty.

A wise and necessary policy required, he thought, the removal of these apprehensions; and, at the general meeting in May, the hereditary principle, and the power of adopting honorary members, were relinquished. The result demonstrated the propriety of this alteration. Although a few who always perceive most danger where none exists, and the visionaries then abounding in Europe, continued their prophetic denunciations against the order, America dismissed her fears; and, notwithstanding the refusal of one or two of the state societies to adopt the measures recommended by the general meeting, the members of the Cincinnati were received as brethren into the bosom of their country.

The causes which led to a change of the government of the United States.

While General Washington thus devoted a great part of his time to rural pursuits, to the duties of friendship, and to institutions of public utility, the political state of his country, becoming daily more embarrassed, attracted more and more deeply the anxious solicitude of every enlightened and virtuous patriot. From peace, from independence, and from governments of their own choice, the United States had confidently anticipated every blessing. The glorious termination of their contest with one of the most powerful nations of the earth; the steady and persevering courage with which that contest had been maintained; and the unyielding firmness with which the privations attending it had been supported, had surrounded the infant republics with a great degree of splendour, and had bestowed upon them a character which could be preserved only by a national and dignified system of conduct. A very short time was sufficient to demonstrate, that something not yet possessed was requisite, to insure the public and private prosperity expected to flow from self government. After a short struggle so to administer the existing system, as to make it competent to the great objects for which it was instituted, the effort became apparently desperate; and American affairs were impelled rapidly to a crisis, on which the continuance of the United States, as a nation, appeared to depend.

In tracing the causes which led to this interesting state of things, it will be necessary to carry back our attention to the conclusion of the war.

A government authorized to declare war, but relying on independent states for the means of prosecuting it; capable of contracting debts, and of pledging the public faith for their payment, but depending on thirteen distinct sovereignties for the preservation of that faith, could not be rescued from ignominy and contempt, but by finding those sovereignties administered by men exempt from the passions incident to human nature.

The debts of the union were computed, on the first of January, 1783, at somewhat more than forty millions of dollars. "If," say congress, in an address to the states, urging that the means of payment should be placed in their hands, "other motives than that of justice could be requisite on this occasion, no nation could ever feel stronger; for to whom are the debts to be paid?

"*To an ally*, in the first place, who to the exertion of his arms in support of our cause has added the succours of his treasure; who to his important loans has added liberal donations, and whose loans themselves carry the impression of his magnanimity and friendship.

"*To individuals in a foreign country*, in the next place, who were the first to give so precious a token of their confidence in our justice, and of their friendship for our cause, and who are members of a republic which was second in espousing our rank among nations.

Another class of creditors is, that *illustrious and patriotic band of fellow citizens*, whose blood and whose bravery have defended the liberties of their country, who have patiently borne, among other distresses, the privation of their stipends, whilst the distresses of their country disabled it from bestowing them: and who, even now, ask for no more than such a portion of their dues, as will enable them to retire from the field of victory and glory, into the bosom of peace and private citizenship, and for such effectual security for the residue of their claims, as their country is now unquestionably able to provide.

"The remaining class of creditors is composed partly of such of our fellow citizens as originally lent to the public the use of their funds, or have since manifested most confidence in their country, by receiving transfers from the lenders; and partly of those whose property has been either advanced or assumed for the public service. To discriminate the merits of these several descriptions of creditors, would be a task equally unnecessary and invidious. If the voice of humanity plead more loudly in favour of some than of others, the voice of policy, no less than of justice, pleads in favour of all. A wise nation will never permit those who relieve the wants of their country, or who rely most on its faith, its firmness, and its resources, when either of them is distrusted, to suffer by the event."

In a government constituted like that of the United States, it would readily be expected that great contrariety of sentiment would prevail, respecting the principles on which its affairs should be conducted. It has been already stated that the continent was divided into two great political parties, the one of which contemplated America as a nation, and laboured incessantly to invest the federal head with powers competent to the preservation of the union. The other attached itself to the state government, viewed all the powers of congress with jealousy, and assented reluctantly to measures which would enable the head to act, in any respect, independently of the members. Men of enlarged and liberal minds who, in the imbecility of a general government, by which alone the capacities of the nation could be efficaciously exerted, could discern the imbecility of the nation itself; who, viewing the situation of the world, could perceive the dangers to which these young republics were exposed, if not held together by a cement capable of preserving a beneficial connexion; who felt the full value of national honour, and the full obligation of national faith; and who were persuaded of the insecurity of both, if resting for their preservation on the concurrence of thirteen distinct sovereigns; arranged themselves generally in the first party. The officers of the army, whose local prejudices had been weakened by associating with each other, and whose experience had furnished lessons on the inefficacy of requisitions which were not soon to be forgotten, threw their weight almost universally into the same scale.

The other party, if not more intelligent, was more numerous, and more powerful. It was sustained by prejudices and feelings which grew without effort, and gained strength from the intimate connexions subsisting between a state and its citizens. It required a concurrence of extrinsic circumstances to force on minds unwilling to receive the

43

demonstration, a conviction of the necessity of an effective national government, and to give even a temporary ascendency to that party which had long foreseen and deplored the crisis to which the affairs of the United States were hastening.

Sensible that the character of the government would be decided, in a considerable degree, by the measures which should immediately follow the treaty of peace, gentlemen of the first political abilities and integrity sought a place in the congress of 1783. Combining their efforts for the establishment of principles on which the honour and the interest of the nation were believed to depend, they exerted all their talents to impress on the several states, the necessity of conferring on the government of the union, powers which might be competent to its preservation, and which would enable it to comply with the engagements it had formed. With unwearied perseverance they digested and obtained the assent of congress to a system, which, though unequal to what their wishes would have prepared, or their judgments have approved, was believed to be the best that was attainable. The great object in view was, "to restore and support public credit," to effect which it was necessary, "to obtain from the states substantial funds for funding the whole debt of the United States."

The committee[26] to whom this interesting subject was referred, reported sundry resolutions, recommending it to the several states, to vest in congress permanent and productive funds adequate to the immediate payment of the interest on the national debt, and to the gradual extinction of the principal. A change in the rule by which the proportions of the different states were to be ascertained, was also recommended. In lieu of that article of the confederation which apportions on them the sums required for the public treasury, according to the value of their located lands with the improvements thereon, it was proposed to substitute another more capable of execution, which should make the population of each state the measure of its contribution.[27]

To the application which congress had made during the war for power to levy an impost of five per cent on imported and prize goods, one state had never assented, and another had withdrawn the assent it had previously given.

It was impossible to yield to some of the objections which had been made to this measure, because they went to the certain destruction of the system itself; but in points where the alterations demanded, though mischievous, were not fatal to the plan, it was thought adviseable to accommodate the recommendations of the government to the prejudices which had been disclosed. It had been insisted that the power of appointing persons to collect the duties, would enable congress to introduce into a state, officers unknown and unaccountable to the government thereof; and that a power to collect an indefinite sum for an indefinite time, for the expenditure of which that body could not be accountable to the states, would render it independent of its constituents, and would be dangerous to liberty. To obviate these objections, the proposition now made was so modified, that the grant was to be limited to twenty-five years; was to be strictly appropriated to the debt contracted on account of the war; and was to be collected by persons to be appointed by the respective states.

After a debate, which the tedious mode of conducting business protracted for several weeks, the report was adopted; and a committee, consisting of Mr. Madison, Mr. Hamilton, and Mr. Ellsworth, was appointed to prepare an address, which should accompany the recommendation to the several states.

After a full explanation of the principles on which the system had been framed, this address proceeds:—"The plan thus communicated and explained by congress, must now receive its fate from their constituents. All the objects comprised in it are conceived to be of great importance to the happiness of this confederated republic, are necessary to render the fruits of the revolution a full reward for the blood, the toils, the cares and the calamities which have purchased it. But the object of which the necessity will be peculiarly felt, and which it is peculiarly the duty of congress to inculcate, is the provision recommended for the national debt. Although this debt is greater than could have been wished, it is still less on the whole than could have been expected; and when referred to the cause in which it has been incurred, and compared with the burthens which wars of ambition and of vain glory have entailed on other nations, ought to be borne not only with cheerfulness but with pride. But the magnitude of the debt makes no part of the question. It is sufficient that the debt has been fairly contracted, and that justice and good faith demand that it should be fully discharged. Congress had no option but between different modes of discharging it. The same option is the only one that can exist with the states. The mode which has, after long and elaborate discussion, been preferred, is, we are persuaded, the least objectionable of any that would have been equal to the purpose. Under this persuasion, we call upon the justice and plighted faith of the several states to give it its proper effect, to reflect on the consequences of rejecting it, and to remember that congress will not be answerable for them."

After expatiating on the merits of the several creditors, the report concludes, "let it be remembered finally, that it ever has been the pride and boast of America, that the rights for which she contended, were the rights of human nature. By the blessing of the Author of these rights, on the means exerted for their defence, they have prevailed against all opposition, and formed the basis of thirteen independent states. No instance has heretofore occurred, nor can any instance be expected hereafter to occur, in which the unadulterated forms of republican government can pretend to so fair an opportunity of justifying themselves by their fruits. In this view, the citizens of the United States are responsible for the greatest trust ever confided to a political society. If justice, good faith, honour, gratitude, and all the other good qualities which ennoble the character of a nation, and fulfil the ends of government, be the fruits of our establishments, the cause of liberty will acquire a dignity and lustre which it has never yet enjoyed; and an example will be set, which can not but have the most favourable influence on the rights of mankind. If, on the other side, our governments should be unfortunately blotted with the reverse of these cardinal and essential virtues, the great cause which we have engaged to vindicate will be dishonoured and betrayed; the last and fairest experiment in favour of the rights of human nature will be turned against them, and their patrons and friends exposed to be insulted and silenced by the votaries of tyranny and usurpation."

For the complete success of the plan recommended by congress, no person felt more anxious solicitude than General Washington. Of the vital importance of UNION, no man could be more entirely persuaded; and of the obligations of the government to its creditors, no man could feel a stronger conviction. His conspicuous station had rendered him peculiarly sensible to their claims; and he had unavoidably been personally instrumental in the creation of a part of them. All the feelings of his heart were deeply engaged in the payment of some of the creditors, and that high sense of national honour, of national justice, and of national faith, of which elevated minds endowed with integrity can never be divested, impelled him to take a strong interest in the security of all. Availing himself of the usage of communicating on national subjects with the state governments, and of the opportunity, which his approaching resignation of the command of the army gave, impressively to convey his sentiments to them, he had determined to employ all the influence which the circumstances of his life had created, in a solemn recommendation of measures, on which he believed the happiness and prosperity of his country to depend. On the eighth of June, 1783, he addressed to the governors of the several states respectively, the paternal and affectionate letter which follows.

Letters of General Washington to the governors of the several states.
"Sir,
"The great object for which I had the honour to hold an appointment in the service of my country being accomplished, I am now preparing to resign it into the hands of congress, and to return to that domestic retirement which, it is well known, I left with the greatest reluctance; a retirement for which I have never ceased to sigh through a long and painful absence, and in which (remote from the noise and trouble of the world) I meditate to pass the remainder of life in a state of undisturbed repose. But before I carry this resolution into effect, I think it a duty incumbent upon me, to make this my last official communication; to congratulate you on the glorious events which heaven has been pleased to produce in our favour; to offer my sentiments respecting some important subjects which appear to me to be intimately connected with the tranquillity of the United States: to take my leave of your excellency as a public character: and to give my final blessing to that country in whose service I have spent the prime of my life, for whose sake I have consumed so many

anxious days and watchful nights, and whose happiness, being extremely dear to me, will always constitute no inconsiderable part of my own.

"Impressed with the liveliest sensibility on this pleasing occasion, I will claim the indulgence of dilating the more copiously on the subjects of our mutual felicitation. When we consider the magnitude of the prize we contended for, the doubtful nature of the contest, and the favourable manner in which it has terminated, we shall find the greatest possible reason for gratitude and rejoicing. This is a theme that will afford infinite delight to every benevolent and liberal mind, whether the event in contemplation be considered as the source of present enjoyment, or the parent of future happiness: and we shall have equal occasion to felicitate ourselves on the lot which Providence has assigned us, whether we view it in a natural, a political, or moral point of light.

"The citizens of America, placed in the most enviable condition, as the sole lords and proprietors of a vast tract of continent, comprehending all the various soils and climates of the world, and abounding with all the necessaries and conveniencies of life, are now, by the late satisfactory pacification, acknowledged to be possessed of absolute freedom and independency. They are from this period, to be considered as the actors on a most conspicuous theatre, which seems to be peculiarly designated by Providence for the display of human greatness and felicity. Here they are not only surrounded with every thing which can contribute to the completion of private and domestic enjoyment; but heaven has crowned all its other blessings, by giving a fairer opportunity for political happiness, than any other nation has ever been favoured with. Nothing can illustrate these observations more forcibly, than a recollection of the happy conjuncture of times and circumstances, under which our republic assumed its rank among the nations. The foundation of our empire was not laid in the gloomy age of ignorance and superstition, but at an epoch when the rights of mankind were better understood, and more clearly defined, than at any former period. The researches of the human mind after social happiness have been carried to a great extent; the treasures of knowledge acquired by the labours of philosophers, sages, and legislators, through a long succession of years, are laid open for our use; and their collected wisdom may be happily employed in the establishment of our forms of government. The free cultivation of letters; the unbounded extension of commerce; the progressive refinement of manners; the growing liberality of sentiment; and above all, the pure and benign light of revelation; have had a meliorating influence on mankind, and increased the blessings of society. At this auspicious period, the United States came into existence as a nation; and if their citizens should not be completely free and happy, the fault will be entirely their own.

"Such is our situation, and such are our prospects. But notwithstanding the cup of blessing is thus reached out to us; notwithstanding happiness is ours, if we have a disposition to seize the occasion, and make it our own; yet, it appears to me, there is an option still left to the United States of America; that it is in their choice, and depends upon their conduct, whether they will be respectable and prosperous, or contemptible and miserable as a nation. This is the time of their political probation; this is the moment when the eyes of the whole world are turned upon them; this is the moment to establish or ruin their national character forever; this is the favourable moment to give such a tone to our federal government, as will enable it to answer the ends of its institution, or this may be the ill-fated moment for relaxing the powers of the union, annihilating the cement of the confederation, and exposing us to become the sport of European politics, which may play one state against another, to prevent their growing importance, and to serve their own interested purposes. For according to the system of policy the states shall adopt at this moment, they will stand or fall; and by their confirmation or lapse, it is yet to be decided, whether the revolution must ultimately be considered a blessing or a curse:—a blessing or a curse not to the present age alone, for with our fate will the destiny of unborn millions be involved.

"With this conviction of the importance of the present crisis, silence in me would be a crime. I will therefore speak to your excellency the language of freedom and of sincerity, without disguise. I am aware, however, that those who differ from me in political sentiment, may perhaps remark that I am stepping out of the proper line of my duty, and may possibly ascribe to arrogance or ostentation, what I know is alone the result of the purest intentions. But the rectitude of my own heart, which disdains such unworthy motives; the part I have hitherto acted in life; the determination I have formed of not taking any share in public business hereafter; the ardent desire I feel, and shall continue to manifest, of quietly enjoying, in private life, after all the toils of war, the benefits of a wise and liberal government: will, I flatter myself, sooner or later convince my countrymen, that I could have no sinister views in delivering with so little reserve the opinions contained in this address.

"There are four things which I humbly conceive are essential to the well being, I may even venture to say, to the existence of the United States as an independent power.

1st. An indissoluble union of the states under one federal head.

2d. A sacred regard to public justice.

3d. The adoption of a proper peace establishment, and,

4th. The prevalence of that pacific and friendly disposition, among the people of the United States, which will induce them to forget their local prejudices and politics, to make those mutual concessions which are requisite to the general prosperity, and in some instances, to sacrifice their individual advantages to the interest of the community.

"These are the pillars on which the glorious fabric of our independency and national character must be supported. Liberty is the basis, and whoever would dare to sap the foundation, or overturn the structure, under whatever specious pretext he may attempt it, will merit the bitterest execration, and the severest punishment, which can be inflicted by his injured country.

"On the three first articles, I will make a few observations, leaving the last to the good sense and serious consideration of those immediately concerned.

"Under the first head, although it may not be necessary or proper for me, in this place, to enter into a particular disquisition of the principles of the union, and to take up the great question which has frequently been agitated, whether it be expedient and requisite for the states to delegate a larger proportion of power to congress or not; yet it will be a part of my duty, and that of every true patriot, to assert without reserve, and to insist upon the following positions: that unless the states will suffer congress to exercise those prerogatives they are undoubtedly invested with by the constitution, every thing must very rapidly tend to anarchy and confusion: that it is indispensable to the happiness of the individual states, that there should be lodged somewhere a supreme power to regulate and govern the general concerns of the confederated republic, without which the union can not be of long duration: that there must be a faithful and pointed compliance, on the part of every state, with the late proposals and demands of congress, or the most fatal consequences will ensue: that whatever measures have a tendency to dissolve the union, or contribute to violate or lessen the sovereign authority, ought to be considered as hostile to the liberty and independence of America, and the authors of them treated accordingly: and lastly, that unless we can be enabled, by the concurrence of the states, to participate of the fruits of the revolution, and enjoy the essential benefits of civil society, under a form of government so free and uncorrupted, so happily guarded against the danger of oppression as has been devised and adopted by the articles of confederation, it will be a subject of regret, that so much blood and treasure have been lavished for no purpose; that so many sufferings have been encountered without a compensation; and that so many sacrifices have been made in vain. Many other considerations might here be adduced to prove, that without an entire conformity to the spirit of the union, we can not exist as an independent power. It will be sufficient for my purpose to mention one or two, which seem to me of the greatest importance. It is only in our united character that we are known as an empire, that our independence is acknowledged, that our power can be regarded, or our credit supported among foreign nations. The treaties of the European powers with the United States of America, will have no validity on a dissolution of the union. We shall be left nearly in a state of nature, or we may find, by our own unhappy experience, that there is a natural and necessary progression from the extreme of anarchy to the extreme of tyranny; and that arbitrary power is most easily established on the ruins of liberty abused to licentiousness.

"As to the second article, which respects the performance of public justice, congress have in their late address to the United States, almost exhausted the subject. They have explained their ideas so fully, and have enforced the obligations the states are under, to render complete justice to all the public creditors, with so much dignity and energy, that in my opinion, no real friend to the honour and independency of America, can hesitate a single moment respecting the propriety of complying with the just and honourable measures proposed. If their arguments do not produce conviction, I know of nothing that will have greater influence; especially when we recollect that the system referred to, being the result of the collected wisdom of the continent, must be esteemed, if not perfect, certainly the least objectionable of any that could be devised; and that if it should not be carried into immediate execution, a national bankruptcy, with all its deplorable consequences, will take place before any different plan can possibly be proposed and adopted. So pressing are the present circumstances, and such is the alternative now offered to the states.

"The ability of the country to discharge the debts which have been incurred in its defence is not to be doubted; an inclination I flatter myself will not be wanting. The path of our duty is plain before us—honesty will be found, on every experiment, to be the best and only true policy. Let us then as a nation, be just; let us fulfil the public contracts which congress had undoubtedly a right to make, for the purpose of carrying on the war, with the same good faith we suppose ourselves bound to perform our private engagements. In the mean time, let an attention to the cheerful performance of their proper business as individuals, and as members of society, be earnestly inculcated on the citizens of America. Then will they strengthen the hands of government, and be happy under its protection. Every one will reap the fruit of his labours; every one will enjoy his own acquisitions, without molestation, and without danger.

"In this state of absolute freedom and perfect security, who will grudge to yield a very little of his property to support the common interest of society, and insure the protection of government? Who does not remember the frequent declarations, at the commencement of the war, that we should be completely satisfied, if at the expense of one half, we could defend the remainder of our possessions? Where is the man to be found who wishes to remain indebted for the defence of his own person and property, to the exertions, the bravery, and the blood of others, without making one generous effort to repay the debt of honour and of gratitude? In what part of the continent shall we find any man or body of men, who would not blush to stand up and propose measures purposely calculated to rob the soldier of his stipend, and the public creditor of his due? And were it possible that such a flagrant instance of injustice could ever happen, would it not excite the general indignation, and tend to bring down upon the authors of such measures, the aggravated vengeance of heaven? If, after all, a spirit of disunion, or a temper of obstinacy and perverseness, should manifest itself in any of the states; if such an ungracious disposition should attempt to frustrate all the happy effects that might be expected to flow from the union; if there should be a refusal to comply with the requisitions for funds to discharge the annual interest of the public debts; and if that refusal should revive again all those jealousies, and produce all those evils, which are now happily removed; congress, who have in all their transactions, shown a great degree of magnanimity and justice, will stand justified in the sight of God and man; and the state alone which puts itself in opposition to the aggregate wisdom of the continent, and follows such mistaken and pernicious counsels, will be responsible for all the consequences.

"For my own part, conscious of having acted while a servant of the public, in the manner I conceived best suited to promote the real interests of my country; having, in consequence of my fixed belief, in some measure pledged myself to the army, that their country would finally do them complete and ample justice; and not wishing to conceal any instance of my official conduct from the eyes of the world; I have thought proper to transmit to your excellency the enclosed collection of papers, relative to the half pay and commutation granted by congress to the officers of the army. From these communications, my decided sentiments will be clearly comprehended, together with the conclusive reasons which induced me, at an early period, to recommend the adoption of the measure, in the most earnest and serious manner. As the proceedings of congress, the army, and myself, are open to all, and contain, in my opinion, sufficient information to remove the prejudices, and errors, which may have been entertained by any, I think it unnecessary to say any thing more than just to observe, that the resolutions of congress now alluded to, are undoubtedly as absolutely binding upon the United States, as the most solemn acts of confederation or legislation. As to the idea which I am informed, has in some instances prevailed, that the half pay and commutation are to be regarded merely in the odious light of a pension, it ought to be exploded for ever. That provision should be viewed as it really was, a reasonable compensation offered by congress, at a time when they had nothing else to give to the officers of the army, for services then to be performed. It was the only means to prevent a total dereliction of the service.—It was a part of their hire.—I may be allowed to say it was the price of their blood, and of your independence. It is therefore more than a common debt; it is a debt of honour. It can never be considered as a pension, or gratuity; nor be cancelled until it is fairly discharged.

"With regard to a distinction between officers and soldiers, it is sufficient that the uniform experience of every nation of the world, combined with your own, proves the utility and propriety of the discrimination. Rewards in proportion to the aids the public derives from them, are unquestionably due to all its servants. In some lines, the soldiers have perhaps generally had as ample a compensation for their services, by the large bounties which have been paid to them, as their officers will receive in the proposed commutation; in others, if besides the donation of lands, the payment of arrearages, of clothing and wages, (in which articles all the component parts of the army must be put upon the same footing,) we take into the estimate the bounties many of the soldiers have received, and the gratuity of one year's full pay which is promised to all, possibly their situation (every circumstance duly considered) will not be deemed less eligible than that of the officers. Should a further reward, however, be judged equitable, I will venture to assert, no one will enjoy greater satisfaction than myself, on seeing an exemption from taxes for a limited time, (which has been petitioned for in some instances,) or any other adequate immunity or compensation, granted to the brave defenders of their country's cause. But neither the adoption nor rejection of this proposition will in any manner affect, much less militate against, the act of congress, by which they have offered five years full pay, in lieu of the half pay for life, which had been before promised to the officers of the army.

"Before I conclude the subject of public justice, I can not omit to mention the obligations this country is under to that meritorious class of veteran non-commissioned officers and privates who have been discharged for inability, in consequence of the resolution of congress of the 23d April, 1782, on an annual pension for life. Their peculiar sufferings, their singular merits, and claims to that provision, need only be known, to interest all the feelings of humanity in their behalf. Nothing but a punctual payment of their annual allowance can rescue them from the most complicated misery, and nothing could be a more melancholy and distressing sight, than to behold those who have shed their blood or lost their limbs in the service of their country, without a shelter, without a friend, and without the means of obtaining any of the necessaries or comforts of life; compelled to beg their daily bread from door to door. Surfer me to recommend those of this description, belonging to your state, to the warmest patronage of your excellency and your legislature.

"It is necessary to say but a few words on the third topic which was proposed, and which regards particularly the defence of the republic, as there can be little doubt but congress will recommend a proper peace establishment for the United States, in which a due attention will be paid to the importance of placing the militia of the union upon a regular and respectable footing. If this should be the case, I would beg leave to urge the great advantage of it in the strongest terms. The militia of this country must be considered as the palladium of our security, and the first effectual resort in case of hostility. It is essential, therefore, that the same system should pervade the whole; that the formation and discipline of the militia of the continent should be absolutely uniform, and that the same species of arms, accoutrements, and military apparatus should be introduced in every part of the United States. No one who has not learned it from experience, can conceive the difficulty, expense, and confusion, which result from a contrary system, or the vague arrangements which have hitherto prevailed.

"If in treating of political points, a greater latitude than usual has been taken in the course of this address, the importance of the crisis, and magnitude of the objects in discussion, must be my apology. It is, however, neither my wish nor expectation, that the preceding observations should claim any regard, except so far as they shall appear to be dictated by a good intention, consonant to the immediate rules of justice, calculated to produce a liberal system of policy, and founded on whatever experience may have been acquired by a long and close attention to public business. Here I might speak with the more confidence, from my actual observations; and, if it would not swell this letter (already too prolix) beyond the bounds I had prescribed myself, I could demonstrate to every mind open to conviction, that in less time, and with much less expense than has been incurred, the war might have been brought to the same happy conclusion, if the resources of the continent could have been properly drawn forth; that the distresses and disappointments which have very often occurred, have, in too many instances, resulted more from a want of energy in the continental government, than a deficiency of means in the particular states: that the inefficacy of measures, arising from the want of an adequate authority in the supreme power, from a partial compliance with the requisitions of congress in some of the states, and from a failure of punctuality in others, while it tended to damp the zeal of those which were more willing to exert themselves, served also to accumulate the expenses of the war, and to frustrate the best concerted plans; and that the discouragement occasioned by the complicated difficulties and embarrassments in which our affairs were by this means involved, would have long ago produced the dissolution of any army less patient, less virtuous, and less persevering, than that which I have had the honour to command. But while I mention these things which are notorious facts, as the defects of our federal constitution, particularly in the prosecution of a war, I beg it may be understood, that as I have ever taken a pleasure in gratefully acknowledging the assistance and support I have derived from every class of citizens, so shall I always be happy to do justice to the unparalleled exertions of the individual states, on many interesting occasions.

"I have thus freely disclosed what I wished to make known before I surrendered up my public trust to those who committed it to me. The task is now accomplished. I now bid adieu to your excellency as the chief magistrate of your state; at the same time I bid a last farewell to the cares of office and all the employments of public life.

"It remains then to be my final and only request, that your excellency will communicate these sentiments to your legislature at their next meeting; and that they may be considered as the legacy of one who has ardently wished, on all occasions, to be useful to his country; and who, even in the shade of retirement, will not fail to implore the divine benediction upon it.

"I now make it my earnest prayer that God would have you, and the state over which you preside, in his holy protection, that he would incline the hearts of the citizens to cultivate a spirit of subordination and obedience to government; to entertain a brotherly affection and love for one another, for their fellow citizens of the United States at large, and particularly for their brethren who have served in the field, and finally, that he would most graciously be pleased to dispose us all to do justice, to love mercy, and to demean ourselves with that charity, humility, and pacific temper of mind, which were the characteristics of the Divine Author of our blessed religion; without an humble imitation of whose example in these things we can never hope to be a happy nation."

The impression made by this solemn and affecting admonition could not be surpassed. The circumstances under which it was given, added to the veneration with which it was received; and, like the counsel of a parent on whom the grave is about to close forever, it sunk deep into the hearts of all. But, like the counsels of a parent withdrawn from view, the advice was too soon forgotten, and the impression it had made was too soon effaced.

The recommendations of congress did not receive that prompt consideration which the public exigence demanded, nor did they meet that universal assent which was necessary to give them effect.

Not immediately perceiving that the error lay in a system which was unfit for use, the distinguished patriots of the revolution contemplated with increasing anxiety, the anti-American temper which displayed itself in almost every part of the union. The letters addressed to the late Commander-in-chief, by many of those who had borne a conspicuous part in the arduous struggle for independence, manifest the disappointment and chagrin occasioned by this temper. The venerable Trumbull, who had rendered great service to the cause of united America; who, like Washington, had supported the burden of office throughout a hazardous contest, and like Washington, had determined to withdraw from the cares of a public station when that contest should be terminated, in a letter communicating to his friend and compatriot the resolution he had taken, thus disclosed the fears which the dispositions manifested by many of his countrymen inspired. "The fruits of our peace and independence do not at present wear so promising an appearance as I had fondly painted to my mind. The prejudices, the jealousies, and turbulence of the people, at times, almost stagger my confidence in our political establishments; and almost occasion me to think that they will show themselves unworthy of the noble prize for which we have contended, and which, I had pleased myself with the hope, we were so near enjoying. But again, I check this rising impatience, and console myself under the present prospect with the consideration, that the same beneficent and wise Providence which has done so much for this country, will not eventually leave us to ruin our own happiness, to become the sport of chance, or the scoff of a once admiring world; but that great things are yet in store for this people, which time, and the wisdom of the Great Director will produce in its best season."

"It is indeed a pleasure," said General Washington in reply, "from the walks of private life to view in retrospect the difficulties through which we have waded, and the happy haven into which our ship has been brought. Is it possible after this that it should founder? will not the all wise and all powerful Director of human events preserve it? I think he will. He may, however, for some wise purpose of his own, suffer our indiscretions and folly to place our national character low in the political scale;—and this, unless more wisdom and less prejudice take the lead in our government, will most certainly happen."

That the imbecility of the federal government, the impotence of its requisitions, and the inattention of some of the states to its recommendations, would, in the estimation of the world, abase the American character, could scarcely be termed a prediction. That course of national degradation had already commenced.

As the system recommended to the states on the 18th of April, 1783, had been matured by the best wisdom in the federal councils, a compliance with it was the last hope of the government; and congress continued to urge its adoption on the several states. While its fate remain undecided, requisitions for the intermediate supply of the national demands were annually repeated, and were annually neglected. Happily, a loan had been negotiated in Holland by Mr. Adams, after the termination of the war, out of which the interest of the foreign debt had been partly paid; but that fund was exhausted, and the United States possessed no means of replacing it. Unable to pay the interest, they would, in the course of the succeeding year, be liable for the first instalment of the principal; and the humiliating circumstance was to be encountered of a total failure to comply with the most solemn engagements, unaccompanied with the prospect of being enabled to give assurances, that, at any future time, their situation would be more eligible. If the condition of the domestic creditors was not absolutely desperate, the prospect of obtaining satisfaction for their claims was so distant and uncertain, that their evidences of debt were transferred at an eighth, and even at a tenth of their nominal value. The distress consequent on this depreciation was great and afflicting. "The requisitions of congress for eight years past," say the committee in February, 1786, to whom the subject of the revenue had been referred, "have been so irregular in their operation, so uncertain in their collection, and so evidently unproductive, that a reliance on them in future as a source from whence moneys are to be drawn to discharge the engagements of the confederacy, definite as they are in time and amount, would be not less dishonourable to the understandings of those who entertain such confidence, than it would be dangerous to the welfare and peace of the union." Under public embarrassments which were daily increasing, it had become, it was said, "the duty of congress to declare most explicitly that the crisis *had* arrived, when the people of the United States, by whose will, and for whose benefit, the federal government was instituted, must decide whether they will support their rank as a nation, by maintaining the public faith at home and abroad, or whether, for want of a timely exertion in establishing a general revenue, and thereby giving strength to the confederacy, they will hazard not only the existence of the union, but of those great and invaluable privileges for which they have so arduously and so honourably contended."

The revenue system of the 18th of April, 1783, was again solemnly recommended to the consideration of the several states, and their unanimous and early accession to it was declared to be the only measure which could enable congress to preserve the public faith, and to avoid the fatal evils which will inevitably flow from "a violation of those principles of justice which are the only solid basis of the honour and prosperity of nations."

In framing this system, a revenue adequate to the funding of the whole national debt had been contemplated, and no part of it was to go into operation until the whole should be adopted. By suspending partial relief to the pressing necessities of the government, it was believed that complete relief would be the more certainly secured.

The enlightened and virtuous statesmen with whom that measure originated, thought it impossible that their countrymen would be so unmindful of the obligations of honour and of justice, or could so mistake their real interests, as to withhold their assent from the entire plan, if convinced that no partial compliance with it would be received. In the progress of the business, however, there was reason to believe that the impost might be conceded, but that the application for internal taxes would encounter difficulties not to be surmounted. In the impoverished state of the federal treasury, an incompetent revenue was preferred to no revenue; and it was deemed more adviseable to accept a partial compliance with the recommendations of congress, than, by inflexibly adhering to the integrity of the system, to lose the whole. The states therefore, were requested to enable congress, "to carry into effect that part which related to impost so soon as it should be acceded to." In the course of the year 1786, every state in the union had acted upon the recommendation, and, with the exception of New York, had granted the impost duty which had been required. New York had passed an act upon the subject; but, influenced by its jealousy of the federal government, had not vested in congress the power of collection, but had reserved to itself the sole right of levying the duties according to its own laws. Neither did the act permit the collectors to be made accountable to congress. To the state only were they amenable. In addition to these deviations from the plan recommended, New York had emitted bills of credit, which were liable to depreciation, and in them the duties were payable. As the failure on the part of this single state, suspended the operation of the grants made by all the others, the executive thereof was requested again to convene the legislature, in order to lay the subject once more before them. To a similar resolution Governor Clinton had already replied, that "he had not power to convene the legislature before the time fixed by law for their stated meeting, except on extraordinary occasions, and as the present business proposed for their consideration had already been repeatedly laid before them, and so recently as at their last session had received their determination, it could not come within that description." This second resolution was not more successful than that which preceded it, and thus was finally defeated the laborious and persevering effort made by the federal government to obtain from the states the means of preserving, in whole or in part, the faith of the nation. General Washington's letters of that period abound with passages showing the solicitude with which he watched the progress of this recommendation, and the chagrin with which he viewed the obstacles to its adoption. In a letter of October, 1785, he said, "the war, as you have very justly observed, has terminated most advantageously for America, and a fair field is presented to our view; but I confess to you freely, my dear sir, that I do not think we possess wisdom or justice enough to cultivate it properly. Illiberality, jealousy, and local policy, mix too much in our public councils, for the good government of the union. In a word, the confederation appears to me to be little more than a shadow without the substance; and congress a nugatory body, their ordinances being little attended to. To *me*, it is a solecism in politics:—indeed it is one of the most extraordinary things in nature, that we should confederate as a nation, and yet be afraid to give the rulers of that nation, who are the creatures of our own making, appointed for a limited and short duration, and who are amenable for every action, recallable at any moment, and subject to all the evils which they may be instrumental in producing,—sufficient powers to order and direct the affairs of the same. By such policy as this, the wheels of government are clogged, and our brightest prospects, and that high expectation which was entertained of us by the wondering world, are turned into astonishment; and from the high ground on which we stood, we are descending into the vale of confusion and darkness.

"That we have it in our power to become one of the most respectable nations upon earth, admits, in my humble opinion, of no doubt, if we would but pursue a wise, just, and liberal policy towards one another, and would keep good faith with the rest of the world:—that our resources are ample and increasing, none can deny; but while they are grudgingly applied, or not applied at all, we give a vital stab to public faith, and will sink in the eyes of Europe, into contempt."

CHAPTER IV.

Differences between Great Britain and the United States.... Mr. Adams appointed minister to Great Britain.... Discontents excited by the commercial regulations of Britain.... Parties in the United States.... The convention at Annapolis.... Virginia appoints deputies to a convention at Philadelphia.... General Washington chosen one of them.... Insurrection at Massachusetts.... Convention at Philadelphia.... A form of government submitted to the respective states, as ratified by eleven of them.... Correspondence of General Washington respecting the chief magistracy.... He is elected president.... Meeting of the first congress.

1783 to 1787

WHILE the friends of the national government were making these unavailing efforts to invest it with a revenue which might enable it to preserve the national faith, many causes concurred to prepare the public mind for some great and radical change in the political system of America.

Misunderstandings between Great Britain and the United States.

Scarcely had the war of the revolution terminated, when the United States and Great Britain reciprocally charged each other with violations of the treaty of peace. On the construction of that part of the seventh article which stipulates against the "destruction or carrying away of any negroes, or other property of the American inhabitants," a serious difference of opinion prevailed which could not be easily accommodated. As men seldom allow much weight to the reasoning of an adversary, the construction put upon that article by the cabinet of London was generally treated in America as a mere evasion; and the removal of the negroes who had joined the British army on the faith of a proclamation offering them freedom, was considered as a flagrant breach of faith. In addition to this circumstance, the troops of his Britannic Majesty still retained possession of the posts on the American side of the great lakes. As those posts gave their possessors a decided influence over the warlike tribes of Indians in their neighbourhood, this was a subject to which the United States were peculiarly sensible.

On the other hand, the United States were charged with infringing the fourth, fifth, and sixth articles, which contain agreements respecting the payment of debts, the confiscation of property, and prosecution of individuals for the part taken by them during the war.

On the 14th of January, 1784, the day on which the definitive articles were ratified, congress passed a resolution containing a recommendation in the words of the treaty, respecting confiscated property, which was transmitted without delay to the several states. They considered this resolution as merely formal; and contended that neither the American nor the British government expected from it any beneficial results. But other stipulations which are explicit, the performance of which was not to rest on the recommendation of the government, especially that respecting the payment of debts, were also neglected. These causes of mutual complaint being permitted to rankle for some time in the bosoms of both nations, produced a considerable degree of irritation. The British merchants had large credits in America. Those engaged in the colonial trade had been nearly ruined by the rupture between the two countries; and, without taking into the account the embarrassments in which the war had involved their debtors, they calculated, after the restoration of peace, on the prompt collection of the vast sums which were due to them. But the impediments to the recovery of debts were, in many instances, permitted to remain; and the dispositions manifested by those states in which they were chiefly due, did not authorize a belief that any favourable change of measures was about to take place. The complaints of the creditors were loud and incessant. They openly charged the American government with violating the most solemn obligations which public and private contract could create; and this charge affected the national character the more seriously, because the terms of the treaty were universally deemed highly advantageous to the United States. The recriminations on the part of individuals in America, were also uttered with the angry vehemence of men who believe themselves to be suffering unprovoked injuries. The negroes in possession of the British armies at the restoration of peace, belonged, in many cases, to actual debtors; and in all, to persons who required the labour of which they were thus deprived, to repair the multiplied losses produced by the war. To the detention of the posts on the lakes was ascribed the hostile temper manifested by the Indians; and thus, to the indignity of permitting a foreign power to maintain garrisons within the limits of the nation, were superadded the murders perpetrated by the savages, and the consequent difficulty of settling the fertile and vacant lands of the west.[28] On the north-eastern frontier too, the British were charged with making encroachments on the territory of the United States. On that side, the river St. Croix, from its source to its mouth in the bay of Passamaquoddy, is the boundary between the two nations. Three rivers of that name empty into the bay. The Americans claimed the most eastern, as the real St. Croix, while settlements were actually made under the authority of the government of Nova Scotia to the middle river, and the town of St. Andrews was established on its banks.

Mr. Adams appointed to negotiate with the British cabinet.

But the cause of most extensive disquiet was the rigorous commercial system pursued by Great Britain. While colonists, the Americans had carried on a free and gainful trade with the British West Indies. Those ports were closed against them as citizens of an independent state; and their accustomed intercourse with other parts of the empire also was interrupted by the navigation act. To explore new channels for the commerce of the nation was, in the actual state of things, opposed by obstacles which almost discouraged the attempt. On every side they met with rigorous and unlooked for restrictions. Their trade with the colonies of other powers, as well as with those of England, was prohibited; and in all the ports of Europe they encountered regulations which were extremely embarrassing. From the Mediterranean, they were excluded by the Barbary powers, whose hostility they had no force to subdue, and whose friendship they had no money to purchase. Thus, the characteristic enterprise of their merchants, which, in better times, has displayed their flag in every ocean, was then in a great measure restrained from exerting itself by the scantiness of their means. These commercial difficulties suggested the idea of compelling Great Britain to relax the rigour of her system, by opposing it with regulations equally restrictive; but to render success in such a conflict possible, it was necessary that the whole power of regulating commerce should reside in a single legislature. Few were so sanguine as to hope that thirteen independent governments, jealous of each other, could be induced to concur for a length of time, in measures capable of producing the desired effect. With many, therefore, the desire of counteracting a system which appeared to them so injurious, triumphed over their attachment to state sovereignty; and the converts to the opinion that congress ought to be empowered to regulate trade, were daily multiplied. Meanwhile, the United States were unremitting in their endeavours to form commercial treaties in Europe. Three commissioners had been appointed for that purpose; and at length, as the trade with England was peculiarly important, and the growing misunderstandings between the two countries threatened serious consequences should their adjustment be much longer delayed, Mr. John Adams was appointed minister plenipotentiary to the court of St. James. His endeavours to form a commercial treaty were not successful. His overtures were declined by the cabinet of London, because the government of the United States was unable to secure the observance of any general commercial regulations; and it was deemed unwise to enter into stipulations which could not be of reciprocal obligation. In fact, it is not probable that, had even this difficulty been surmounted, Britain could have been induced to grant advantages that would have been satisfactory to America. The latter expected great relaxations of the navigation act, and a free admission into the colonies of the former; and believed its commerce of sufficient importance to obtain these objects, if it could be regulated by a single legislature. The reflecting part of America did not require this additional evidence of the sacrifice which had been made of national interest on the altars of state jealousy, to demonstrate the defectiveness of the existing system. On the mind of no person had this impression been more strongly made, than on that of General Washington. His extensive correspondence bears ample testimony to the solicitude with which he contemplated the proceedings of the states on this interesting subject.

The opinion he sought to inculcate was, that the trade between the United States and Great Britain was equally important to each; and therefore, that a commercial intercourse between the two nations might be established on equal terms, if the political arrangements in America would enable its government to guard its interests; but without such arrangements, those interests could not be protected, and America must appear in a very contemptible point of view to those with whom she was endeavouring to form commercial treaties, without possessing the means of carrying them into effect:—who "must see and feel that the union, or the states individually are sovereign as best suits their purposes:—in a word, that we are one nation to day, and thirteen to-morrow. Who," he added, "will treat with us on such terms?"

About this time, General Washington received a long and affectionate letter from the Marquis de Lafayette, who had just returned from a tour through the north of Europe. In communicating the occurrences at the courts he had visited, and especially at that of Prussia, whose aged and distinguished monarch, uniting the acquirements of the scholar and the statesman with the most profound skill in the art of war, could confer either literary or military fame, he dwelt with enthusiasm on the plaudits which were universally bestowed on his military patron and paternal friend. "I wish," he added, "the other sentiments I have had occasion to discover with respect to America, were equally satisfactory with those that are personal to yourself. I need not say that the spirit, the firmness, with which the revolution was conducted, has excited universal admiration:—That every friend to the rights of mankind is an enthusiast for the principles on which those constitutions are built:—but I have often had the mortification to hear, that the want of powers in congress, of union between the states, of energy in their government, would make the confederation very insignificant. By their conduct in the revolution," he added, "the citizens of America have commanded the respect of the world; but it grieves me to think they will in a measure lose it, unless they strengthen the confederation, give congress power to regulate their trade, pay off their debt, or at least the interest of it, establish a well regulated militia, and, in a word, complete all those measures which you have recommended to them."

"Unhappily for us," said the general in reply, "though the reports you mention are greatly exaggerated, our conduct has laid the foundation for them. It is one of the evils of democratic governments, that the people, not always seeing, and frequently misled, must often feel before they act right. But evils of this nature seldom fail to work their own cure. It is to be lamented, nevertheless, that the remedies are so slow, and that those who wish to apply them seasonably, are not attended to before they suffer in person, in interest, and in reputation. I am not without hopes that matters will soon take a favourable turn in the federal constitution. The discerning part of the community have long since seen the necessity of giving adequate powers to congress for national purposes, and those of a different description must yield to it ere long."

Discontents of the Americans against the commercial regulations of Britain.

While the recommendation of the 30th of April, 1784, was before the states, many causes contributed to diffuse through the community such a general dissatisfaction with the existing state of things, as to prepare the way for some essential change in the American system. In the course of the long war which had been carried on in the bosom of their country, the people of the United States had been greatly impoverished. Their property had been seized for the support of both armies; and much of their labour had been drawn from agriculture for the performance of military service. The naval power of their enemy had almost annihilated their commerce; from which resulted the two-fold calamity, that imported commodities were enhanced to an enormous price, while those for exportation were reduced much below their ordinary value. The inevitable consequence was, that those consumable articles which habit had rendered necessary, were exhausted; and peace found the American people, not only destitute of the elegancies, and even of the conveniences of life, but also without the means of procuring them, otherwise than by anticipating the proceeds of future industry. On opening their ports, an immense quantity of foreign merchandise was introduced into the country, and they were tempted by the sudden cheapness of imported goods, and by their own wants, to purchase beyond their capacities for payment. Into this indiscretion, they were in some measure beguiled by their own sanguine calculations on the value which a free trade would bestow on the produce of their soil, and by a reliance on those evidences of the public debt which were in the hands of most of them. So extravagantly too did many estimate the temptation which equal liberty and vacant lands would hold out to emigrants from the old world, as to entertain the opinion that Europe was about to empty itself into America, and that the United States would derive from that source such an increase of population, as would enhance their lands to a price heretofore not even conjectured. Co-operating with the cause last mentioned, was the impression which had been made by paper money on public morals, and on public opinion. It had not escaped observation that every purchaser on credit, however excessive the price might apparently be, had not only been relieved by the depreciation, but had derived great gains from his contract. Speculating on a similar course of things, many individuals had made extensive purchases at high prices; and had thus contributed to continue for a time, the deception imposed on themselves by those who supposed that the revolution was a talisman, whose magic powers were capable of changing the nature of things. The delusive hopes created by these visionary calculations were soon dissipated, and a great proportion of the inhabitants found themselves involved in debts they were unable to discharge. One of the consequences resulting from this unprosperous state of things was a general discontent with the course of trade. It had commenced with the native merchants of the north, who found themselves incapable of contending in their own ports with foreigners; and was soon communicated to others. The gazettes of Boston contained some very animated and angry addresses, which produced resolutions for the government of the citizens of that town, applications to their state legislature, a petition to congress, and a circular letter to the merchants of the several sea-ports throughout the United States. After detailing the disadvantages under which the trade and navigation of America laboured, and expressing their confidence that the necessary powers to the federal government would be soon, if not already, delegated, the petition to congress thus concludes: "Impressed with these ideas, your petitioners beg leave to request of the very august body which they have now the honour to address, that the numerous impositions of the British, on the trade and exports of these states, may be forthwith contravened by similar expedients on our part: else may it please your excellency and honours, the commerce of this country, and of consequence its wealth, and perhaps the union itself, may become victims to the artifice of a nation whose arms have been in vain exerted to accomplish the ruin of America."

The merchants of the city of Philadelphia presented a memorial to the legislature of that state, in which, after lamenting it as a fundamental defect in the constitution that full and entire power over the commerce of the United States had not been originally vested in congress, "as no concern common to many could be conducted to a good end, but by a unity of councils;" they say, "hence it is that the intercourses of the states are liable to be perplexed and injured by various and discordant regulations, instead of that harmony of measures on which the particular, as well as general interests depend; productive of mutual disgusts, and alienation among the several members of the empire.

"But the more certain inconveniences foreseen and now experimentally felt, flow from the unequal footing this circumstance puts us on with other nations, and by which we stand in a very singular and disadvantageous situation; for while the whole of our trade is laid open to these nations, they are at liberty to limit us to such branches of theirs as interest or policy may dictate:—unrestrained by any apprehensions, as long as the power remains severally with the states, of being met and opposed by any consistent and effectual restrictions on our part."

This memorial prayed that the legislature would endeavour to procure from congress, a recommendation to the several states, to vest in that body the necessary powers over the commerce of the United States.

It was immediately taken into consideration, and resolutions were passed conforming to its prayer. Similar applications were made by other commercial towns.

From these proceedings, and from the general representations made by the American merchants, General Washington had augured the most happy effects.

In a letter to the Marquis de Lafayette, he thus expressed his hope of the consequences which would attend the efforts then making to enlarge the powers of congress. "However unimportant America may be considered at present, and however Britain may affect to despise her trade, there will assuredly come a day when this country will have some weight in the scale of empires."

But a concurrence of the states in granting to the general government the beneficial powers in question, was not so near being effected as was hoped by its friends. A resolution was moved in congress, recommending it to the several states to vest in that body full authority to regulate their commerce, both external and internal, and to impose such duties as might be necessary for that purpose. This power was to be fettered with several extraordinary limitations, which might render it more acceptable to the governments who were asked to bestow it, among which was a provision that the duties should be "collectible under the authority, and accrue to the use of the state in which the same should be made payable." Notwithstanding these restrictions, marking the keen sighted jealousy with which any diminution of state sovereignty was watched, this resolution encountered much opposition even in congress.

During these transactions, the public attention was called to another subject which served to impress still more powerfully on every reflecting mind, the necessity of enlarging the powers of the general government, were it only to give efficacy to those which in theory it already possessed.

The uneasiness occasioned by the infractions of the treaty of peace on the part of Great Britain, has been already noticed. To obtain its complete execution, constituted one of the objects for which Mr. Adams had been deputed to the court of St. James. A memorial presented by that minister in December, 1785, urging the complaints of America, and pressing for a full compliance with the treaty, was answered by an enumeration of the violations of that compact on the part of the United States. The Marquis of Carmarthen acknowledged explicitly the obligation created by the seventh article to withdraw the British garrisons from every post within the United States; but insisted that the obligation created by the fourth article, to remove every lawful impediment to the recovery of *bona fide* debts, was equally clear and explicit.

"The engagements entered into by a treaty ought," he said, "to be mutual, and equally binding on the respective contracting parties. It would, therefore, be the height of folly as well as injustice, to suppose one party alone obliged to a strict observance of the public faith, while the other might remain free to deviate from its own engagements as often as convenience might render such deviation necessary, though at the expense of its own credit and importance."

He concluded with the assurance, "that whenever America should manifest a real determination to fulfil her part of the treaty, Great Britain would not hesitate to prove her sincerity to co-operate in whatever points depended upon her, for carrying every article of it into real and complete effect."

This letter was accompanied by a statement of the infractions of the fourth article.

Copies of both documents were immediately transmitted by Mr. Adams to congress, by whom they were referred to Mr. Jay, the secretary for foreign affairs. The report of that upright minister did not, by contravening facts, affect to exculpate his country. "Some of the facts," said he in a letter to General Washington, written after permission to communicate the papers had been given, "are inaccurately stated and improperly coloured; but it is too true that the treaty has been violated. On such occasions, I think it better fairly to confess and correct errors, than attempt to deceive ourselves and others, by fallacious though plausible palliations and excuses.

"To oppose popular prejudices, to censure the proceedings and expose the impropriety of states, is an unpleasant task, but it must be done."[29]

That the United States might with reason be required to fulfil the treaty before they could entitle themselves to demand a strict performance of it on the part of Great Britain, was a position the propriety of which they were prevented from contesting by the miserably defective organization of the government. If their treaties were obligatory in theory, the inability of congress to enforce their execution had been demonstrated in practice. Restrained by this defect in the constitution from insisting that the evacuation of the western posts should precede the removal of the impediments to the *bona fide* execution of the treaty on the part of America, government exerted its earnest endeavours to prevail on the several states to repeal all existing laws which might be repugnant to that compact. The resolutions which were passed on that subject, and the circular letters which accompanied them to the several governors, contain arguments which ought to have demonstrated to all, the constitutional obligation of a treaty negotiated under the authority of congress, and the real policy, as well as the moral duty of faithfully executing that which had been formed with Great Britain. To the deep mortification of those who respected the character of the nation, these earnest representations did not produce the effect which was expected from them. "It was impolitic and unfortunate, if not unjust in these states," said General Washington to a member of congress by whom the objectionable conduct of America was first intimated to him, "to pass laws which by fair construction might be considered as infractions of the treaty of peace. It is good policy at all times to place one's adversary in the wrong. Had we observed good faith, and the western posts had been withheld from us by Great Britain, we might have appealed to God and man for justice."

"What a misfortune it is," said he in reply to the secretary for foreign affairs, "that the British should have so well grounded a pretext for their palpable infractions, and what a disgraceful part, out of the choice of difficulties before us, are we to act!"

Rise of parties in the United States.

The discontents arising from the embarrassments in which individuals were involved, continued to increase. At length, two great parties were formed in every state, which were distinctly marked, and which pursued distinct objects, with systematic arrangement.

The one struggled with unabated zeal for the exact observance of public and private engagements. By those belonging to it, the faith of a nation, or of a private man was deemed a sacred pledge, the violation of which was equally forbidden by the principles of moral justice, and of sound policy. The distresses of individuals were, they thought, to be alleviated only by industry and frugality, not by a relaxation of the laws, or by a sacrifice of the rights of others. They were consequently the uniform friends of a regular administration of justice, and of a vigorous course of taxation which would enable the state to comply with its engagements. By a natural association of ideas, they were also, with very few exceptions, in favour of enlarging the powers of the federal government, and of enabling it to protect the dignity and character of the nation abroad, and its interests at home.

The other party marked out for themselves a more indulgent course. Viewing with extreme tenderness the case of the debtor, their efforts were unceasingly directed to his relief. To exact a faithful compliance with contracts was, in their opinion, a harsh measure which the people would not bear. They were uniformly in favour of relaxing the administration of justice, of affording facilities for the payment of debts, or of suspending their collection, and of remitting taxes. The same course of opinion led them to resist every attempt to transfer from their own hands into those of congress, powers, which by others were deemed essential to the preservation of the union. In many of these states, the party last mentioned, constituted a decided majority of the people; and in all of them, it was very powerful. The emission of paper money, the delay of legal proceedings, and the suspension of the collection of taxes, were the fruits of their rule wherever they were completely predominant. Even where they failed to carry their measures, their strength was such as to encourage the hope of succeeding in a future attempt; and annual elections held forth to them the prospect of speedily repairing the loss of a favourite question. Throughout the union, the contest between these parties was periodically revived; and the public mind was perpetually agitated with hopes and fears on subjects which essentially affected the fortunes of a considerable proportion of the society.

These contests were the more animated, because, in the state governments generally, no principle had been introduced which could resist the wild projects of the moment, give the people an opportunity to reflect, and allow the good sense of the nation time for exertion. This uncertainty with respect to measures of great importance to every member of the community, this instability in principles which ought, if possible, to be rendered immutable, produced a long train of ills; and is seriously believed to have been among the operating causes of those pecuniary embarrassments, which, at that time, were so general as to influence the legislation of almost every state in the union. Its direct consequence was the loss of confidence in the government, and in individuals. This, so far as respected the government, was peculiarly discernible in the value of state debts.

The war having been conducted by nations in many respects independent of each other, the debts contracted in its prosecution were due, in part from the United States, and in part from the individual states who became immediately responsible to the creditors, retaining their claim against the government of the union for any balances which might appear to be due on a general settlement of accounts.

That the debt of the United States should have greatly depreciated will excite no surprise, when it is recollected that the government of the union possessed no funds, and, without the assent of jealous and independent sovereigns, could acquire none, to pay the accruing interest: but the depreciation of the debt due from those states which made an annual and adequate provision for the interest, can be ascribed only to a want of confidence in governments which were controlled by no fixed principles; and it is therefore not entirely unworthy of attention. In many of those states which had repelled every attempt to introduce into circulation a depreciated medium of commerce, or to defeat the annual provision of funds for the payment of the interest, the debt sunk in value to ten, five, and even less than four shillings in the pound. However unexceptionable might be the conduct of the existing legislature, the hazard from those which were to follow was too great to be encountered without an immense premium. In private transactions, an astonishing degree of distrust also prevailed. The bonds of men whose ability to pay their debts was unquestionable, could not be negotiated but at a discount of thirty, forty, and fifty *per centum.* real property was scarcely vendible; and sales of any article for ready money could be made only at a ruinous loss. The prospect of extricating the country from these embarrassments was by no means flattering. Whilst every thing else fluctuated, some of the causes which produced this calamitous state of things were permanent. The hope and fear still remained, that the debtor party would obtain the victory at the elections; and instead of making the painful effort to obtain relief by industry and economy, many rested all their hopes on legislative interference. The mass of national labour, and of national wealth, was consequently diminished. In every quarter were found those who asserted it to be impossible for the people to pay their public or private debts; and in some instances, threats were uttered of suspending the administration of justice by violence.

By the enlightened friends of republican government, this gloomy state of things was viewed with deep chagrin. Many became apprehensive that those plans from which so much happiness to the human race had been anticipated, would produce only real misery; and would maintain but a short and a turbulent existence. Meanwhile, the wise and thinking part of the community, who could trace evils to their source, laboured unceasingly to inculcate opinions favourable to the incorporation of some principles into the political system, which might correct the obvious vices, without endangering the free spirit of the existing institutions.

While the advocates for union were exerting themselves to impress its necessity on the public mind, measures were taken in Virginia, which, though originating in different views, terminated in a proposition for a general convention to revise the state of the union.

To form a compact relative to the navigation of the rivers Potomac and Pocomoke, and of part of the bay of Chesapeake, commissioners were appointed by the legislatures of Virginia and Maryland, who assembled in Alexandria, in March, 1785. While at Mount Vernon on a visit, they agreed to propose to their respective governments, the appointment of other commissioners, with power to make conjoint arrangements, to which the assent of congress was to be solicited, for maintaining a naval force in the Chesapeake; and to establish a tariff of duties on imports, to which the laws of both states should conform. When these propositions received the assent of the legislature of Virginia, an additional resolution was passed, directing that which respected the duties on imports to be communicated to all the states in the union, who were invited to send deputies to the meeting.

On the 21st of January, 1786, a few days after the passage of these resolutions, another was adopted appointing certain commissioners,[30] "who were to meet such as might be appointed by the other states in the union, at a time and place to be agreed on, to take into consideration the trade of the United States; to examine the relative situation and trade of the said states; to consider how far a uniform system in their commercial relations may be necessary to their common interest, and their permanent harmony; and to report to the several states such an act relative to this great object, as, when unanimously ratified by them, will enable the United States in congress assembled effectually to provide for the same."

In the circular letter transmitting these resolutions to the respective states, Annapolis in Maryland was proposed as the place, and the ensuing September as the time of meeting.

Before the arrival of the period at which these commissioners were to assemble, the idea was carried by those who saw and deplored the complicated calamities which flowed from the intricacy of the general government, much further than was avowed by the resolution of Virginia. "Although," said one of the most conspicuous patriots[31] of the revolution, in a letter to General Washington, dated the 16th of March, 1786, "you have wisely retired from public employments, and calmly view from the temple of fame, the various exertions of that sovereignty and independence which Providence has enabled you to be so greatly and gloriously instrumental in securing to your country, yet I am persuaded you can not view them with the eye of an unconcerned spectator.

"Experience has pointed out errors in our national government which call for correction, and which threaten to blast the fruit we expected from our tree of liberty. The convention proposed by Virginia may do some good, and would perhaps do more, if it comprehended more objects. An opinion begins to prevail that a general convention for revising the articles of confederation would be expedient. Whether the people are yet ripe for such a measure, or whether the system proposed to be attained by it is only to be expected from calamity and commotion, is difficult to ascertain.

"I think we are in a delicate situation, and a variety of considerations and circumstances give me uneasiness. It is in contemplation to take measures for forming a general convention. The plan is not matured. If it should be well connected and take effect, I am fervent in my wishes that it may comport with the line of life you have marked out for yourself, to favour your country with your counsels on such an important and *single* occasion. I suggest this merely as a hint for consideration."

In the moment of tranquillity, and of real or imaginary security, the mind delights to retrace the intricate path by which this point of repose has been attained. The patriots who accomplished that great revolution which has given to the American people a national government capable of maintaining the union of the states, and of preserving republican liberty, must be gratified with the review of that arduous and doubtful struggle, which terminated in the triumph of human reason, and the establishment of that government. Even to him who was not an actor in the busy scene, who enjoys the fruits of the labour without participating in the toils or the fears of the patriots who have preceded him, the sentiments entertained by the most enlightened and virtuous of America at the eventful period between the restoration of peace and the adoption of our present free and effective constitution, can not be uninteresting.

"Our affairs," said the same gentleman in a letter of the 27th of June, "seem to lead to some crisis, some revolution—something that I can not foresee or conjecture. I am uneasy and apprehensive, more so than during the war. *Then*, we had a fixed object, and though the means and time of obtaining it were often problematical, yet I did firmly believe that we should ultimately succeed, because I did firmly believe that justice was with us. The case is now altered; we are going, and doing wrong, and therefore I look forward to evils and calamities, but without being able to guess at the instrument, nature, or measure of them.

"That we shall again recover, and things again go well, I have no doubt. Such a variety of circumstances would not, almost miraculously, have combined to liberate and make us a nation, for transient and unimportant purposes. I therefore believe we are yet to become a great and respectable people—but when or how, only the spirit of prophecy can discern.

"There doubtless is much reason to think and to say that we are wofully, and, in many instances, wickedly misled. Private rage for property suppresses public considerations, and personal rather than national interests have become the great objects of attention. Representative bodies will ever be faithful copies of their originals, and generally exhibit a chequered assemblage of virtue and vice, of abilities and weakness. The mass of men are neither wise nor good, and the virtue, like the other resources of a country, can only be drawn to a point by strong circumstances, ably managed, or strong governments, ably administered. New governments have not the aid of habit and hereditary respect, and being generally the result of preceding tumult and confusion, do not immediately acquire stability or strength. Besides, in times of commotion, some men will gain confidence and importance who merit neither; and who, like political mountebanks, are less solicitous about the health of the credulous crowd, than about making the most of their nostrums and prescriptions.

"What I most fear is, that the better kind of people (by which I mean the people who are orderly and industrious, who are content with their situations, and not uneasy in their circumstances) will be led by the insecurity of property, the loss of confidence in their rulers, and the want of public faith and rectitude, to consider the charms of liberty as imaginary and delusive. A state of uncertainty and fluctuation must disgust and alarm such men, and prepare their minds for almost any change that may promise them quiet and security."

To this interesting letter, General Washington made the following reply: "Your sentiments that our affairs are drawing rapidly to a crisis, accord with my own. What the event will be is also beyond the reach of my foresight. We have errors to correct; we have probably had too good an opinion of human nature in forming our confederation. Experience has taught us that men will not adopt and carry into execution measures the best calculated for their own good, without the intervention of coercive power. I do not conceive we can exist long as a nation, without lodging somewhere a power which will pervade the whole union in as energetic a manner, as the authority of the state governments extends over the several states. To be fearful of investing congress, constituted as that body is, with ample authorities for national purposes, appears to me the very climax of popular absurdity and madness. Could congress exert them for the detriment of the people, without injuring themselves in an equal or greater proportion? Are not their interests inseparably connected with those of their constituents? By the rotation of appointment, must they not mingle frequently with the mass of citizens? Is it not rather to be apprehended, if they were possessed of the powers before described, that the individual members would be induced to use them, on many occasions, very timidly and inefficaciously, for fear of losing their popularity and future election? We must take human nature as we find it: perfection falls not to the share of mortals. Many are of opinion that congress have too frequently made use of the suppliant humble tone of requisition in applications to the states, when they had a right to assert their imperial dignity, and command obedience. Be that as it may, requisitions are a perfect nullity, where thirteen sovereign, independent, disunited states, are in the habit of discussing, and refusing or complying with them at their option. Requisitions are actually little better than a jest and a bye-word throughout the land. If you tell the legislatures they have violated the treaty of peace, and invaded the prerogatives of the confederacy, they will laugh in your face. What then is to be done? Things can not go on in the same train for ever. It is much to be feared, as you observe, that the better kind of people, being disgusted with these circumstances, will have their minds prepared for any revolution whatever. We are apt to run from one extreme into another. To anticipate and prevent disastrous contingencies, would be the part of wisdom and patriotism.

"What astonishing changes a few years are capable of producing! I am told that even respectable characters speak of a monarchical form of government without horror. From thinking, proceeds speaking, thence to acting is often but a single step. But how irrevocable and tremendous! what a triumph for our enemies to verify their predictions!—what a triumph for the advocates of despotism to find that we are incapable of governing ourselves, and that systems founded on the basis of equal liberty are merely ideal and fallacious! Would to God that wise measures may be taken in time to avert the consequences we have but too much reason to apprehend.

"Retired as I am from the world, I frankly acknowledge I can not feel myself an unconcerned spectator. Yet having happily assisted in bringing the ship into port, and having been fairly discharged, it is not my business to embark again on a sea of troubles.

"Nor could it be expected that my sentiments and opinions would have much weight on the minds of my countrymen.—They have been neglected, though given as a last legacy in the most solemn manner.—I had then perhaps some claims to public attention.—I consider myself as having none at present."

The convention at Annapolis.

The convention at Annapolis was attended by commissioners from only six states.[32] These, after appointing Mr. Dickinson their chairman, proceeded to discuss the objects for which they had convened. Perceiving that more ample powers would be required to effect the beneficial purposes which they contemplated, and hoping to procure a representation from a greater number of states, the convention determined to rise without coming to any specific resolutions on the particular subject which had been referred to them. Previous to their adjournment, however, they agreed on a report to be made to their respective states, in which they represented the necessity of extending the revision of the federal system to all its defects, and recommended that deputies for that purpose be appointed by the several legislatures, to meet in convention in the city of Philadelphia, on the second day of the ensuing May.

The reasons for preferring a convention to a discussion of this subject in congress were stated to be, "that in the latter body, it might be too much interrupted by the ordinary business before them, and would, besides, be deprived of the valuable counsels of sundry individuals who were disqualified by the constitution or laws of particular states, or by peculiar circumstances, from a seat in that assembly."

A copy of this report was transmitted to congress in a letter from the chairman, stating the inefficacy of the federal government, and the necessity of devising such further provisions as would render it adequate to the exigencies of the union.

Virginia appoints deputies to meet those of other states at Philadelphia for the purpose of revising the federal system.

On receiving this report, the legislature of Virginia passed an act for the appointment of deputies to meet such as might be appointed by other states; to assemble in convention at Philadelphia, at the time, and for the purposes, specified in the recommendation from the convention which had met at Annapolis.

In communicating this act to General Washington, its principal advocate[33] thus intimated the intention of aiding it by the influence and character of the chief of the revolution. "It has been thought adviseable to give the subject a very solemn dress, and all the weight which could be derived from a single state. This idea will also be pursued in the selection of characters to represent Virginia in the federal convention. You will infer our earnestness on this point, from the liberty which will be used of placing your name at the head of them. How far this liberty may correspond with the ideas by which you ought to be governed, will be best decided where it must ultimately be decided. In every event it will assist powerfully in marking the zeal of our legislature, and its opinion of the magnitude of the occasion."

"Although," said the general in reply, "I have bid a public adieu to the public walks of life, and had resolved never more to tread that theatre; yet, if upon an occasion so interesting to the well being of the confederacy, it had been the wish of the assembly that I should be an associate in the business of revising the federal system, I should from a sense of the obligation I am under for repeated proofs of confidence in me, more than from any opinion I could entertain of my usefulness, have obeyed its call; but it is now out of my power to do this with any degree of consistency—the cause I will mention.

"I presume you heard, sir, that I was first appointed, and have since been rechosen president of the society of the Cincinnati; and you may have understood also, that the triennial general meeting of this body is to be held in Philadelphia the first Monday in May next. Some particular reasons combining with the peculiar situation of my private concerns, the necessity of paying attention to them, a wish for retirement and relaxation from public cares, and rheumatic pains which I begin to feel very sensibly, induced me, on the 31st ultimo, to address a circular letter to each state society, informing them of my intention not to be at the next meeting, and of my desire not to be rechosen president. The vice-president is also informed of this, that the business of the society may not be impeded by my absence. Under these circumstances, it will readily be perceived that I could not appear at the same time and place on any other occasion, without giving offence to a very respectable and deserving part of the community—the late officers of the American army."

Washington chosen one of them.

Notwithstanding this letter, the name of General Washington was not withdrawn, and he was unanimously chosen a member of the convention. On receiving private information of this appointment, he addressed a second letter to his confidential friend, in which he detailed more at large, the motives which induced him to decline a service, the importance of which he felt sensibly, and which he would willingly have undertaken but for the peculiar circumstances which were stated.

His name, however, was continued in the appointment. The gloomy aspect of affairs in the north rendered this the more necessary, and it was thus explained by his correspondent. "I have considered well the circumstances which it (your letter) confidentially discloses, as well as those contained in your preceding favour. The difficulties which they oppose to an acceptance of the appointment in which you are included, can as little be denied, as they can fail to be regretted. But I still am inclined to think, that the posture of our affairs, if it should continue, would prevent any criticism on the situation which the contemporary meetings would place you in; and wish that at least a door could be kept open for your acceptance hereafter, in case the gathering clouds should become so dark and menacing as to supersede every consideration but that of our national existence or safety. A suspense of your ultimate determination would be nowise inconvenient in a public view, as the executive are authorized to fill vacancies, and can fill them at any time; and in any event, three out of seven deputies are authorized to represent the state. How far it may be admissible in another view, will depend perhaps in some measure on the chance of your finally undertaking the service, but principally on the correspondence which is now passing on the subject, between yourself and the governor."

The governor of Virginia,[34] who was himself also elected to the convention, transmitted to General Washington the act, and the vote of the assembly in the following letter. "By the enclosed act you will readily discover that the assembly are alarmed at the storms which threaten the United States. What our enemies have foretold seems to be hastening to its accomplishment, and can not be frustrated but by an instantaneous, zealous, and steady union among the friends of the federal government. To you I need not press our present dangers. The inefficiency of congress you have often felt in your official character; the increasing languor of our associated republics you hourly see; and a dissolution would be, I know, to you, a source of the deepest mortification.

"I freely then entreat you to accept the unanimous appointment of the general assembly to the convention at Philadelphia. For the gloomy prospect still admits one ray of hope, that those who began, carried on, and consummated the revolution, can yet rescue America from the impending ruin."

"Sensible as I am," said the general in reply, "of the honour conferred on me by the general assembly of this commonwealth, in appointing me one of the deputies to a convention proposed to be held in the city of Philadelphia in May next, for the purpose of revising the federal constitution; and desirous as I am on all occasions of testifying a ready obedience to the calls of my country—yet, sir, there exist at this moment, circumstances which I am persuaded will render this fresh instance of confidence incompatible with other measures which I had previously adopted, and from which seeing little prospect of disengaging myself, it would be disingenuous not to express a wish that some other character, on whom greater reliance can be had, may be substituted in my place, the probability of my non-attendance being too great to continue my appointment.

"As no mind can be more deeply impressed than mine is with the critical situation of our affairs, resulting in a great measure from the want of efficient powers in the federal head, and due respect to its ordinances, so consequently those who do engage in the important business of removing these defects, will carry with them every good wish of mine, which the best dispositions towards their attainment can bestow."

The executive, unwilling to relinquish the advantages which the legislature had expected to derive from exhibiting the name of Washington at the head of the Virginia delegation, refused to consider him as having declined the appointment. That his judgment had not completely decided on the course which duty and patriotism required him to pursue; that in a crisis on which probably depended the union of the states, and the happiness of America, he refused himself reluctantly to the anxious wishes of his countrymen; were too apparent not to leave a hope that events might yet determine him to yield to their desires. He was therefore emphatically requested not to decide absolutely, and was informed that as no inconvenience would result from not appointing a successor, the option of complying with the earnest solicitations of those who considered the effort about to be made as the last hope of the union, would, as long as possible, be permitted to remain with him. In the mean time, those who persuaded themselves that much good might result from the proposed convention, continued to urge him with delicacy but with earnestness, not to withhold on this great and particular occasion, those inestimable services which the confidence so justly reposed by the public in his talents and character, enabled him alone to render.

Placed in these circumstances, General Washington weighed deliberately in his own mind the arguments for and against accepting the appointment which was so seriously pressed upon him. That the proposed convention was, in any point of view in which it could be contemplated, an object of the first magnitude, appeared to him to be undeniable. It was apparent that the actual government could not exist much longer without additional means. It was therefore necessary to meet the solemn question whether it ought to be supported or annihilated. Those who embraced the former part of the alternative must consider the convention as the only remaining experiment from which the federal government could derive powers sufficiently ample for its preservation. Those who embraced the latter, who thought that on a full and dispassionate revision of the system, its continuance would be adjudged impracticable or unwise, could not hesitate to admit that their opinion would derive great additional weight from the sanction of so respectable a body as that which was about to assemble: and that in such an event, it was greatly desirable, and would afford some security against civil discord, to put the public in possession of a plan prepared and digested by such high authority. "I must candidly confess," he added in a letter to Colonel Humphries, "as we could not remain quiet more than three or four years in time of peace, under the constitutions of our own choosing, which were believed in many states to have been formed with deliberation and wisdom, I see little prospect either of our agreeing on any other, or that we should remain long satisfied under it, if we could. Yet I would wish any thing and every thing essayed to prevent the effusion of blood, and to avert the humiliating and contemptible figure we are about to make in the annals of mankind!"

Earnestly as General Washington wished success to the experiment about to be made, he could not surrender his objections to the step its friends urged him to take, without the most serious consideration. In addition to that which grew out of his connexion with the Cincinnati, and to the reluctance with which he could permit himself to be drawn, on any occasion, into a political station, there were others which could not be disregarded. A convention, not originating in a recommendation of congress, was deemed by many an illegitimate meeting; and as the New England states had neglected the invitation to appear by their representatives at Annapolis, there was reason to apprehend they might be equally inattentive to the request now made them to assemble at Philadelphia. To appear in a public character, for a purpose not generally deemed of the utmost importance, would not only be unpleasant to himself, but might diminish his capacity to be useful on occasions which subsequent events might produce. "If," said he in a private letter to a military friend, "this second attempt to convene the states for the purposes proposed by the report of the partial representation at Annapolis in September, should also prove abortive, it may be considered as unequivocal evidence that the states are not likely to agree on any general measure which is to pervade the union, and of course, that there is an end of the federal government. The states which make this last dying essay to avoid this misfortune would be mortified at the issue, and their deputies would return home chagrined at their ill success and disappointment. This would be a disagreeable circumstance to any one of them, but more particularly to a person in my situation." His letters of consultation therefore, with a few confidential friends, also requested information respecting those points on which his own judgment might ultimately be formed. He was particularly desirous of knowing how the proposition made by Virginia was received in the other states, and what measures were taken to contravene, or to give it effect. He inquired too with the utmost solicitude how the members of the Cincinnati would receive his appearance in convention, after declining to be rechosen the president of that society.

The enlightened friends of the union and of republican government, generally regarded the convention as a measure which afforded the best chance for preserving liberty and internal peace. And those whose hopes predominated over their fears, were anxious to increase the probability of deriving from it every practicable good, by retaining on the list of its members, the most conspicuous name of which America could boast. But this opinion was not universal. Among those who felt the importance of the crisis, and who earnestly wished that a free government, competent to the preservation of the union, might be established, there were some who despaired of a favourable issue to the attempt, and who were therefore anxious to rescue their general from the increased mortification which would attend its failure, should he be personally engaged in it. They believed that all the states would not be represented in the convention. In a letter of the 20th of January, 1787, Colonel Humphries, who was himself under this impression, thus accounts for the omission of the federal men in the assembly of Connecticut, to press the appointment of deputies. "The reason," he said, "was a conviction that the persons who could be elected were some of the best anti-federal men in the state, who believed, or acted as if they believed, that the powers of congress were already too unlimited, and who would wish, apparently, to see the union dissolved. These demagogues," continued the letter, "really affect to persuade the people (to use their own phraseology) that they are only in danger of having their liberties stolen away by an artful designing aristocracy. But should the convention be formed under the most favourable auspices, and should the members be unanimous in recommending, in the most forcible, the most glowing, and the most pathetic terms which language can afford, that it is indispensable to the salvation of the country, congress should be clothed with more ample powers, the states," he thought, "would not all comply with the recommendation. They have a mortal reluctance to divest themselves of the smallest attribute of independent separate sovereignties." After assigning many reasons against accepting the appointment, this gentleman added: "the result of the convention may not perhaps be so important as is expected, in which case your character would be materially affected. Other people can work up the present scene. I know your personal influence and character is justly considered the last stake which America has to play. Should you not reserve yourself for the united call of a continent entire?

"If you should attend on this convention, and concur in recommending measures which should be generally adopted, but opposed in some parts of the union, it would doubtless be understood that you had in a degree pledged yourself for their execution. This would at once sweep you back inevitably into the tide of public affairs."

The same opinion was also intimated by another military friend[35] who had always possessed a large portion of the esteem and affection of his general. After stating the various and contradictory plans of government which were suggested by the schemers of the day, he added: "you will see by this sketch, my dear sir, how various are the opinions of men, and how difficult it will be to bring them to concur in any effective government. I am persuaded, if you were determined to attend the convention, and it should be generally known, it would induce the eastern states to send delegates to it. I should therefore be much obliged for information of your decision on this subject. At the same time, the principles of the purest and most respectful friendship induce me to say, that however strongly I wish for measures which would lead to national happiness and glory, yet I do not wish you to be concerned in any political operations, of which there are such various opinions. There may indeed arise

65

some solemn occasion, in which you may conceive it to be your duty again to exert your utmost talents to promote the happiness of your country. But this occasion must be of an unequivocal nature, in which the enlightened and virtuous citizens should generally concur."

While the confidential friends of General Washington were thus divided on the part which it behoved him to act, there was much reason to fear that a full representation of the states would not be obtained. Among those who were disinclined to a convention, were persons who were actuated by different, and even by opposite motives. There were probably some who believed that a higher toned[36] government than was compatible with the opinions generally prevailing among the friends of order, of real liberty, and of national character, was essential to the public safety. They believed that men would be conducted to that point only through the road of misery into which their follies would lead them, and that "times must be worse before they could be better." Many had sketched in their own minds a plan of government strongly resembling that which had been actually adopted, but despaired of seeing so rational a system accepted, or even recommended; "some gentlemen," said the correspondent last mentioned, "are apprehensive that a convention of the nature proposed to meet in May next, might devise some expedient to brace up the present defective confederation, so as just to serve to keep us together, while it would prevent those exertions for a national character which are essential to our happiness: that in this point of view it might be attended with the bad effect of assisting us to creep on in our present miserable condition, without a hope of a generous constitution, that should, at the same time, shield us from the effects of faction, and of despotism."[37] Many discountenanced the convention, because the mode of calling it was deemed irregular, and some objected to it, because it was not so constituted as to give authority to the plan which should be devised. But the great mass of opposition originated in a devotion to state sovereignty, and in hostility to any considerable augmentation of federal power.

The ultimate decision of the states on this interesting proposition seems to have been in no inconsiderable degree influenced by the commotions which about that time agitated all New England, and particularly Massachusetts.

Insurrection in Massachusetts.

Those causes of discontent which existed, after the restoration of peace, in every part of the union, were particularly operative in New England. The great exertions which had been made by those states in the course of the war, had accumulated a mass of debt, the taxes for the payment of which were the more burdensome, because their fisheries had become unproductive. The restlessness produced by the uneasy situation of individuals, connected with lax notions concerning public and private faith, and erroneous opinions which confound liberty with an exemption from legal control, produced a state of things which alarmed all reflecting men, and demonstrated to many the indispensable necessity of clothing government with powers sufficiently ample for the protection of the rights of the peaceable and quiet, from the invasions of the licentious and turbulent part of the community.

This disorderly spirit was cherished by unlicensed conventions, which, after voting their own constitutionality, and assuming the name of the people, arrayed themselves against the legislature, and detailed at great length the grievances by which they alleged themselves to be oppressed. Its hostility was principally directed against the compensation promised to the officers of the army, against taxes, and against the administration of justice: and the circulation of a depreciated currency was required, as a relief from the pressure of public and private burdens which had become, it was alleged, too heavy to be borne. Against lawyers and courts, the strongest resentments were manifested; and to such a dangerous extent were these dispositions indulged, that, in many instances, tumultuous assemblages of people arrested the course of law, and restrained the judges from proceeding in the execution of their duty. The ordinary recourse to the power of the country was found an insufficient protection, and the appeals made to reason were attended with no beneficial effect. The forbearance of the government was attributed to timidity rather than to moderation, and the spirit of insurrection appeared to be organized into a regular system for the suppression of courts.

In the bosom of Washington, these tumults excited attention and alarm. "For God's sake tell me," said he in a letter to Colonel Humphries, "what is the cause of all these commotions? Do they proceed from licentiousness, British influence disseminated by the tories, or real grievances which admit of redress? if the latter, why was redress delayed until the public mind had become so much agitated? if the former, why are not the powers of government tried at once? It is as well to be without, as not to exercise them. Commotions of this sort, like snow-balls, gather strength as they roll, if there is no opposition in the way to divide and crumble them."

"As to your question, my dear general," said Colonel Humphries in reply, "respecting the cause and origin of these commotions, I hardly find myself in condition to give a certain answer. If from all the information I have been able to obtain, I might be authorized to hazard an opinion, I should attribute them to all the three causes which you have suggested. In Massachusetts particularly, I believe there are a few real grievances; and also some wicked agents or emissaries who have been busy in magnifying the positive evils, and fomenting causeless jealousies and disturbances. But it rather appears to me, that there is a licentious spirit prevailing among many of the people; a levelling principle; a desire of change; and a wish to annihilate all debts, public and private." "It is indeed a fact," said General Knox, after returning from a visit to the eastern country, "that high taxes are the ostensible cause of the commotion, but that they are the real cause, is as far remote from truth, as light is from darkness. The people who are the insurgents have never paid any, or but very little taxes. But they see the weakness of government. They feel at once their own poverty compared with the opulent, and their own force; and they are determined to make use of the latter, in order to remedy the former. Their creed is, that the property of the United States has been protected from confiscation by the joint exertions of all, and therefore ought to be common to all. And he that attempts opposition to this creed is an enemy to equity and justice, and ought to be swept from the face of the earth."

The force of this party throughout New England was computed by General Knox at twelve or fifteen thousand men. "They were chiefly," he said, "of the young and active part of the community, who were more easily collected than kept together. Desperate and unprincipled, they would probably commit overt acts of treason which would compel them, for their own safety, to embody and submit to discipline. Thus would there be a formidable rebellion against reason, the principle of all government, and the very name of liberty. This dreadful situation," he added, "has alarmed every man of principle and property in New England. They start as from a dream, and ask—what has been the cause of our delusion? What is to afford us security against the violence of lawless men? Our government must be braced, changed, or altered, to secure our lives and our property. We imagined that the mildness of the government, and the virtue of the people were so correspondent, that we were not as other nations, requiring brutal force to support the laws. But we find that we are men, actual men, possessing all the turbulent passions belonging to that animal; and that we must have a government proper and adequate for him. Men of reflection and principle are determined to endeavour to establish a government which shall have the power to protect them in their lawful pursuits, and which will be efficient in cases of internal commotions, or foreign invasions. They mean that liberty shall be the basis, a liberty resulting from the equal and firm administration of the laws."

Deeply affected by these commotions, General Washington continued his anxious inquiries respecting the course they threatened to take. "I feel, my dear General Knox," said he, in answer to the letter from which the foregoing extracts are taken, "infinitely more than I can express to you, for the disorders which have arisen in these states. Good God! who besides a tory could have foreseen, or a Briton have predicted them? I do assure you that even at this moment, when I reflect upon the present aspect of our affairs, it seems to me like the visions of a dream. My mind can scarcely realize it as a thing in actual existence:—so strange, so wonderful does it appear to me. In this, as in most other matters, we are too slow. When this spirit first dawned, it might probably have been easily checked; but it is scarcely within the reach of human ken, at this moment, to say when, where, or how it will terminate. There are combustibles in every state, to which a spark might set fire.

"In bewailing, which I have often done with the keenest sorrow, the death of our much lamented friend General Greene,[38] I have accompanied my regrets of late with a query, whether he would not have preferred such an exit to the scenes which it is more than probable, many of his compatriots may live to bemoan."

Ostensibly, on account of the danger which threatened the frontiers, but, really, with a view to the situation of Massachusetts, congress had agreed to augment the military establishment to a legionary corps of two thousand and forty men, and had detached the secretary of war, General Knox, to that state, with directions to concert measures with its government for the safety of the arsenal at Springfield. So inauspicious was the aspect of affairs, as to inspire serious fears that the torch of civil discord, about to be lighted up in Massachusetts, would communicate its flame to all New England, and perhaps to the union. Colonel Lee, a member of congress, drew the following picture of the condition of the eastern country at that time. "General Knox has just returned, and his report, grounded on his own knowledge, is replete with melancholy information. A majority of the people of Massachusetts are in opposition to the government. Some of the leaders avow the subversion of it to be their object, together with the abolition of debts, the division of property, and a reunion with Great Britain. In all the eastern states, same temper prevails more or less, and will certainly break forth whenever the opportune moment may arrive. The malcontents are in close connexion with Vermont, and that district, it is believed, is in negotiation with the government of Canada. In one word, my dear general, we are all in dire apprehension that a beginning of anarchy with all its calamities is made, and we have no means to stop the dreadful work. Knowing your unbounded influence, and believing that your appearance among the seditious might bring them back to peace and reconciliation, individuals suggest the propriety of an invitation to you from congress to pay us a visit. This is only a surmise, and I take the liberty to mention it to you, that, should the conjuncture of affairs induce congress to make this request, you may have some previous time for reflection on it."

"The picture which you have exhibited," replied the general, "and the accounts which are published of the commotions and temper of numerous bodies in the eastern country, present a state of things equally to be lamented and deprecated. They exhibit a melancholy verification of what our transatlantic foes have predicted; and of another thing perhaps which is still more to be regretted, and is yet more unaccountable—that mankind when left to themselves are unfit for their own government. I am mortified beyond expression when I view the clouds which have spread over the brightest morn that ever dawned upon any country. In a word, I am lost in amazement when I behold what intrigue, the interested views of desperate characters, ignorance and jealousy of the minor part, are capable of effecting as a scourge on the major part of our fellow citizens of the union; for it is hardly to be supposed that the great body of the people, though they will not act, can be so short sighted or enveloped in darkness, as not to see rays of a distant sun through all this mist of intoxication and folly.

"You talk, my good sir, of employing influence to appease the present tumults in Massachusetts. I know not where that influence is to be found; nor if attainable, that it would be a proper remedy for these disorders. *Influence* is not *government*. Let us have a *government*, by which our lives, liberties, and properties will be secured; or let us know the worst at once. Under these impressions, my humble opinion is, that there is a call for decision. Know precisely what the insurgents aim at. If they have *real* grievances, redress them if possible; or acknowledge the justice of them, and your inability to do it in the present moment. If they have not, employ the force of the government against them at once. If this is inadequate, *all* will be convinced that the superstructure is bad, or wants support. To be more exposed in the eyes of the world, and more contemptible than we already are, is hardly possible. To delay one or the other of these expedients, is to exasperate on the one hand, or to give confidence on the other, and will add to their numbers; for like snow-balls, such bodies increase by every movement, unless there is something in the way to obstruct and crumble them before their weight is too great and irresistible.

"These are my sentiments. Precedents are dangerous things. Let the reins of government then be braced, and held with a steady hand; and every violation of the constitution be reprehended. If defective, let it be amended, but not suffered to be trampled upon while it has an existence."

In a letter written about the same period, Colonel Humphries, after stating his apprehensions that the insurgents would seize the continental magazine at Springfield, proceeded to add: "a general failure to comply with the requisitions of congress for money, seems to prognosticate that we are rapidly advancing to a crisis. The wheels of the great political machine can scarcely continue to move much longer, under their present embarrassment. Congress, I am told, are seriously alarmed, and hardly know which way to turn, or what to expect. Indeed, my dear general, nothing but a good Providence can extricate us from our present difficulties, and prevent some terrible conclusion.

"In case of civil discord I have already told you it was seriously my opinion that you could not remain neuter; and that you would be obliged in self defence, to take part on one side or the other, or withdraw from the continent. Your friends are of the same opinion; and I believe you are convinced that it is impossible to have more disinterested or zealous friends, than those who have been about your person."

"It is," said the general in reply, "with the deepest and most heartfelt concern, I perceive by some late paragraphs extracted from the Boston papers, that the insurgents of Massachusetts, far from being satisfied with the redress offered by their general court, are still acting in open violation of law and government, and have obliged the chief magistrate, in a decided tone, to call upon the militia of the state to support the constitution. What, gracious God, is man! that there should be such inconsistency and perfidiousness in his conduct. It is but the other day that we were shedding our blood to obtain the constitutions under which we now live—constitutions of our own choice and making—and now, we are unsheathing the sword to overturn them. The thing is so unaccountable, that I hardly know how to realize it; or to persuade myself that I am not under the illusion of a dream.

"My mind, previous to the receipt of your letter of the first ultimo, had often been agitated by a thought similar to the one you expressed respecting an old friend of yours: but heaven forbid that a crisis should come when he shall be driven to the necessity of making a choice of either of the alternatives there mentioned."

Finding that the lenient measures which had been taken by the legislature to reclaim the insurgents, only enlarged their demands; and that they were proceeding systematically to organize a military force for the subversion of the constitution; Governor Bowdoin determined, with the advice of council, on a vigorous exertion of all the powers he possessed, for the protection and defence of the commonwealth. Upwards of four thousand militia were ordered into service, and were placed under the command of the veteran General Lincoln. "His military reputation," says Mr. Minot, "and mildness of temper, rendered him doubly capacitated for so delicate and important a trust." But the public treasury did not afford the means of keeping this force in the field a single week; and, the legislature not being in session, the government was incapable of putting the troops in motion. This difficulty was removed by individual patriotism. From the commencement of the commotions, the citizens of Boston had manifested, unequivocally, their fidelity to the constitution. On this occasion, a number of gentlemen, preceded by the governor, subscribed, in a few hours, a sufficient sum to carry on the proposed expedition.

In the depth of winter, the troops from the eastern part of the state assembled near Boston, and marched towards the scene of action. Those from the western counties met in arms under General Shepard, and took possession of the arsenal at Springfield. Before the arrival of Lincoln, a party of the insurgents attempted to dislodge Shepard, but were repulsed with some loss. Not being pursued by that officer, who could not venture to weaken his post by detachments, they continued embodied, but did not venture again to undertake offensive operations.

Urging his march with the utmost celerity, Lincoln soon came up; and, pressing the insurgent army, endeavoured, by a succession of rapid movements, in which the ardour of his troops triumphed over the severity of the season, to disperse, or to bring it to action. Their generals retreated from post to post with a rapidity which for some time eluded his designs; and, rejecting every proposition to lay down their arms, used all their address to produce a suspension of hostilities until an accommodation might be negotiated with the legislature. "Applications were also made," says General Lincoln, "by committees and select men of the several towns in the counties of Worcester and Hampshire, praying that the effusion of blood might be avoided, while the real design of these applications was supposed to be, to stay our operations until a new court should be elected. They had no doubt, if they could keep up their influence until another choice of the legislature and of the executive, that matters might be moulded in general court to their wishes. To avoid this, was the duty of government." In answer to these applications, Lincoln exhorted those towns who sincerely wished to put an end to the rebellion without the effusion of blood, "to recall their men now in arms, and to aid in apprehending all abettors of those who should persist in their treason, and all who should yield them any comfort or supplies."

The army of government continued to brave the rigours of the climate, and to press the insurgents without intermission. At length, with the loss of a few killed, and several prisoners, the rebels were dispersed, their leaders driven out of the state, and this formidable and wicked rebellion was quelled.

The same love of country which had supported the officers and soldiers of the late army through a perilous war, still glowed in their bosoms; and the patriot veterans of the revolution, uninfected by the wide spreading contagion of the times, arranged themselves almost universally under the banners of the constitution and of the laws. This circumstance lessened the prejudices which had been excited against them as creditors of the public, and diminished the odium which, in the eastern states, especially, had been directed against the order of the Cincinnati. But the most important effect of this unprovoked rebellion was, a deep conviction of the necessity of enlarging the powers of the general government; and the consequent direction of the public mind towards the convention which was to assemble at Philadelphia.

In producing this effect, a resolution of congress had also considerable influence. New York had given her final *veto* to the impost system, and in doing so, had virtually decreed the dissolution of the existing government. The confederation was apparently expiring from mere debility. The last hope of its friends having been destroyed, the vital necessity of some measure which might prevent the separation of the integral parts of which the American empire was composed, became apparent even to those who had been unwilling to perceive it; and congress was restrained from giving its sanction to the proposed convention, only by an apprehension that their taking an interest in the measure would impede rather than promote it. From this embarrassment, the members of that body were relieved by the legislature of New York. A vote of that state, which passed in the senate by a majority of only one voice, instructed its delegation to move in congress, a resolution, recommending to the several states, to appoint deputies to meet in convention, for the purpose of revising and proposing amendments to the federal constitution. On the 21st of February, 1787, the day succeeding the instructions given by New York, the subject, which had been for some time under consideration, was finally acted upon: and it was declared, "in the opinion of congress, to be expedient that, on the second Monday in May next, a convention of delegates, who shall have been appointed by the several states, be held at Philadelphia, for the sole and express purpose of revising the articles of confederation, and reporting to congress and the several legislatures, such alterations and provisions therein, as shall, when agreed to in congress, and confirmed by the states, render the federal constitution adequate to the exigencies of government, and the preservation of the union."

This recommendation removed all objections to the regularity of the convention; and co-operated with the impressions made by the licentious and turbulent spirit which had lately endangered the peace and liberty of New England, to incline those states to favour the measure. By giving the proposed meeting a constitutional sanction, and by postponing it to a day subsequent to that on which the Cincinnati were to assemble, it also removed one impediment, and diminished another, to the attendance of General Washington as a member. He persuaded himself that by repairing to Philadelphia previous to the second Monday in May, in order to attend the general meeting of the Cincinnati, he should efface any impressions unfavourable to the attachment he felt to his military friends, which might otherwise be excited in their bosoms by his appearing in a public character, after declining the presidency of their society. The increasing probability that the convention would be

70

attended by a full representation of the states, and would propose a scheme of government which, if accepted, might conduce to the public happiness, and would not be unworthy of his character, had also its influence on his mind. An opinion too began to prevail, that the government must be invigorated by agreement or by force, and that a part of the opposition to the convention originated in a desire to establish a system of greater energy than could spring from consent. The idea that his refusing his aid in the present crisis might be attributed to a dereliction of republican principles, furnished additional motives for yielding to the wishes of his fellow citizens. On the 28th of March, he addressed a letter to the governor of Virginia, in which, after stating the reasons which had induced him to decline attending the convention, the influence of which he still felt, he added—"However, as my friends, with a degree of solicitude which is unusual, seem to wish for my attendance on this occasion, I have come to a resolution to go if my health will permit, provided from the lapse of time between your excellency's letter and this reply, the executive may not (the reverse of which would be highly pleasing to me) have turned their thoughts to some other character."

After communicating this determination to the executive of Virginia, he received a letter from the secretary of war, one of the small number of his friends who had endeavoured to dissuade him from the resolution he had ultimately taken, in which that officer avowed an entire change of opinion on this subject. "It is," said he, "the general wish that you should attend. It is conceived to be highly important to the success of the propositions which may be made by the convention.

"The mass of the people feel the inconvenience of the present government, and ardently wish for such alterations as would remedy them. These must be effected by reason and by agreement, or by force. The convention appears to be the only mean by which to effect them peaceably. If it should not be attended by a proper weight of wisdom and character to carry into execution its propositions, we are to look to events, and to force, for a remedy. Were you not then to attend the convention, slander and malice might suggest that force would be the most agreeable mode of reform to you. When civil commotion rages, no purity of character, no services, however exalted, can afford a secure shield from the shafts of calumny.

"On the other hand, the unbounded confidence the people have in your tried patriotism and wisdom, would exceedingly facilitate the adoption of any important alterations that might be proposed by a convention of which you were a member; and (as I before hinted) the president."

Convention at Philadelphia.

At the time and place appointed, the representatives of twelve states convened. In Rhode Island alone a spirit sufficiently hostile to every species of reform was found, to prevent the election of deputies on an occasion so generally deemed momentous. Having unanimously chosen General Washington for their president, the convention proceeded, with closed doors, to discuss the interesting and extensive subject submitted to their consideration.

On the great principles which should constitute the basis of their system, not much contrariety of opinion is understood to have prevailed. But on the various and intricate modifications of those principles, an equal degree of harmony was not to be expected. More than once, there was reason to fear that the rich harvest of national felicity, which had been anticipated from the ample stock of worth collected in convention, would all be blasted by the rising of that body without effecting the object for which it was formed. At length the high importance attached to union triumphed over local interests; and, on the 17th of September, that constitution which has been alike the theme of panegyric and invective, was presented to the American public.

The instrument with its accompanying resolutions was by the unanimous order of the convention, transmitted to congress in a letter subscribed by the president, in which it was said to be, "the result of a spirit of amity, and of that mutual deference and concession, which the peculiarity of their political situation rendered indispensable.

A form of government for the United States is submitted to the respective states, which is ratified by eleven of them.

"That it will meet the full and entire approbation of every state," continued the letter, "is not, perhaps, to be expected; but each will doubtless consider, that had her interests been alone consulted, the consequences might have been particularly disagreeable or injurious to others. That it is liable to as few exceptions as could reasonably have been expected, we hope and believe; that it may promote the lasting welfare of that country so dear to us all, and secure her freedom and happiness, is our most ardent wish."

Congress resolved unanimously, that the report with the letter accompanying it be transmitted to the several legislatures, in order to be submitted to a convention of delegates chosen in each state by the people thereof.

Neither the intrinsic merits of the constitution nor the imposing weight of character by which it was supported, gave assurance to its friends that it would be ultimately adopted. A comparison of the views and interests by which a powerful party was actuated, with particular provisions in the constitution which were especially designed to counteract those views and interests, prepared them to expect a mass of zealous and active opposition, against which the powers of reason would be in vain directed, because the real motives in which it originated would not be avowed. There were also many individuals, possessing great influence and respectable talents, who, from judgment, or from particular causes, seemed desirous of retaining the sovereignty of the states unimpaired, and of reducing the union to an alliance between independent nations. To these descriptions of persons, joined by those who supposed that an opposition of interests existed between different parts of the continent, was added a numerous class of honest men, many of whom possessed no inconsiderable share of intelligence, who could identify themselves perfectly with the state government, but who considered the government of the United States as in some respects foreign. The representation of their particular state not composing a majority of the national legislature, they could not consider that body as safely representing the people, and were disposed to measure out power to it with the same sparing hand with which they would confer it on persons not chosen by themselves, not accountable to them for its exercise, nor having any common interest with them. That power might be abused, was, to persons of this opinion, a conclusive argument against its being bestowed; and they seemed firmly persuaded that the cradle of the constitution would be the grave of republican liberty. The friends and the enemies of that instrument were stimulated to exertion by motives equally powerful; and, during the interval between its publication and adoption, every faculty of the mind was strained to secure its reception or rejection. The press teemed with the productions of temperate reason, of genius, and of passion; and it was apparent that each party believed power, sovereignty, liberty, peace, and security;—things most dear to the human heart;—to be staked on the question depending before the public. From that oblivion which is the common destiny of fugitive pieces, treating on subjects which agitate only for the moment, was rescued, by its peculiar merit, a series of essays which first appeared in the papers of New York. To expose the real circumstances of America, and the dangers which hung over the republic; to detect the numerous misrepresentations of the constitution; to refute the arguments of its opponents; and to confirm, and increase, its friends, by a full and able development of its principles; three gentlemen,[39] distinguished for their political experience, their talents, and their love of union, gave to the public a series of numbers which, collected in two volumes under the title of the FEDERALIST, will be read and admired when the controversy in which that valuable treatise on government originated, shall be no longer remembered.

To decide the interesting question which agitated a continent, the best talents of the several states were assembled in their respective conventions. So balanced were parties in some of them, that, even after the subject had been discussed for a considerable time, the fate of the constitution could scarcely be conjectured; and so small, in many instances, was the majority in its favour, as to afford strong ground for the opinion that, had the influence of character been removed, the intrinsic merits of the instrument would not have secured its adoption. Indeed, it is scarcely to be doubted that, in some of the adopting states, a majority of the people were in the opposition. In all of them, the numerous amendments which were proposed, demonstrate the reluctance with which the new government was accepted; and that a dread of dismemberment, not an approbation of the particular system under consideration, had induced an acquiescence in it. The interesting nature of the question, the equality of the parties, the animation produced inevitably by ardent debate, had a necessary tendency to embitter the dispositions of the vanquished, and to fix more deeply, in many bosoms, their prejudices against a plan of government, in opposition to which all their passions were enlisted.

1788

At length, the conventions of eleven states[40] assented to and ratified the constitution; and the preparatory measures were taken for bringing it into operation.

From the moment the public was possessed of this new arrangement of their political system, the attention of all was directed to General Washington as the first President of the United States. He alone was believed to fill so pre-eminent a station in the public opinion, that he might be placed at the head of the nation without exciting envy; and he alone possessed the confidence of the people in so unlimited a degree that under his auspices, the friends of the government might hope to see it introduced with a degree of firmness which would enable it to resist the open assaults, and secret plots of its numerous adversaries. By all who knew him, fears were entertained that his preference for private life would prevail over the wishes of the public; and, soon after the adoption of the constitution was ascertained, his correspondents began to press him on a point which was believed essential to the completion of the great work on which the grandeur and happiness of America was supposed to depend. "We can not," said Mr. Johnson, a gentleman of great political eminence in Maryland, "do without you, and I, and thousands more can explain to any body but yourself, why we can not do without you." "I have ever thought," said Mr. Gouverneur Morris, a gentleman who had been among the most valuable members of congress through great part of the war, and who had performed a most splendid part in the general convention, "and have ever said that you must be president; no other man can fill that office. No other man can draw forth the abilities of our country into the various departments of civil life. You alone can awe the insolence of opposing factions, and the greater insolence of assuming adherents. I say nothing of foreign powers, nor of their ministers. With these last you will have some plague. As to your feelings on this occasion, they are, I know, both deep and affecting; you embark property most precious on a most tempestuous ocean: for, as you possess the highest reputation, so you expose it to the perilous chance of popular opinion. On the other hand, you will, I firmly expect, enjoy the inexpressible felicity of contributing to the happiness of all your countrymen. You will become the father of more than three millions of children; and while your bosom glows with parental tenderness, in theirs, or at least in a majority of them, you will excite the duteous sentiments of filial affection. This, I repeat it, is what I firmly expect; and my views are not directed by that enthusiasm which your public character has impressed on the public mind. Enthusiasm is generally short sighted and too often blind. I form my conclusions from those talents and virtues which the world *believes*, and which your friends *know* you possess."

To those who attribute human action in every case to the motives which most usually guide the human mind, it will appear scarcely possible that the supreme magistracy could possess no charms for a man long accustomed to command others; and that ambition had no share in tempting the hero of the American revolution to tread once more the paths of public life. Yet, if his communications to friends to whom he unbosomed the inmost sentiments of his soul be inspected, it will be difficult to resist the conviction that the struggle produced by the occasion was unaffected, and that, in accepting the presidency of the United States, no private passion was gratified; but a decided preference for private life yielded to a sense of duty, and a deep conviction of his obligations to his country.

As this is an important æra in the life of Washington, and the motives by which he was actuated will assist in developing his real character, the American reader, at least, will be gratified at seeing copious extracts from his correspondence on this interesting occasion.

In a letter detailing those arrangements which were making for the introduction of the new government, Colonel Lee proceeded thus to speak of the presidency of the United States. "The solemnity of the moment, and its application to yourself, have fixed my mind in contemplations of a public and a personal nature, and I feel an involuntary impulse which I can not resist, to communicate without reserve to you some of the reflections which the hour has produced. Solicitous for our common happiness as a people, and convinced as I continue to be that our peace and prosperity depend on the proper improvement of the present period, my anxiety is extreme that the new government may have an auspicious beginning. To effect this, and to perpetuate a nation formed under your auspices, it is certain that again you will be called forth.

"The same principles of devotion to the good of mankind, which have invariably governed your conduct, will no doubt continue to rule your mind, however opposite their consequences may be to your repose and happiness. It may be wrong, but I can not suppress, in my wishes for national felicity, a due regard for your personal fame and content.

"If the same success should attend your efforts on this important occasion which has distinguished you hitherto, then, to be sure, you will have spent a life which Providence rarely if ever before gave to the lot of one man. It is my anxious hope, it is my belief, that this will be the case; but all things are uncertain, and perhaps nothing more so than political events." He then proceeded to state his apprehensions, that the government might sink under the active hostility of its foes, and in particular, the fears which he entertained from the circular letter of New York, around which the minorities in the several states might be expected to rally.

To counteract its baneful influence with the legislature of Virginia, he expressed his earnest wish, that Mr. Madison might be prevailed on to take a seat in that assembly, and then added,

"It would certainly be unpleasant to you, and obnoxious to all who feel for your just fame, to see you at the head of a trembling system. It is a sacrifice on your part unjustifiable in any point of view. But on the other hand no alternative seems to be presented.

"Without you, the government can have but little chance of success; and the people, of that happiness which its prosperity must yield."

1789

Letters from Gen. Washington respecting the chief magistracy of the new government.

In reply to this letter General Washington said, "Your observations on the solemnity of the crisis, and its application to myself, bring before me subjects of the most momentous and interesting nature. In our endeavours to establish a new general government, the contest, nationally considered, seems not to have been so much for glory, as existence. It was for a long time doubtful whether we were to survive as an independent republic, or decline from our federal dignity into insignificant and wretched fragments of empire. The adoption of the constitution so extensively, and with so liberal an acquiescence on the part of the minorities in general, promised the former; but lately, the circular letter of New York has manifested, in my apprehension, an unfavourable, if not an insidious tendency to a contrary policy. I still hope for the best; but before you mentioned it, I could not help fearing it would serve as a standard to which the disaffected might resort. It is now evidently the part of all honest men, who are friends to the new constitution, to endeavour to give it a chance to disclose its merits and defects, by carrying it fairly into effect, in the first instance.

"The principal topic of your letter, is to me a point of great delicacy indeed;— insomuch that I can scarcely, without some impropriety, touch upon it. In the first place, the event to which you allude may never happen, among other reasons, because, if the partiality of my fellow citizens conceive it to be a mean by which the sinews of the new government would be strengthened, it will of consequence be obnoxious to those who are in opposition to it, many of whom, unquestionably, will be placed among the electors.

"This consideration alone would supersede the expediency of announcing any definitive and irrevocable resolution. You are among the small number of those who know my invincible attachment to domestic life, and that my sincerest wish is to continue in the enjoyment of it solely, until my final hour. But the world would be neither so well instructed, nor so candidly disposed, as to believe me to be uninfluenced by sinister motives, in case any circumstance should render a deviation from the line of conduct I had prescribed for myself indispensable. Should the contingency you suggest take place, and (for argument sake alone, let me say) should my unfeigned reluctance to accept the office be overcome by a deference for the reasons and opinions of my friends; might I not, after the declarations I have made, (and heaven knows they were made in the sincerity of my heart,) in the judgment of the impartial world, and of posterity, be chargeable with levity and inconsistency, if not with rashness and ambition? Nay, farther, would there not even be some apparent foundation for the two former charges? Now, justice to myself, and tranquillity of conscience require that I should act a part, if not above imputation, at least capable of vindication. Nor will you conceive me to be too solicitous for reputation. Though I prize as I ought the good opinion of my fellow citizens, yet, if I know myself, I would not seek or retain popularity at the expense of one social duty, or moral virtue. While doing what my conscience informed me was right, as it respected my God, my country, and myself, I could despise all the party clamour and unjust censure which must be expected from some, whose personal enmity might be occasioned by their hostility to the government. I am conscious, that I fear alone to give any real occasion for obloquy, and that I do not dread to meet with unmerited reproach. And certain I am, whensoever I shall be convinced the good of my country requires my reputation to be put in risque, regard for my own fame will not come in competition with an object of so much magnitude.

"If I declined the task, it would be upon quite another principle. Notwithstanding my advanced season of life, my increasing fondness for agricultural amusements, and my growing love of retirement, augment and confirm my decided predilection for the character of a private citizen, yet it will be no one of these motives, nor the hazard to which my former reputation might be exposed, or the terror of encountering new fatigues and troubles, that would deter me from an acceptance;—but a belief that some other person, who had less pretence and less inclination to be excused, could execute all the duties full as satisfactorily as myself. To say more would be indiscreet; as a disclosure of a refusal before hand might incur the application of the fable, in which the fox is represented as undervaluing the grapes he could not reach. You will perceive, my dear sir, by what is here observed (and which you will be pleased to consider in the light of a confidential communication), that my inclinations will dispose and decide me to remain as I am, unless a clear and insurmountable conviction should be impressed on my mind, that some very disagreeable consequences must in all human probability result from the indulgence of my wishes."

About the same time, Colonel Hamilton concluded a letter on miscellaneous subjects with the following observations. "I take it for granted, sir, you have concluded to comply with what will, no doubt, be the general call of your country in relation to the new government. You will permit me to say that it is indispensable you should lend yourself to its first operations. It is to little purpose to have introduced a system, if the weightiest influence is not given to its firm establishment in the outset."

"On the delicate subject," said General Washington in reply, "with which you conclude your letter, I can say nothing; because the event alluded to may never happen; and because in case it should occur, it would be a point of prudence to defer forming one's ultimate and irrevocable decision, so long as new data might be afforded for one to act with the greater wisdom and propriety. I would not wish to conceal my prevailing sentiment from you. For you know me well enough, my good sir, to be persuaded that I am not guilty of affectation, when I tell you it is my great and sole desire to live and die in peace and retirement on my own farm. Were it even indispensable a different line of conduct should be adopted, while you and some others who are acquainted with my heart would *acquit*, the world and posterity might probably *accuse* me of *inconsistency* and *ambition*. Still I hope, I shall always possess firmness and virtue enough to maintain (what I consider the most enviable of all titles) the character of *an honest man*."

This answer drew from Colonel Hamilton the following reply: "I should be deeply pained, my dear sir, if your scruples in regard to a certain station should be matured into a resolution to decline it; though I am neither surprised at their existence, nor can I but agree in opinion that the caution you observe in deferring the ultimate determination is prudent. I have, however, reflected maturely on the subject, and have come to a conclusion (in which I feel no hesitation) that every public and personal consideration will demand from you an acquiescence in what will *certainly* be the unanimous wish of your country.

"The absolute retreat which you meditated at the close of the late war was natural and proper. Had the government produced by the revolution gone on in a *tolerable* train, it would have been most adviseable to have persisted in that retreat. But I am clearly of opinion that the crisis which brought you again into public view left you no alternative but to comply; and I am equally clear in the opinion that you are by that act *pledged* to take a part in the execution of the government. I am not less convinced that the impression of the necessity of your filling the station in question is so universal, that you run no risk of any uncandid imputation by submitting to it. But even if this were not the case, a regard to your own reputation, as well as to the public good, calls upon you in the strongest manner to run that risk.

"It can not be considered as a compliment to say, that on your acceptance of the office of president, the success of the new government in its commencement may materially depend. Your agency and influence will be not less important in preserving it from the future attacks of its enemies, than they have been in recommending it in the first instance to the adoption of the people. Independent of all considerations drawn from this source, the point of light in which you stand at home and abroad, will make an infinite difference in the respectability with which the government will begin its operations, in the alternative of your being or not being at the head of it. I forbear to mention considerations which might have a more personal application. What I have said will suffice for the inferences I mean to draw.

"First. In a matter so essential to the well being of society as the prosperity of a newly instituted government, a citizen of so much consequence as yourself to its success, has no option but to lend his services if called for. Permit me to say, it would be inglorious, in such a situation, not to hazard the glory, however great, which he might have previously acquired.

"Secondly. Your signature to the proposed system, pledges your judgment for its being such an one as upon the whole was worthy of the public approbation. If it should miscarry, (as men commonly decide from success or the want of it) the blame will in all probability be laid on the system itself. And the framers of it will have to encounter the disrepute of having brought about a revolution in government, without substituting any thing that was worthy of the effort; they pulled down one Utopia, it will be said, to build up another. This view of the subject, if I mistake not, my dear sir, will suggest to your mind greater hazard to that fame, which must be, and ought to be dear to you, in refusing your future aid to the system, than in affording it. I will only add, that in my estimate of the matter, that aid is indispensable.

"I have taken the liberty to express these sentiments, and to lay before you my view of the subject. I doubt not the considerations mentioned have fully occurred to you, and I trust, they will finally produce in your mind the same result which exists in mine. I flatter myself the frankness with which I have delivered myself, will not be displeasing to you. It has been prompted by motives which you would not disapprove."

In answer to this letter General Washington opened himself without reserve. "In acknowledging," said he, "the receipt of your candid and kind letter by the last post, little more is incumbent on me than to thank you sincerely for the frankness with which you communicated your sentiments, and to assure you that the same manly tone of intercourse will always be more than barely welcome,—indeed it will be highly acceptable to me.

"I am particularly glad, in the present instance, that you have dealt thus freely and like a friend. Although I could not help observing from several publications and letters that my name had been sometimes spoken of, and that it was possible the *contingency* which is the subject of your letter might happen, yet I thought it best to maintain a guarded silence, and to lack the counsel of my best friends (which I certainly hold in the highest estimation) rather than to hazard an imputation unfriendly to the delicacy of my feelings. For, situated as I am, I could hardly bring the question into the slightest discussion, or ask an opinion even in the most confidential manner, without betraying, in my judgment, some impropriety of conduct, or without feeling an apprehension that a premature display of anxiety, might be construed into a vain glorious desire of pushing myself into notice as a candidate. Now; if I am not grossly deceived in myself, I should unfeignedly rejoice, in case the electors, by giving their votes in favour of some other person, would save me from the dreadful dilemma of being forced to accept or refuse. If that may not be, I am in the next place, earnestly desirous of searching out the truth, and of knowing whether there does not exist a probability that the government would be just as happily and effectually carried into execution without my aid, as with it. I am *truly* solicitous to obtain all the previous information which the circumstances will afford, and to determine (when the determination can with propriety be no longer postponed) according to the principles of right reason, and the dictates of a clear conscience; without too great a reference to the unforeseen consequences which may affect my person or reputation. Until that period, I may fairly hold myself open to conviction, though I allow your sentiments to have weight in them; and I shall not pass by your arguments without giving them as dispassionate a consideration as I can possibly bestow upon them.

"In taking a survey of the subject, in whatever point of light I have been able to place it, I will not suppress the acknowledgment, my dear sir, that I have always felt a kind of gloom upon my mind, as often as I have been taught to expect I might, and perhaps must ere long be called to make a decision. You will, I am well assured, believe the assertion (though I have little expectation it would gain credit from those who are less acquainted with me) that if I should receive the appointment, and should be prevailed upon to accept it; the acceptance would be attended with more diffidence and reluctance, than ever I experienced before in my life. It would be, however, with a fixed and sole determination of lending whatever assistance might be in my power to promote the public weal, in hopes that at a convenient and an early period, my services might be dispensed with; and that I might be permitted once more to retire—to pass an unclouded evening after the stormy day of life, in the bosom of domestic tranquillity."

This correspondence was thus closed by Colonel Hamilton. "I feel a conviction that you will finally see your acceptance to be indispensable. It is no compliment to say that no other man can sufficiently unite the public opinion, or can give the requisite weight to the office, in the commencement of the government. These considerations appear to me of themselves decisive. I am not sure that your refusal would not throw every thing into confusion. I am sure that it would have the worst effect imaginable.

"Indeed, as I hinted in a former letter, I think circumstances leave no option."

Although this correspondence does not appear to have absolutely decided General Washington on the part he should embrace, it could not have been without its influence on his judgment, nor have failed to dispose him to yield to the wish of his country. "I would willingly," said he to his estimable friend General Lincoln, who had also pressed the subject on him, "pass over in silence that part of your letter, in which you mention the persons who are candidates for the two first offices in the executive, if I did not fear the omission might seem to betray a want of confidence. Motives of delicacy have prevented me hitherto from conversing or writing on this subject, whenever I could avoid it with decency. I may, however, with great sincerity, and I believe without offending against modesty or propriety, *say* to *you*, that I most heartily wish the choice to which you allude might not fall upon me: and that if it should, I must reserve to myself the right of making up my final decision, at the last moment, when it can be brought into one view, and when the expediency or inexpediency of a refusal can be more judiciously determined than at present. But be assured, my dear sir, if from any inducement I shall be persuaded ultimately to accept, it will not be (so far as I know my own heart) from any of a private or personal nature. Every personal consideration conspires, to rivet me (if I may use the expression) to retirement. At my time of life, and under my circumstances, nothing in this world can ever draw me from it, unless it be a *conviction* that the partiality of my countrymen had made my services absolutely necessary, joined to a *fear* that my refusal might induce a belief that I preferred the conservation of my own reputation and private ease, to the good of my country. After all, if I should conceive myself in a manner constrained to accept, I call heaven to witness, that this very act would be the greatest sacrifice of my personal feelings and wishes, that ever I have been called upon to make. It would be to forego repose and domestic enjoyment for trouble, perhaps for public obloquy: for I should consider myself as entering upon an unexplored field, enveloped on every side with clouds and darkness.

"From this embarrassing situation I had naturally supposed that my declarations at the close of the war would have saved me; and that my sincere intentions, then publicly made known, would have effectually precluded me forever afterwards from being looked upon as a candidate for any office. This hope, as a last anchor of worldly happiness in old age, I had still carefully preserved; until the public papers and private letters from my correspondents in almost every quarter, taught me to apprehend that I might soon be obliged to answer the question, whether I would go again into public life or not?"

"I can say little or nothing new," said he in a letter to the Marquis de Lafayette, "in consequence of the repetition of your opinion on the expediency there will be, for my accepting the office to which you refer. Your sentiments indeed coincide much more nearly with those of my other friends, than with my own feelings. In truth, my difficulties increase and magnify as I draw towards the period, when, according to the common belief, it will be necessary for me to give a definitive answer in one way or other. Should circumstances render it, in a manner, inevitably necessary to be in the affirmative, be assured, my dear sir, I shall assume the task with the most unfeigned reluctance, and with a real diffidence, for which I shall probably receive no credit from the world. If I know my own heart, nothing short of a conviction of duty will induce me again to take an active part in public affairs. And in that case, if I can form a plan for my own conduct, my endeavours shall be unremittingly exerted (even at the hazard of former fame or present popularity) to extricate my country from the embarrassments in which it is entangled through want of credit; and to establish a general system of policy, which, if pursued, will ensure permanent felicity to the commonwealth. I think I see a path, as clear and as direct as a ray of light, which leads to the attainment of that object. Nothing but harmony, honesty, industry, and frugality, are necessary to make us a great and happy people. Happily, the present posture of affairs, and the prevailing disposition of my countrymen, promise to co-operate in establishing those four great and essential pillars of public felicity."

The Room in Which the First Constitutional Convention Met in Philadelphia

Delegates from twelve of the thirteen States (Rhode Island alone being unrepresented) assembled at Philadelphia, where the opening sessions of the first Constitutional Convention were held in this room in Independence Hall, May 14, 1787. George Washington presided during the four months taken to draft the Constitution of the United States. When it was completed on September 17th, it is said that many of the delegates seemed awe-struck and that Washington himself sat with his head bowed in deep meditation. As the Convention adjourned, Franklin, who was then over eighty-one years of age, arose and pointing to the President's quaint armchair on the back of which was emblazoned a half sun, brilliant with gilded rays, observed: "As I have been sitting here all these weeks, I have often wondered whether yonder sun is rising or setting, but now I know that it is a rising sun."

He is unanimously elected president.

After the elections had taken place, a general persuasion prevailed that the public will, respecting the chief magistrate of the union, had been too unequivocally manifested not to be certainly obeyed; and several applications were made to General Washington for those offices in the respective states, which would be in the gift of the president of the United States.

As marking the frame of mind with which he came into the government, the following extract is given from one of the many letters written to persons whose pretensions he was disposed to favour. "Should it become absolutely necessary for me to occupy the station in which your letter presupposes me, I have determined to go into it, perfectly free from all engagements of every nature whatsoever.—A conduct in conformity to this resolution, would enable me, in balancing the various pretensions of different candidates for appointments, to act with a sole reference to justice and the public good. This is, in substance, the answer that I have given to all applications (and they are not few) which have already been made. Among the places sought after in these applications, I must not conceal that the office to which you particularly allude is comprehended. This fact I tell you merely as matter of information. My general manner of thinking, as to the propriety of holding myself totally disengaged, will apologize for my not enlarging farther on the subject.

"Though I am sensible that the public suffrage which places a man in office, should prevent him from being swayed, in the execution of it, by his private inclinations, yet he may assuredly, without violating his duty, be indulged in the continuance of his former attachments."

Meeting of the first congress.

The impotence of the late government, added to the dilatoriness inseparable from its perplexed mode of proceeding on the public business, and to its continued session, had produced among the members of congress such an habitual disregard of punctuality in their attendance on that body, that, although the new government was to commence its operations on the 4th of March, 1789, a house of representatives was not formed until the first, nor a senate until the 6th day of April.

At length, the votes for the president and vice president of the United States were opened and counted in the senate. Neither the animosity of parties, nor the preponderance of the enemies of the new government in some of the states, could deprive General Washington of a single vote. By the unanimous voice of an immense continent, he was called to the chief magistracy of the nation. The second number of votes was given to Mr. John Adams. George Washington and John Adams were therefore declared to be duly elected president and vice president of the United States, to serve for four years from the 4th of March, 1789.[41]

CHAPTER V.

The election of General Washington officially announced to him.... His departure for the seat of government.... Marks of affection shown him on his journey.... His inauguration and speech to Congress.... His system of intercourse with the world.... Letters on this and other subjects.... Answer of both houses of Congress to the speech.... Domestic and foreign relations of the United States.... Debates on the impost and tonnage bills.... On the power of removal from office.... On the policy of the secretary of the treasury reporting plans of revenue.... On the style of the President.... Amendments to the constitution.... Appointment of executive officers, and of the judges.... Adjournment of the first session of Congress.... The President visits New England.... His reception.... North Carolina accedes to the union.

1789
The election of General Washington officially announced to him.

THE election of General Washington to the office of chief magistrate of the United States, was announced to him at Mount Vernon on the 14th of April, 1789. Accustomed to respect the wishes of his fellow citizens, he did not think himself at liberty to decline an appointment conferred upon him by the suffrage of an entire people. His acceptance of it, and his expressions of gratitude for this fresh proof of the esteem and confidence of his country, were connected with declarations of diffidence in himself. "I wish," he said, "that there may not be reason for regretting the choice,—for indeed, all I can promise, is to accomplish that which can be done by an honest zeal."

His departure for the seat of government.

As the public business required the immediate attendance of the president at the seat of government, he hastened his departure; and, on the second day after receiving notice of his appointment, took leave of Mount Vernon.

In an entry made by himself in his diary, the feelings inspired by an occasion so affecting to his mind are thus described, "About ten o'clock I bade adieu to Mount Vernon, to private life, and to domestic felicity; and with a mind oppressed with more anxious and painful sensations than I have words to express, set out for New York in company with Mr. Thompson, and Colonel Humphries, with the best dispositions to render service to my country in obedience to its call, but with less hope of answering its expectations."

Marks of respect and affection shown him on his journey.

He was met by a number of gentlemen residing in Alexandria, and escorted to their city, where a public dinner had been prepared to which he was invited. The sentiments of veneration and affection which were felt by all classes of his fellow citizens for their patriot chief, were manifested by the most flattering marks of heartfelt respect; and by addresses which evinced the unlimited confidence reposed in his virtues and his talents. A place can not be given to these addresses: but that from the citizens of Alexandria derives such pretensions to particular notice from the recollection that it is to be considered as an effusion from the hearts of his neighbours and private friends, that its insertion may be pardoned. It is in the following words:

"Again your country commands your care. Obedient to its wishes, unmindful of your ease, we see you again relinquishing the bliss of retirement; and this too at a period of life, when nature itself seems to authorize a preference of repose!

"Not to extol your glory as a soldier; not to pour forth our gratitude for past services; not to acknowledge the justice of the unexampled honour which has been conferred upon you by the spontaneous and unanimous suffrages of three millions of freemen, in your election to the supreme magistracy; nor to admire the patriotism which directs your conduct, do your neighbours and friends now address you. Themes less splendid but more endearing, impress our minds. The first and best of citizens must leave us: our aged must lose their ornament; our youth their model; our agriculture its improver; our commerce its friend; our infant academy its protector; our poor their benefactor; and the interior navigation of the Potomac (an event replete with the most extensive utility, already, by your unremitted exertions, brought into partial use) its institutor and promoter.

"Farewell!—go! and make a grateful people happy, a people, who will be doubly grateful when they contemplate this recent sacrifice for their interest.

"To that Being who maketh and unmaketh at his will, we commend you; and after the accomplishment of the arduous business to which you are called, may he restore to us again, the best of men, and the most beloved fellow citizen!"

To this affectionate address General Washington returned the following answer:
"Gentlemen,

"Although I ought not to conceal, yet I can not describe the painful emotions which I felt in being called upon to determine whether I would accept or refuse the presidency of the United States. The unanimity in the choice, the opinion of my friends communicated from different parts of Europe, as well as from America, the apparent wish of those who were not entirely satisfied with the constitution in its present form; and an ardent desire on my own part to be instrumental in connecting the good will of my countrymen towards each other, have induced an acceptance. Those who know me best (and you my fellow citizens are, from your situation, in that number) know better than any others, my love of retirement is so great, that no earthly consideration, short of a conviction of duty, could have prevailed upon me to depart from my resolution, 'never more to take any share in transactions of a public nature.' For, at my age, and in my circumstances, what prospects or advantages could I propose to myself, from embarking again on the tempestuous and uncertain ocean of public life?

"I do not feel myself under the necessity of making public declarations, in order to convince you, gentlemen, of my attachment to yourselves, and regard for your interests. The whole tenor of my life has been open to your inspection; and my past actions, rather than my present declarations, must be the pledge of my future conduct.

"In the mean time, I thank you most sincerely for the expressions of kindness contained in your valedictory address. It is true, just after having bade adieu to my domestic connexions, this tender proof of your friendships is but too well calculated still further to awaken my sensibility, and increase my regret at parting from the enjoyments of private life.

"All that now remains for me is to commit myself and you to the protection of that beneficent Being who, on a former occasion, hath happily brought us together, after a long and distressing separation. Perhaps, the same gracious Providence will again indulge me. Unutterable sensations must then be left to more expressive silence; while from an aching heart, I bid you all, my affectionate friends, and kind neighbours, farewell!"

In the afternoon of the same day, he left Alexandria, and was attended by his neighbours to Georgetown, where a number of citizens from the state of Maryland had assembled to receive him.

Throughout his journey the people continued to manifest the same feeling. Crowds flocked around him wherever he stopped; and corps of militia, and companies of the most respectable citizens, escorted him through their respective streets. At Philadelphia, he was received with peculiar splendour. Gray's bridge, over the Schuylkill, was highly decorated. In imitation of the triumphal exhibitions of ancient Rome, an arch, composed of laurel, in which was displayed the simple elegance of true taste, was erected at each end of it, and on each side was a laurel shrubbery. As the object of universal admiration passed under the arch, a civic crown was, unperceived by him, let down upon his head by a youth ornamented with sprigs of laurel, who was assisted by machinery. The fields and avenues leading from the Schuylkill to Philadelphia, were crowded with people, through whom General Washington was conducted into the city by a numerous and respectable body of citizens; and at night the town was illuminated. The next day, at Trenton, he was welcomed in a manner as new as it was pleasing. In addition to the usual demonstrations of respect and attachment which were given by the discharge of cannon, by military corps, and by private persons of distinction, the gentler sex prepared in their own taste, a tribute of applause indicative of the grateful recollection in which they held their deliverance twelve years before from a formidable enemy. On the bridge over the creek which passes through the town, was erected a triumphal arch highly ornamented with laurels and flowers: and supported by thirteen pillars, each entwined with wreaths of evergreen. On the front arch was inscribed in large gilt letters,

THE DEFENDER OF THE MOTHERS
WILL BE THE
PROTECTOR OF THE DAUGHTERS.

On the centre of the arch above the inscription, was a dome or cupola of flowers and evergreens, encircling the dates of two memorable events which were peculiarly interesting to New Jersey. The first was the battle of Trenton, and the second the bold and judicious stand made by the American troops at the same creek, by which the progress of the British army was arrested on the evening preceding the battle of Princeton.

At this place, he was met by a party of matrons leading their daughters dressed in white, who carried baskets of flowers in their hands, and sang, with exquisite sweetness, an ode of two stanzas composed for the occasion.

At Brunswick, he was joined by the governor of New Jersey, who accompanied him to Elizabethtown Point. A committee of congress received him on the road, and conducted him with military parade to the Point, where he took leave of the governor and other gentlemen of Jersey, and embarked for New York in an elegant barge of thirteen oars, manned by thirteen branch pilots prepared for the purpose by the citizens of New York.

"The display of boats," says the general, in his private journal, "which attended and joined on this occasion, some with vocal, and others with instrumental music on board, the decorations of the ships, the roar of cannon, and the loud acclamations of the people, which rent the sky as I passed along the wharves, filled my mind with sensations as painful (contemplating the reverse of this scene, which may be the case after all my labours to do good) as they were pleasing."

At the stairs on Murray's wharf, which had been prepared and ornamented for the purpose, he was received by the governor of New York, and conducted with military honours, through an immense concourse of people, to the apartments provided for him. These were attended by all who were in office, and by many private citizens of distinction, who pressed around him to offer their congratulations, and to express the joy which glowed in their bosoms at seeing the man in whom all confided, at the head of the American empire. This day of extravagant joy was succeeded by a splendid illumination.

It is no equivocal mark of the worth of Washington, and of the soundness of his judgment, that it could neither be corrupted nor misguided by these flattering testimonials of attachment.

Two days before the arrival of the President, the Vice President took his seat in the senate, and addressed that body in a dignified speech adapted to the occasion, in which, after manifesting the high opinion that statesman always entertained of his countrymen, he thus expressed his sentiments of the executive magistrate.

"It is with satisfaction that I congratulate the people of America on the formation of a national constitution, and the fair prospect of a consistent administration of a government of laws: on the acquisition of a house of representatives, chosen by themselves; of a senate thus composed by their own state legislatures; and on the prospect of an executive authority, in the hands of one whose portrait I shall not presume to draw.—Were I blessed with powers to do justice to his character, it would be impossible to increase the confidence or affection of his country, or make the smallest addition to his glory. This can only be effected by a discharge of the present exalted trust on the same principles, with the same abilities and virtues which have uniformly appeared in all his former conduct, public or private. May I nevertheless be indulged to inquire, if we look over the catalogue of the first magistrates of nations, whether they have been denominated presidents or consuls, kings, or princes, where shall we find one, whose commanding talents and virtues, whose overruling good fortune, have so completely united all hearts and voices in his favour? who enjoyed the esteem and admiration of foreign nations, and fellow citizens, with equal unanimity? qualities so uncommon, are no common blessings to the country that possesses them. By these great qualities, and their benign effects, has Providence marked out the head of this nation, with a hand so distinctly visible, as to have been seen by all men, and mistaken by none."

Washington Taking the Oath of Office
From the painting by Alonzo Chappell

On the balcony of the old City Hall, Broad and Wall Streets, New York, Washington was sworn in as first President of the United States, April 30, 1789. The artist here accurately depicts him wearing a suit of dark brown, at his side a dress sword, and his hair powdered in the fashion of the period. White silk stockings and shoes with simple silver buckles completed his attire. On one side of him stood Chancellor Livingstone, who administered the oath. On the other side was Vice-President John Adams. Washington solemnly repeated the words of the oath, clearly enunciating, "I swear"; adding in a whisper, with closed eyes, "So help me, God".

He forms a system of conduct to be observed in his intercourse with the world.

A President of the United States being a new political personage, to a great portion of whose time the public was entitled, it became proper to digest a system of conduct to be observed in his intercourse with the world, which would keep in view the duties of his station, without entirely disregarding his personal accommodation, or the course of public opinion. In the interval between his arrival in New York, and entering on the duties of his office, those most capable of advising on the subject were consulted; and some rules were framed by General Washington for his government in these respects. As one of them, the allotment of a particular hour for receiving visits not on business, became the subject of much animadversion; and, being considered merely as an imitation of the levee days established by crowned heads, has constituted not the least important of the charges which have been made against this gentleman. The motives assigned by himself for the rule may not be unworthy of attention.

Letters from him on this and other subjects.

Not long after the government came into operation, Doctor Stuart, a gentleman nearly connected with the President in friendship and by marriage, addressed to him a letter stating the accusations which were commonly circulating in Virginia on various subjects, and especially against the regal manners of those who administered the affairs of the nation. In answer to this letter the President observed, "while the eyes of America, perhaps of the world, are turned to this government, and many are watching the movements of all those who are concerned in its administration, I should like to be informed, through so good a medium, of the public opinion of both men and measures, and of none more than myself;— not so much of what may be thought commendable parts, if any, of my conduct, as of those which are conceived to be of a different complexion. The man who means to commit no wrong will never be guilty of enormities, consequently can never be unwilling to learn what are ascribed to him as foibles.—If they are really such, the knowledge of them in a well disposed mind will go half way towards a reform.—If they are not errors, he can explain and justify the motives of his actions.

"At a distance from the theatre of action, truth is not always related without embellishment, and sometimes is entirely perverted from a misconception of the causes which produced the effects that are the subject of censure.

"This leads me to think that a system which I found it indispensably necessary to adopt upon my first coming to this city, might have undergone severe strictures, and have had motives very foreign from those that governed me, assigned as causes thereof.—I mean first, returning *no* visits: second, appointing certain days to receive them generally (not to the exclusion however of visits on any other days under particular circumstances;) and third, at first entertaining no company, and afterwards (until I was unable to entertain any at all) confining it to official characters. A few days evinced the necessity of the two first in so clear a point of view, that had I not adopted it, I should have been unable to have attended to any sort of business, unless I had applied the hours allotted to rest and refreshment to this purpose; for by the time I had done breakfast, and thence until dinner—and afterwards until bed-time, I could not get relieved from the ceremony of one visit before I had to attend to another. In a word, I had no leisure to read or to answer the despatches that were pouring in upon me from all quarters."

In a subsequent letter written to the same gentleman, after his levees had been openly-censured by the enemies of his administration, he thus expressed himself:

"Before the custom was established, which now accommodates foreign characters, strangers, and others who from motives of curiosity, respect to the chief magistrate, or any other cause, are induced to call upon me, I was unable to attend to any business whatsoever. For gentlemen, consulting their own convenience rather than mine, were calling from the time I rose from breakfast—often before—until I sat down to dinner. This, as I resolved not to neglect my public duties, reduced me to the choice of one of these alternatives; either to refuse them *altogether*, or to appropriate a time for the reception of them. The first would, I well knew, be disgusting to many;—the latter I expected, would undergo animadversion from those who would find fault with or without cause. To please every body was impossible. I therefore adopted that line of conduct which combined public advantage with private convenience, and which, in my judgment, was unexceptionable in itself.

"These visits are optional. They are made without invitation. Between the hours of three and four every Tuesday, I am prepared to receive them. Gentlemen, often in great numbers, come and go;—chat with each other;—and act as they please. A porter shows them into the room; and they retire from it when they choose, and without ceremony. At their first entrance, they salute me, and I them, and as many as I can talk to, I do. What pomp there is in all this I am unable to discover. Perhaps it consists in not sitting. To this two reasons are opposed: first, it is unusual; secondly, (which is a more substantial one) because I have no room large enough to contain a third of the chairs which would be sufficient to admit it. If it is supposed that ostentation, or the fashions of courts (which by the by I believe originate oftener in convenience, not to say necessity, than is generally imagined) gave rise to this custom, I will boldly affirm that *no* supposition was ever more erroneous; for were I to indulge my inclinations, every moment that I could withdraw from the fatigues of my station should be spent in retirement. That they are not, proceeds from the sense I entertain of the propriety of giving to every one as free access as consists with that respect which is due to the chair of government;—and that respect, I conceive, is neither to be acquired nor preserved, but by maintaining a just medium between too much state, and too great familiarity.

"Similar to the above, but of a more familiar and sociable kind, are the visits every Friday afternoon to Mrs. Washington, where I always am. These public meetings, and a dinner once a week to as many as my table will hold, with the references to and from the different departments of state, and other communications with all parts of the union, is as much if not more than I am able to undergo; for I have already had within less than a year, two severe attacks;—the last worse than the first,—a third, it is more than probable will put me to sleep with my fathers—at what distance this may be, I know not."

His inauguration and speech to congress.

The ceremonies of the inauguration having been adjusted by congress, the President attended in the senate chamber, on the 30th of April, in order to take, in the presence of both houses, the oath prescribed by the constitution.

To gratify the public curiosity, an open gallery adjoining the senate chamber had been selected by congress, as the place in which the oath should be administered. Having taken it in the view of an immense concourse of people, whose loud and repeated acclamations attested the joy with which his being proclaimed President of the United States inspired them, he returned to the senate chamber, where he delivered the following address:

"*Fellow citizens of the Senate and of the House of Representatives:*

"Among the vicissitudes incident to life, no event could have filled me with greater anxieties than that of which the notification was transmitted by your order, and received on the 14th day of the present month. On the one hand, I was summoned by my country, whose voice I can never hear but with veneration and love, from a retreat which I had chosen with the fondest predilection, and, in my flattering hopes, with an immutable decision, as the asylum of my declining years: a retreat which was rendered every day more necessary as well as more dear to me, by the addition of habit to inclination, and of frequent interruptions in my health to the gradual waste committed on it by time. On the other hand, the magnitude and difficulty of the trust to which the voice of my country called me, being sufficient to awaken in the wisest and most experienced of her citizens a distrustful scrutiny into his qualifications, could not but overwhelm with despondence, one, who, inheriting inferior endowments from nature, and unpractised in the duties of civil administration, ought to be peculiarly conscious of his own deficiencies. In this conflict of emotions, all I dare aver is, that it has been my faithful study to collect my duty from a just appreciation of every circumstance by which it might be effected. All I dare hope is, that, if in accepting this task, I have been too much swayed by a grateful remembrance of former instances, or by an affectionate sensibility to this transcendent proof of the confidence of my fellow citizens: and have thence too little consulted my incapacity, as well as disinclination for the weighty and untried cares before me; my ERROR will be palliated by the motives which misled me, and its consequences be judged by my country, with some share of the partiality in which they originated.

"Such being the impressions under which I have, in obedience to the public summons, repaired to the present station, it will be peculiarly improper to omit in this first official act, my fervent supplications to that Almighty Being who rules over the universe— who presides in the councils of nations—and whose providential aids can supply every human defect, that his benediction may consecrate to the liberties and happiness of the people of the United States, a government instituted by themselves for these essential purposes: and may enable every instrument employed in its administration, to execute with success, the functions allotted to his charge. In tendering this homage to the great Author of every public and private good, I assure myself that it expresses your sentiments not less than my own; nor those of my fellow citizens at large, less than either. No people can be bound to acknowledge and adore the invisible hand which conducts the affairs of men, more than the people of the United States. Every step by which they have advanced to the character of an independent nation seems to have been distinguished by some token of providential agency; and in the important revolution just accomplished in the system of their united government, the tranquil deliberations and voluntary consent of so many distinct communities, from which the event has resulted, can not be compared with the means by which most governments have been established, without some return of pious gratitude along with an humble anticipation of the future blessings which the past seem to presage. These reflections, arising out of the present crisis, have forced themselves too strongly on my mind to be suppressed. You will join with me, I trust, in thinking that there are none, under the influence of which the proceedings of a new and free government can more auspiciously commence.

"By the article establishing the executive department, it is made the duty of the President 'to recommend to your consideration, such measures as he shall judge necessary and expedient.' The circumstances under which I now meet you will acquit me from entering into that subject, farther than to refer to the great constitutional charter under which you are assembled, and which in defining your powers, designates the objects to which your attention is to be given. It will be more consistent with those circumstances, and far more congenial with the feelings which actuate me, to substitute in place of a recommendation of particular measures, the tribute that is due to the talents, the rectitude, and the patriotism, which adorn the characters selected to devise and adopt them. In these honourable qualifications, I behold the surest pledges that, as on one side, no local prejudices or attachments, no separate views nor party animosities, will misdirect the comprehensive and equal eye which ought to watch over this great assemblage of communities and interests: so, on another, that the foundations of our national policy will be laid in the pure and immutable principles of private morality; and the pre-eminence of free government be exemplified by all the attributes which can win the affections of its citizens, and command the respect of the world. I dwell on this prospect with every satisfaction which an ardent love for my country can inspire, since there is no truth more thoroughly established than that there exists, in the economy and course of nature, an indissoluble union between virtue and happiness—between duty and advantage—between the genuine maxims of an honest and magnanimous policy, and the solid rewards of public prosperity and felicity; since we ought to be no less persuaded that the propitious smiles of heaven can never be expected on a nation that disregards the eternal rules of order and right which heaven itself has ordained: and since the preservation of the sacred fire of liberty, and the destiny of the republican model of government, are justly considered as DEEPLY, perhaps as FINALLY staked, on the experiment entrusted to the hands of the American people.

"Besides the ordinary objects submitted to your care, it will remain with your judgment to decide, how far an exercise of the occasional power delegated by the fifth article of the constitution is rendered expedient, at the present juncture, by the nature of objections which have been urged against the system, or by the degree of inquietude which has given birth to them. Instead of undertaking particular recommendations on this subject, in which I could be guided by no lights derived from official opportunities, I shall again give way to my entire confidence in your discernment and pursuit of the public good: for I assure myself that whilst you carefully avoid every alteration which might endanger the benefits of a united and effective government, or which ought to await the future lessons of experience, a reverence for the characteristic rights of freemen, and a regard for the public harmony, will sufficiently influence your deliberations on the question how far the former can be more impregnably fortified, or the latter be safely and advantageously promoted.

"To the preceding observations I have one to add, which will be most properly addressed to the house of representatives. It concerns myself, and will therefore be as brief as possible. When I was first honoured with a call into the service of my country, then on the eve of an arduous struggle for its liberties, the light in which I contemplated my duty required that I should renounce every pecuniary compensation. From this resolution I have in no instance departed. And being still under the impressions which produced it, I must decline, as inapplicable to myself, any share in the personal emoluments which may be indispensably included in a permanent provision for the executive department; and must accordingly pray that the pecuniary estimates for the station in which I am placed, may, during my continuance in it, be limited to such actual expenditures as the public good may be thought to require.

"Having thus imparted to you my sentiments, as they have been awakened by the occasion which brings us together, I shall take my present leave; but not without resorting once more to the benign Parent of the human race, in humble supplication, that since he has been pleased to favour the American people with opportunities for deliberating in perfect tranquillity, and dispositions for deciding with unparalleled unanimity on a form of government, for the security of their union, and the advancement of their happiness, so his divine blessing may be equally *conspicuous* in the enlarged views, the temperate consultations, and the wise measures on which the success of this government must depend."

Answer of both houses of congress to the speech.

In their answer to this speech, the senate say: "The unanimous suffrage of the elective body in your favour, is peculiarly expressive of the gratitude, confidence, and affection of the citizens of America, and is the highest testimonial at once of your merit, and their esteem.

We are sensible, sir, that nothing but the voice of your fellow citizens could have called you from a retreat, chosen with the fondest predilection, endeared by habit, and consecrated to the repose of declining years. We rejoice, and with us all America, that, in obedience to the call of our common country, you have returned once more to public life. In you all parties confide; in you all interests unite; and we have no doubt that your past services, great as they have been, will be equalled by your future exertions; and that your prudence and sagacity, as a statesman, will tend to avert the dangers to which we were exposed, to give stability to the present government, and dignity and splendour to that country, which your skill and valour as a soldier, so eminently contributed to raise to independence and to empire."

The affection for the person and character of the President with which the answer of the house of representatives glowed, promised that between this branch of the legislature also and the executive, the most harmonious co-operation in the public service might be expected.

"The representatives of the people of the United States," says this address, "present their congratulations on the event by which your fellow citizens have attested the pre-eminence of your merit. You have long held the first place in their esteem. You have often received tokens of their affection. You now possess the only proof that remained of their gratitude for your services, of their reverence for your wisdom, and of their confidence in your virtues. You enjoy the highest, because the truest honour, of being the first magistrate, by the unanimous choice of the freest people on the face of the earth."

After noticing the several communications made in the speech, intense of deep felt respect and affection, the answer concludes thus:

"Such are the sentiments with which we have thought fit to address you. They flow from our own hearts, and we verily believe that among the millions we represent, there is not a virtuous citizen whose heart will disown them.

"All that remains is, that we join in your fervent supplications for the blessing of heaven on our country; and that we add our own for the choicest of these blessings on the most beloved of her citizens."

Situation of the United States at this period in their domestic and foreign relations.

A perfect knowledge of the antecedent state of things being essential to a due administration of the executive department, its attainment engaged the immediate attention of the President; and he required the temporary heads of departments to prepare and lay before him such statements and documents as would give this information.

But in the full view which it was useful to take of the interior, many objects were to be contemplated, the documents respecting which were not to be found in official records. The progress which had been made in assuaging the bitter animosities engendered in the sharp contest respecting the adoption of the constitution, and the means which might be used for conciliating the affections of all good men to the new government, without enfeebling its essential principles, were subjects of the most interesting inquiry.

The agitation had been too great to be suddenly calmed; and for the active opponents of the system to become suddenly its friends, or even indifferent to its fate, would have been a victory of reason over passion, or a surrender of individual judgment to the decision of a majority, examples of which are rarely given in the progress of human affairs.

In some of the states, a disposition to acquiesce in the decision which had been made, and to await the issue of a fair experiment of the constitution, was avowed by the minority. In others, the chagrin of defeat seemed to increase the original hostility to the instrument; and serious fears were entertained by its friends, that a second general convention might pluck from it the most essential of its powers, before their value, and the safety with which they might be confided where they were placed, could be ascertained by experience.

From the same cause, exerting itself in a different direction, the friends of the new system had been still more alarmed. In all those states where the opposition was sufficiently formidable to inspire a hope of success, the effort was made to fill the legislature with the declared enemies of the government, and thus to commit it, in its infancy, to the custody of its foes. Their fears were quieted for the present. In both branches of the legislature, the federalists, an appellation at that time distinguishing those who had supported the constitution, formed the majority; and it soon appeared that a new convention was too bold an experiment to be applied for by the requisite number of states. The condition of individuals too, was visibly becoming more generally eligible. Industry, notwithstanding the causes which had diminished its profits, was gradually improving their affairs; and the new course of thinking, inspired by the adoption of a constitution prohibiting all laws impairing the obligation of contracts, had, in a great measure, restored that confidence which is essential to the internal prosperity of nations. From these, or from other causes, the crisis of the pressure on individuals seemed to be passing away, and brighter prospects to be opening on them.

But, two states still remained out of the pale of the union; and a mass of ill humour existed among those who were included within it, which increased the necessity of circumspection in those who administered the government.

To the western parts of the continent, the attention of the executive was attracted by discontents which were displayed with some violence, and which originated in circumstances, and in interests, peculiar to that country.

Spain, in possession of the mouth of the Mississippi, had refused to permit the citizens of the United States to follow its waters into the ocean; and had occasionally tolerated or interdicted their commerce to New Orleans, as had been suggested by the supposed interest or caprice of the Spanish government, or of its representatives in America. The eyes of the inhabitants adjacent to the waters which emptied into that river, were turned down it, as the only channel through which the surplus produce of their luxuriant soil could be conveyed to the markets of the world. Believing that the future wealth and prosperity of their country depended on the use of that river, they gave some evidence of a disposition to drop from the confederacy, if this valuable acquisition could not otherwise be made. This temper could not fail to be viewed with interest by the neighbouring powers, who had been encouraged by it, and by the imbecility of the government, to enter into intrigues of an alarming nature.

Previous to his departure from Mount Vernon, the President had received intelligence, too authentic to be disregarded, of private machinations by real or pretended agents both of Spain and Great Britain, which were extremely hostile to the peace, and to the integrity of the union.

Spain had intimated that the navigation of the Mississippi could never be conceded, while the inhabitants of the western country remained connected with the Atlantic states, but might be freely granted to them, if they should form an independent empire.

On the other hand, a gentleman from Canada, whose ostensible business was to repossess himself of some lands on the Ohio which had been formerly granted to him, frequently discussed the vital importance of the navigation of the Mississippi, and privately assured several individuals of great influence, that if they were disposed to assert their rights, he was authorized by Lord Dorchester, the governor of Canada, to say, that they might rely confidently on his assistance. With the aid it was in his power to give, they might seize New Orleans, fortify the Balise at the mouth of the Mississippi, and maintain themselves in that place against the utmost efforts of Spain.

The probability of failing in any attempt to hold the mouth of the Mississippi by force, and the resentments against Great Britain which prevailed generally throughout the western country, diminished the danger to be apprehended from any machinations of that power; but against those of Spain, the same security did not exist.

In contemplating the situation of the United States in their relations not purely domestic, the object demanding most immediate consideration was the hostility of several tribes of Indians. The military strength of the nations who inhabited the country between the lakes, the Mississippi, and the Ohio, was computed at five thousand men, of whom about fifteen hundred were at open war with the United States. Treaties had been concluded with the residue; but the attachment of young savages to war, and the provocation given by the undistinguishing vengeance which had been taken by the whites in their expeditions into the Indian country, furnished reasons for apprehending that these treaties would soon be broken.

In the south, the Creeks, who could bring into the field six thousand fighting men, were at war with Georgia. In the mind of their leader, the son of a white man, some irritation had been produced by the confiscation of the lands of his father, who had resided in that state; and several other refugees whose property had also been confiscated, contributed still further to exasperate the nation. But the immediate point in contest between them was a tract of land on the Oconee, which the state of Georgia claimed under a purchase, the validity of which was denied by the Indians.

The regular force of the United States was less than six hundred men.

Not only the policy of accommodating differences by negotiation which the government was in no condition to terminate by the sword; but a real respect for the rights of the natives, and a regard for the claims of justice and humanity, disposed the President to endeavour, in the first instance, to remove every cause of quarrel by a treaty; and his message to congress on this subject evidenced his preference of pacific measures.

Possessing many valuable articles of commerce for which the best market was often found on the coast of the Mediterranean, struggling to export them in their own bottoms, and unable to afford a single gun for their protection, the Americans could not view with unconcern the dispositions which were manifested towards them by the Barbary powers. A treaty had been formed with the emperor of Morocco; but from Algiers, Tunis, and Tripoli, peace had not been purchased; and those regencies consider all as enemies to whom they have not sold their friendship. The unprotected vessels of America presented a tempting object to their rapacity; and their hostility was the more terrible, because by their public law, prisoners became slaves.

The United States were at peace with all the powers of Europe; but controversies of a delicate nature existed with some of them, the adjustment of which required a degree of moderation and firmness, which there was reason to fear, might not, in every instance, be exhibited.

The early apprehensions with which Spain had contemplated the future strength of the United States, and the consequent disposition of the house of Bourbon to restrict them to narrow limits, have been already noticed. After the conclusion of the war, the attempt to form a treaty with that power had been repeated; but no advance towards an agreement on the points of difference between the two governments had been made. A long and intricate negotiation between the secretary of foreign affairs, and Don Guardoqui, the minister of his Catholic majesty, had terminated with the old government; and the result was an inflexible adherence on the part of Mr. Guardoqui to the exclusion of the citizens of the United States from navigating the Mississippi below their southern boundary. On this point there was much reason to fear that the cabinet of Madrid would remain immoveable. The violence with which the discontents of the western people were expressed, furnished Spain with additional motives for perpetuating the evil of which they complained. Aware of the embarrassments which this display of restlessness must occasion, and sensible of the increased difficulty and delay with which a removal of its primary cause must be attended, the executive perceived in this critical state of things, abundant cause for the exercise of its watchfulness, and of its prudence. With Spain, there was also a contest respecting boundaries. The treaty of peace had extended the limits of the United States to the thirty-first degree of north latitude, but the pretensions of the Catholic King were carried north of that line, to an undefined extent. He claimed as far as he had conquered from Britain, but the precise limits of his conquest were not ascertained.

The circumstances attending the points of difference with Great Britain, were still more serious; because, in their progress, a temper unfavourable to accommodation had been uniformly displayed.

The resentments produced by the various calamities war had occasioned, were not terminated with their cause. The idea that Great Britain was the natural enemy of America had become habitual. Believing it impossible for that nation to have relinquished its views of conquest, many found it difficult to bury their animosities, and to act upon the sentiment contained in the declaration of independence, "to hold them as the rest of mankind, enemies in war, in peace friends." In addition to the complaints respecting the violation of the treaty of peace, events were continually supplying this temper with fresh aliment. The disinclination which the cabinet of London had discovered to a commercial treaty with the United States was not attributed exclusively to the cause which had been assigned for it. It was in part ascribed to that jealousy with which Britain was supposed to view the growing trade of America.

The general restrictions on commerce by which every maritime power sought to promote its own navigation, and that part of the European system in particular, by which each aimed at a monopoly of the trade of its colonies, were felt with peculiar keenness when enforced by England. The people of America were perhaps the more sensible to the British resolutions on this subject, because, having composed a part of that empire, they had grown up in the habit of a free intercourse with all its ports; and, without accurately appreciating the cause to which a change of this usage was to be ascribed, they attributed it to a jealousy of their prosperity, and to an inclination to diminish the value of their independence. In this suspicious temper, almost every unfavourable event which occurred was traced up to British hostility.

That an attempt to form a commercial treaty with Portugal had failed, was attributed to the influence of the cabinet of London; and to the machinations of the same power were also ascribed the danger from the corsairs of Barbary, and the bloody incursions of the Indians. The resentment excited by these causes was felt by a large proportion of the American people; and the expression of it was common and public. That correspondent dispositions existed in England is by no means improbable, and the necessary effect of this temper was to increase the difficulty of adjusting the differences between the two nations.

With France, the most perfect harmony subsisted. Those attachments which originated in the signal services received from his most Christian Majesty during the war of the revolution, had sustained no diminution. Yet, from causes which it was found difficult to counteract, the commercial intercourse between the two nations was not so extensive as had been expected. It was the interest, and of consequence the policy of France, to avail herself of the misunderstandings between the United States and Great Britain, in order to obtain such regulations as might gradually divert the increasing trade of the American continent from those channels in which it had been accustomed to flow; and a disposition was felt throughout the United States to co-operate with her, in enabling her merchants, by legislative encouragements, to rival those of Britain in the American market.

A great revolution had commenced in that country, the first stage of which was completed by limiting the powers of the monarch, and by the establishment of a popular assembly. In no part of the globe was this revolution hailed with more joy than in America. The influence it would have on the affairs of the world was not then distinctly foreseen: and the philanthropist, without becoming a political partisan, rejoiced in the event. On this subject, therefore, but one sentiment existed.

The relations of the United States with the other powers of Europe, did not require particular attention. Their dispositions were rather friendly than otherwise; and an inclination was generally manifested to participate in the advantages, which the erection of an independent empire on the western shores of the Atlantic, held forth to the commercial world.

By the ministers of foreign powers in America, it would readily be supposed, that the first steps taken by the new government would, not only be indicative of its present system, but would probably affect its foreign relations permanently, and that the influence of the President would be felt in the legislature. Scarcely was the exercise of his executive functions commenced, when the President received an application from the Count de Moustiers, the minister of France, requesting a private conference. On being told that the department of foreign affairs was the channel through which all official business should pass, the Count replied that the interview he requested was, not for the purpose of actual business, but rather as preparatory to its future transaction.

The next day, at one in the afternoon, was named for the interview. The Count commenced the conversation with declarations of his personal regard for America, the manifestations of which, he said, had been early and uniform. His nation too was well disposed to be upon terms of amity with the United States: but at his public reception, there were occurrences which he thought indicative of coolness in the secretary of foreign affairs, who had, he feared, while in Europe, imbibed prejudices not only against Spain, but against France also. If this conjecture should be right, the present head of that department could not be an agreeable organ of intercourse with the President. He then took a view of the modern usages of European courts, which, he said, favoured the practice he recommended of permitting foreign ministers to make their communications directly to the chief of the executive. "He then presented a letter," says the President in his private journal, "which he termed confidential, and to be considered as addressed to me in my private character, which was too strongly marked with an intention, as well as a wish, to have no person between the Minister and President, in the transaction of business between the two nations."

In reply to these observations, the President gave the most explicit assurances that, judging from his own feelings, and from the public sentiment, there existed in America a reciprocal disposition to be on the best terms with France. That whatever former difficulties might have occurred, he was persuaded the secretary of foreign affairs had offered no intentional disrespect, either to the minister, or to his nation. Without undertaking to know the private opinions of Mr. Jay, he would declare that he had never heard that officer express, directly or indirectly, any sentiment unfavourable to either.

Reason and usage, he added, must direct the mode of treating national and official business. If rules had been established, they must be conformed to. If they were yet to be framed, it was hoped that they would be convenient and proper. So far as ease could be made to comport with regularity, and with necessary forms, it ought to be consulted; but custom, and the dignity of office, were not to be disregarded. The conversation continued upwards of an hour, but no change was made in the resolution of the President.

The subjects which pressed for immediate attention on the first legislature assembled under the new government, were numerous and important. Much was to be created, and much to be reformed.

The subject of revenue, as constituting the vital spring without which the action of government could not long be continued, was taken up in the house of representatives, as soon as it could be introduced. The qualification of the members was succeeded by a motion for the house to resolve itself into a committee of the whole on the state of the union; and in that committee, a resolution was moved by Mr. Madison, declaring the opinion that certain duties ought to be levied on goods, wares, and merchandise, imported into the United States; and on the tonnage of vessels.

As it was deemed important to complete a temporary system in time to embrace the spring importations, Mr. Madison presented the scheme of impost which had been recommended by the former congress, and had already received the approbation of a majority of the states; to which he added a general proposition for a duty on tonnage. By this scheme specific duties were imposed on certain enumerated articles; and an ad-valorem duty on those not enumerated. Mr. Fitzsimmons, of Pennsylvania, moved an amendment, enlarging the catalogue of enumerated articles.

Debates on the impost and tonnage bills.

Mr. Madison having consented to subjoin the amendment proposed by Mr. Fitzsimmons to the original resolution, it was received by the committee; but in proceeding to fill up the blanks with the sum taxable on each article, it was soon perceived that gentlemen had viewed the subject in very different lights. The tax on many articles was believed to press more heavily on some states than on others; and apprehensions were expressed that, in the form of protecting duties, the industry of one part of the union would be encouraged by premiums charged on the labour of another part. On the discrimination between the duty on the tonnage of foreign and American bottoms, a great degree of sensibility was discovered. The citizens of the United States not owning a sufficient number of vessels to export all the produce of the country, it was said that the increased tonnage on foreign bottoms operated as a tax on agriculture, and a premium to navigation. This discrimination, it was therefore contended, ought to be very small.

In answer to these arguments, Mr. Madison said, "If it is expedient for America to have vessels employed in commerce at all, it will be proper that she have enough to answer all the purposes intended; to form a school for seamen; to lay the foundation of a navy: and to be able to support itself against the interference of foreigners. I do not think there is much weight in the observations that the duty we are about to lay in favour of American vessels is a burden on the community, and particularly oppressive to some parts. But if there were, it may be a burden of that kind which will ultimately save us from one that is greater.

"I consider an acquisition of maritime strength essential to this country; should we ever be so unfortunate as to be engaged in war, what but this can defend our towns and cities upon the sea coast? Or what but this can enable us to repel an invading enemy? Those parts which are said to bear an undue proportion of the burden of the additional duty on foreign shipping, are those which will be most exposed to the operations of a predatory war, and will require the greatest exertions of the union in their defence. If therefore some little sacrifice be made by them to obtain this important object, they will be peculiarly rewarded for it in the hour of danger. Granting a preference to our own navigation will insensibly bring it forward to that perfection so essential to American safety; and though it may produce some little inequality at first, it will soon ascertain its level, and become uniform throughout the union."

But no part of the system was discussed with more animation than that which proposed to make discriminations in favour of those nations with whom the United States had formed commercial treaties. In the debate on this subject, opinions and feelings with respect to foreign powers were disclosed, which, strengthening with circumstances, afterwards agitated the whole American continent.

While the resolutions on which the bills were to be framed were under debate, Mr. Benson rose to inquire on what principle the proposed discriminations between foreign nations was founded? "It was certainly proper," he said, "to comply with existing treaties. But those treaties stipulated no such preference. Congress then was at liberty to consult the interests of the United States. If those interests would be promoted by the measure, he should be willing to adopt it, but he wished its policy to be shown."

The resolutions, as reported, were supported by Mr. Madison, Mr. Baldwin, Mr. Fitzsimmons, Mr. Clymer, Mr. Page, and Mr. Jackson.

They relied much upon the public sentiment which had, they said, been unequivocally expressed through the several state legislatures and otherwise, against placing foreign nations generally, on a footing with the allies of the United States. So strong was this sentiment, that to its operation the existing constitution was principally to be ascribed. They thought it important to prove to those nations who had declined forming commercial treaties with them, that the United States possessed and would exercise the power of retaliating any regulations unfavourable to their trade, and they insisted strongly on the advantages of America in a war of commercial regulation, should this measure produce one.

The disposition France had lately shown to relax with regard to the United States, the rigid policy by which her counsels had generally been guided, ought to be cultivated. The evidence of this disposition was an edict by which American built ships purchased by French subjects became naturalized. There was reason to believe that the person charged with the affairs of the United States at that court, had made some favourable impressions, which the conduct of the American government ought not to efface.

With great earnestness it was urged, that from artificial or adventitious causes, the commerce between the United States and Great Britain had exceeded its natural boundary. It was wise to give such political advantages to other nations as would enable them to acquire their due share of the direct trade. It was also wise to impart some benefits to nations that had formed commercial treaties with the United States, and thereby to impress on those powers which had hitherto neglected to form such treaties, the idea that some advantages were to be gained by a reciprocity of friendship.

That France had claims on the gratitude of the American people which ought not to be overlooked, was an additional argument in favour of the principle for which they contended.

The discrimination was opposed by Mr. Benson, Mr. Lawrence, Mr. Wadsworth, and Mr. Sherman.

They did not admit that the public sentiment had been unequivocally expressed; nor did they admit that such benefits had flowed from commercial treaties as to justify a sacrifice of interest to obtain them. There was a commercial treaty with France; but neither that treaty, nor the favours shown to that nation, had produced any correspondent advantages. The license to sell ships could not be of this description, since it was well known that the merchants of the United States did not own vessels enough for the transportation of the produce of the country, and only two, as was believed, had been sold since the license had been granted. The trade with Great Britain, viewed in all its parts, was upon a footing as beneficial to the United States as that with France.

That the latter power had claims upon the gratitude of America was admitted, but that these claims would justify premiums for the encouragement of French commerce and navigation, to be drawn from the pockets of the American people, was not conceded. The state of the revenue, it was said, would not admit of these experiments.

The observation founded on the extensiveness of the trade between the United States and Great Britain was answered by saying, that this was not a subject proper for legislative interposition. It was one of which the merchants were the best judges. They would consult their interest as individuals; and this was a case in which the interest of the nation and of individuals was the same.

At length, the bills passed the house of representatives, and were carried to the senate, where they were amended by expunging the discrimination made in favour of the tonnage and distilled spirits of those nations which had formed commercial treaties with the United States.

These amendments were disagreed to; and each house insisting on its opinion, a conference took place, after which the point was reluctantly yielded by the house of representatives. The proceedings of the senate being at that time conducted with closed doors, the course of reasoning on which this important principle was rejected can not be stated.

This debate on the impost and tonnage bills was succeeded by one on a subject which was believed to involve principles of still greater interest.

On the President's power of removal from office.

In organizing the departments of the executive, the question in what manner the high officers who filled them should be removeable, came on to be discussed. Believing that the decision of this question would materially influence the character of the new government, the members supported their respective opinions with a degree of earnestness proportioned to the importance they attributed to the measure. In a committee of the whole house on the bill "to establish an executive department to be denominated the[42] department of foreign affairs," Mr. White moved to strike out the clause which declared the secretary to be removeable by the President. The power of removal, where no express provision existed, was, he said, in the nature of things, incidental to that of appointment. And as the senate was, by the constitution, associated with the President in making appointments, that body must, in the same degree, participate in the power of removing from office.

Mr. White was supported by Mr. Smith of South Carolina, Mr. Page, Mr. Stone, and Mr. Jackson.

Those gentlemen contended that the clause was either unnecessary or improper. If the constitution gave the power to the President, a repetition of the grant in an act of congress was nugatory: if the constitution did not give it, the attempt to confer it by law was improper. If it belonged conjointly to the President and senate, the house of representatives should not attempt to abridge the constitutional prerogative of the other branch of the legislature. However this might be, they were clearly of opinion that it was not placed in the President alone. In the power over all the executive officers which the bill proposed to confer upon the President, the most alarming dangers to liberty were perceived. It was in the nature of monarchical prerogative, and would convert them into the mere tools and creatures of his will. A dependence so servile on one individual, would deter men of high and honourable minds from engaging in the public service; and if, contrary to expectation, such men should be brought into office, they would be reduced to the necessity of sacrificing every principle of independence to the will of the chief magistrate, or of exposing themselves to the disgrace of being removed from office, and that too at a time when it might be no longer in their power to engage in other pursuits.

Gentlemen they feared were too much dazzled with the splendour of the virtues which adorned the actual President, to be able to look into futurity. But the framers of the constitution had not confined their views to the person who would most probably first fill the presidential chair. The house of representatives ought to follow their example, and to contemplate this power in the hands of an ambitious man, who might apply it to dangerous purposes; who might from caprice remove the most worthy men from office.

View of the Old City or Federal Hall, New York, in 1789

On the balcony of this building, the site of which is now occupied by the United States Sub-Treasury, at the corner of Broad and Wall Streets, George Washington took the oath of office as First President of the United States, April 30, 1789. In the near distance, at the intersection of Wall and Broadway, may be seen the original Trinity Church structure which was completed in 1697. It was replaced by the present edifice in 1846. President Washington, who was an Episcopalian, did not attend Trinity, but maintained a pew in St. Paul's Chapel, Broadway and Vesey Street, which remains as it was when he worshipped there.

By the friends of the original bill, the amendment was opposed with arguments of great force drawn from the constitution and from general convenience. On several parts of the constitution, and especially on that which vests the executive power in the President, they relied confidently to support the position, that, in conformity with that instrument, the power in question could reside only with the chief magistrate: no power, it was said, could be more completely executive in its nature than that of removal from office.

But if it was a case on which the constitution was silent, the clearest principles of political expediency required that neither branch of the legislature should participate in it.

The danger that a President could ever be found who would remove good men from office, was treated as imaginary. It was not by the splendour attached to the character of the present chief magistrate alone that this opinion was to be defended. It was founded on the structure of the office. The man in whose favour a majority of the people of this continent would unite, had probability at least in favour of his principles; in addition to which, the public odium that would inevitably attach to such conduct, would be an effectual security against it.

After an ardent discussion which consumed several days, the committee divided: and the amendment was negatived by a majority of thirty-four to twenty. The opinion thus expressed by the house of representatives did not explicitly convey their sense of the constitution. Indeed the express grant of the power to the President, rather implied a right in the legislature to give or withhold it at their discretion. To obviate any misunderstanding of the principle on which the question had been 'decided, Mr. Benson moved in the house, when the report of the committee of the whole was taken up, to amend the second clause in the bill so as clearly to imply the power of removal to be solely in the President. He gave notice that if he should succeed in this, he would move to strike out the words which had been the subject of debate. If those words continued, he said the power of removal by the President might hereafter appear to be exercised by virtue of a legislative grant only, and consequently be subjected to legislative instability; when he was well satisfied in his own mind, that it was by fair construction, fixed in the constitution. The motion was seconded by Mr. Madison, and both amendments were adopted. As the bill passed into a law, it has ever been considered as a full expression of the sense of the legislature on this important part of the American constitution.

On the policy of the secretary of the treasury reporting plans for the management of the revenue.

The bill to establish the treasury department, contained a clause making it the duty of the secretary "to digest and report plans for the improvement and management of the revenue, and for the support of public credit."

Mr. Page moved to strike out these words, observing, that to permit the secretary to go further than to prepare estimates would be a dangerous innovation on the constitutional privilege of that house. It would create an undue influence within those walls, because members might be led by the deference commonly paid to men of abilities, who gave an opinion in a case they have thoroughly considered, to support the plan of the minister even against their own judgment. Nor would the mischief stop there. A precedent would be established which might be extended until ministers of the government should be admitted on that floor, to explain and support the plans they had digested and reported, thereby laying a foundation for an aristocracy, or a detestable monarchy.

Mr. Tucker seconded the motion of Mr. Page, and observed, that the authority contained in the bill to prepare and report plans would create an interference of the executive with the legislative powers, and would abridge the particular privilege of that house to originate all bills for raising a revenue. How could the business originate in that house, if it was reported to them by the minister of finance? All the information that could be required might be called for without adopting a clause that might undermine the authority of the house, and the security of the people. The constitution has pointed out the proper method of communication between the executive and legislative departments. It is made the duty of the President to give from time to time information to congress of the state of the union, and to recommend to their consideration such measures as he shall judge necessary and expedient. If revenue plans are to be prepared and reported to congress, he is the proper person to perform this service. He is responsible to the people for what he recommends, and will be more cautious than any other person to whom a less degree of responsibility was attached.

He hoped the house was not already weary of executing and sustaining the powers vested in them by the constitution; and yet the adoption of this clause would argue that they thought themselves less adequate than an individual, to determine what burdens their constituents were able to bear. This was not answering the high expectation that had been formed of their exertions for the general good, or of their vigilance in guarding their own and the people's rights.

The arguments of Mr. Page and Mr. Tucker were enforced and enlarged by Mr. Livermore and Mr. Gerry. The latter gentleman said, "that he had no objection to obtaining information, but he could not help observing the great degree of importance gentlemen were giving to this and the other executive officers. If the doctrine of having prime and great ministers of state was once well established, he did not doubt but he should soon see them distinguished by a green or red ribbon, insignia of court favour and patronage."

It was contended that the plans of the secretary, being digested, would be received entire. Members would be informed that each part was necessary to the whole, and that nothing could be touched without injuring the system. Establish this doctrine, and congress would become a useless burden.

The amendment was opposed by Mr. Benson, Mr. Goodhue, Mr. Ames, Mr. Sedgewick, Mr. Boudinot, Mr. Lawrence, Mr. Madison, Mr. Stone, Mr. Sherman, and Mr. Baldwin. It was insisted that to prepare and report plans for the improvement of the revenue, and support of public credit, constituted the most important service which could be rendered by the officer who should be placed at the head of the department of finance. When the circumstances under which the members of that house were assembled, and the various objects for which they were convened were considered, it was no imputation upon them to suppose that they might receive useful information from a person whose peculiar duty it was to direct his attention to systems of finance, and who would be in some measure selected on account of his fitness for that object. It was denied that the privileges of the house would be infringed by the measure. The plans of the secretary could not be termed bills, nor would they even be reported in that form. They would only constitute information which would be valuable, and which could not be received in a more eligible mode. "Certainly," said Mr. Goodhue, "we carry our dignity to the extreme, when we refuse to receive information from any but ourselves."

"If we consider the present situation of our finances," said Mr. Ames, "owing to a variety of causes, we shall no doubt perceive a great though unavoidable confusion throughout the whole scene. It presents to the imagination a deep, dark, and dreary chaos, impossible to be reduced to order, unless the mind of the architect be clear and capacious, and his power commensurate to the object. He must not be the flitting creature of the day; he must have time given him competent to the successful exercise of his authority. It is with the intention of letting a little sunshine into the business, that the present arrangement is proposed."

It was not admitted that the plans of the secretary would possess an influence to which their intrinsic value would not give them a just claim. There would always be sufficient intelligence in that house to detect, and independence to expose any oppressive or injurious scheme which might be prepared for them. Nor would a plan openly and officially reported possess more influence on the mind of any member, than if given privately at the secretary's office.

Mr. Madison said, the words of the bill were precisely those used by the former congress on two occasions. The same power had been annexed to the office of superintendent of the finances; and he had never heard that any inconvenience had been experienced from the regulation. Perhaps if the power had been more fully and more frequently exercised, it might have contributed more to the public good. "There is," continued this gentleman, "a small probability, though it is but small, that an officer may derive weight from this circumstance, and have some degree of influence upon the deliberations of the legislature. But compare the danger likely to result from this cause, with the danger and inconvenience of not having well formed and digested plans, and we shall find infinitely more to apprehend from the latter. Inconsistent, unproductive, and expensive schemes, will produce greater injury to our constituents, than is to be apprehended from any undue influence which the well digested plans of a well informed officer can have. From a bad administration of the government, more detriment will arise than from any other source. Want of information has occasioned much inconvenience, and many unnecessary burdens in some of the state governments. Let it be our care to avoid those rocks and shoals in our political voyage which have injured, and nearly proved fatal to many of our contemporary navigators."

The amendment was rejected.

On the style by which the president should be addressed.

Among the interesting points which were settled in the first congress, was the question by what style the President and Vice President should be addressed. Mr. Benson, from the committee appointed to confer with a committee of the senate on this subject reported, "that it is not proper to annex any style or title to the respective styles or titles of office expressed in the constitution;" and this report was, without opposition, agreed to in the house of representatives. In the senate, the report was disapproved, and a resolution passed requesting the house of representatives to appoint another committee, again to confer with one from the senate, on the same subject. This message being taken up in the house of representatives, a resolution was moved by Mr. Parker, seconded by Mr. Page, declaring that it would be improper to accede to the request of the senate. Several members were in favour of this motion; but others who were opposed to receding from the ground already taken, seemed inclined to appoint a committee as a measure properly respectful to the other branch of the legislature.

After a warm debate, the resolution proposed by Mr. Parker was set aside by the previous question, and a committee of conference was appointed. They could not agree upon a report, in consequence of which the subject was permitted to rest; and the senate, conforming to the precedent given by the house of representatives, addressed the President in their answer to his speech by the terms used in the constitution.

While the representatives were preparing bills for organizing the great executive departments, the senate was occupied with digesting the system of a national judiciary. This complex and extensive subject was taken up in the commencement of the session, and was completed towards its close.

Amendment to the constitution proposed by congress and ratified by the states.

In the course of this session Mr. Madison brought forward a proposition for recommending to the consideration and adoption of the states, several new articles to be added to the constitution.

Many of those objections to it which had been urged with all the vehemence of conviction, and which, in the opinion of some of its advocates, were entitled to serious consideration, were believed by the most intelligent to derive their sole support from erroneous construction of the instrument. Others were upon points on which the objectors might be gratified without injury to the system. To conciliate the affections of their brethren to the government, was an object greatly desired by its friends. Disposed to respect, what they deemed, the errors of their opponents, where that respect could be manifested without a sacrifice of essential principles, they were anxious to annex to the constitution those explanations and barriers against the possible encroachments of rulers on the liberties of the people, which had been loudly demanded, however unfounded, in their judgments, might be the fears by which those demands were suggested. These dispositions were perhaps, in some measure, stimulated to exertion by motives of the soundest policy. The formidable minorities in several of the conventions, which in the legislatures of some powerful states had become majorities, and the refusal of two states to complete the union, were admonitions not to be disregarded, of the necessity of removing jealousies, however misplaced, which operated on so large a portion of society. Among the most zealous friends of the constitution therefore, were found some of the first and warmest advocates for amendments.

To meet the various ideas expressed by the several conventions; to select from the mass of alterations which they had proposed those which might be adopted without stripping the government of its necessary powers; to condense them into a form and compass which would be acceptable to persons disposed to indulge the caprice, and to adopt the language of their particular states; were labours not easily to be accomplished. But the greatest difficulty to be surmounted was, the disposition to make those alterations which would enfeeble, and materially injure, the future operations of the government. At length, ten articles in addition to and amendment of the constitution, were assented to by two-thirds of both houses of congress, and proposed to the legislatures of the several states. Although the necessity of these amendments had been urged by the enemies of the constitution, and denied by its friends, they encountered scarcely any other opposition in the state legislatures, than was given by the leaders of the anti-federal party. Admitting the articles to be good and necessary, it was contended that they were not sufficient for the security of liberty; and the apprehension was avowed that their adoption would quiet the fears of the people, and check the pursuit of those radical alterations which would afford a safe and adequate protection to their rights. They were at length ratified by the legislatures of three-fourths of the states, and probably contributed, in some degree, to diminish the jealousies which had been imbibed against the constitution.

Appointment of the officers of the cabinet, council and of the judges.

The government being completely organized, and a system of revenue established, the important duty of filling the offices which had been created, remained to be performed. In the execution of this delicate trust, the purest virtue and the most impartial judgment were exercised in selecting the best talents, and the greatest weight of character, which the United States could furnish. The unmingled patriotism of the motives by which the President was actuated, would receive its clearest demonstration from a view of all his private letters on this subject: and the success of his endeavours is attested by the abilities and reputation which he drew into the public service.

At the head of the department of foreign affairs, since denominated the department of state, he placed Mr. Jefferson.

This gentleman had been bred to the bar, and at an early period of life, had acquired considerable reputation for extensive attainments in the science of politics. He had been a distinguished member of the second congress, and had been offered a diplomatic appointment, which he had declined. Withdrawing from the administration of continental affairs, he had been elected governor of Virginia, which office he filled for two years. He afterwards again represented his native state in the councils of the union, and in the year 1784, was appointed to succeed Dr. Franklin at the court of Versailles. In that station, he had acquitted himself much to the public satisfaction. His Notes on Virginia, which were read with applause, were believed to evince the soundness of his political opinions; and the Declaration of Independence was universally ascribed to his pen. He had long been placed by America amongst the most eminent of her citizens, and had long been classed by the

President with those who were most capable of serving the nation. Having lately obtained permission to return for a short time to the United States, he was, while on his passage, nominated to this important office; and, on his arrival in Virginia, found a letter from the President, giving him the option of becoming the secretary of foreign affairs, or of retaining his station at the court of Versailles. He appears rather to have inclined to continue in his foreign appointment; and, in changing his situation, to have consulted the wishes of the first magistrate more than the preference of his own mind.

The task of restoring public credit, of drawing order and arrangement from the chaotic confusion in which the finances of America were involved, and of devising means which should render the revenue productive, and commensurate with the demand, in a manner least burdensome to the people, was justly classed among the most arduous of the duties which devolved on the new government. In discharging it, much aid was expected from the head of the treasury. This important, and, at that time, intricate department, was assigned to Colonel Hamilton.

This gentleman was a native of the island of St. Croix, and, at a very early period of life, had been placed by his friends, in New York. Possessing an ardent temper, he caught fire from the concussions of the moment, and, with all the enthusiasm of youth, engaged first his pen, and afterwards his sword, in the stern contest between the American colonies and their parent state. Among the first troops raised by New York was a corps of artillery, in which he was appointed a captain. Soon after the war was transferred to the Hudson, his superior endowments recommended him to the attention of the Commander-in-chief, into whose family, before completing his twenty-first year, he was invited to enter. Equally brave and intelligent, he continued, in this situation, to display a degree of firmness and capacity which commanded the confidence and esteem of his general, and of the principal officers in the army.

After the capitulation at Yorktown, the war languished throughout the American continent, and the probability that its termination was approaching daily increased.

The critical circumstances of the existing government rendered the events of the civil, more interesting than those of the military department; and Colonel Hamilton accepted a seat in the congress of the United States. In all the important acts of the day, he performed a conspicuous part; and was greatly distinguished among those distinguished men whom the crisis had attracted to the councils of their country. He had afterwards been active in promoting those measures which led to the convention at Philadelphia, of which he was a member, and had greatly contributed to the adoption of the constitution by the state of New York. In the pre-eminent part he had performed, both in the military and civil transactions of his country, he had acquired a great degree of well merited fame; and the frankness of his manners, the openness of his temper, the warmth of his feelings, and the sincerity of his heart, had secured him many valuable friends.

To talents equally splendid and useful, he united a patient industry, not always the companion of genius, which fitted him, in a peculiar manner, for subduing the difficulties to be encountered by the man who should be placed at the head of the American finances.

The department of war was already filled by General Knox, and he was again nominated to it.

Throughout the contest of the revolution, this officer had continued at the head of the American artillery, and from being the colonel of a regiment, had been promoted to the rank of a major general. In this important station, he had preserved a high military character; and, on the resignation of General Lincoln, had been appointed secretary of war. To his past services, and to unquestionable integrity, he was admitted to unite a sound understanding; and the public judgment, as well as that of the chief magistrate, pronounced him in all respects competent to the station he filled.

The office of attorney general was filled by Mr. Edmund Randolph. To a distinguished reputation in the line of his profession, this gentleman added a considerable degree of political eminence. After having been for several years the attorney general of Virginia, he had been elected its governor. While in this office, he was chosen a member of the convention which framed the constitution, and was also elected to that which was called by the state for its adoption or rejection. After having served at the head of the executive the term permitted by the constitution of the state, he entered into its legislature, where he preserved a great share of influence.

Such was the first cabinet council of the President. In its composition, public opinion as well as intrinsic worth had been consulted, and a high degree of character had been combined with real talent.

In the selection of persons for high judicial offices, the President was guided by the same principles. At the head of this department he placed Mr. John Jay.

From the commencement of the revolution, this gentleman had filled a large space in the public mind. Remaining, without intermission, in the service of his country, he had passed through a succession of high offices, and, in all of them, had merited the approbation of his fellow citizens. To his pen, while in congress, America was indebted for some of those masterly addresses which reflected most honour upon the government; and to his firmness and penetration, was to be ascribed, in no inconsiderable degree, the happy issue of those intricate negotiations, which were conducted, towards the close of the war, at Madrid, and at Paris. On returning to the United States, he had been appointed secretary of foreign affairs, in which station he had conducted himself with his accustomed ability. A sound judgment improved by extensive reading and great knowledge of public affairs, unyielding firmness, and inflexible integrity, were qualities of which Mr. Jay had given frequent and signal proofs. Although for some years withdrawn from that profession to which he was bred, the acquisitions of his early life had not been lost; and the subjects on which his mind had been exercised, were not entirely foreign from those which would, in the first instance, employ the courts in which he was to preside.

John Rutledge of South Carolina, James Wilson of Pennsylvania, William Cushing of Massachusetts, Robert Harrison of Maryland, and John Blair of Virginia were nominated as associate justices. Some of these gentlemen had filled the highest law offices in their respective states; and all of them had received distinguished marks of the public confidence.

In the systems which had been adopted by the several states, offices corresponding to those created by the revenue laws of congress, had been already established. Uninfluenced by considerations of personal regard, the President could not be induced to change men whom he found in place, if worthy of being employed; and where the man who had filled such office in the former state of things was unexceptionable in his conduct and character, he was uniformly re-appointed. In deciding between competitors for vacant offices, the law he prescribed for his government was to regard the fitness of candidates for the duties they would be required to discharge; and, where an equality in this respect existed, former merits and sufferings in the public service, gave claims to preference which could not be overlooked.

In the legislative, as well as in the executive and judicial departments, great respectability of character was also associated with an eminent degree of talents. The constitutional prohibition to appoint any member of the legislature to an office created during the time for which he had been elected, did not exclude men of the most distinguished abilities from the first congress. Impelled by an anxious solicitude respecting the first measures of the government, its zealous friends had pressed into its service: and, in both branches of the legislature, men were found who possessed the fairest claims to the public confidence.

From the duties attached to his office, the Vice President of the United States, and President of the senate, though not a member of the legislature, was classed, in the public mind, with that department not less than with the executive. Elected by the whole people of America in common with the President, he could not fail to be taken from the most distinguished citizens, and to add to the dignity of the body over which he presided.

Mr. John Adams was one of the earliest and most ardent patriots of the revolution. Bred to the bar, he had necessarily studied the constitution of his country, and was among the most determined asserters of its rights. Active in guiding that high spirit which animated all New England, he became a member of the congress of 1774, and was among the first who dared to avow sentiments in favour of independence. In that body he soon attained considerable eminence; and, at an early stage of the war, was chosen one of the commissioners to whom the interests of the United States in Europe were confided. In his diplomatic character, he had contributed greatly to those measures which drew Holland into the war; had negotiated the treaty between the United States and the Dutch republic: and had, at critical points of time, obtained loans of money which were of great advantage to his country. In the negotiations which terminated the war, he had also rendered important services; and, after the ratification of the definitive articles of peace, had been deputed to Great Britain for the purpose of effecting a commercial treaty with that nation. The political situation of America having rendered this object unattainable, he solicited leave to return, and arrived in the United States soon after the adoption of the constitution.

As a statesman, this gentleman had, at all times, ranked high in the estimation of his countrymen. He had improved a sound understanding by extensive political and historical reading; and perhaps no American had reflected more profoundly on the subject of government. The exalted opinion he entertained of his own country was flattering to his fellow citizens; and the purity of his mind, the unblemished integrity of a life spent in the public service, had gained him their confidence.

A government, supported in all its departments by so much character and talent, at the head of which was placed a man whose capacity was undoubted, whose life had been one great and continued lesson of disinterested patriotism, and for whom almost every bosom glowed with an attachment bordering on enthusiasm, could not fail to make a rapid progress in conciliating the affection of the people. That all hostility to the constitution should subside, that public measures should receive universal approbation; that no particular disgusts and individual irritations should be excited; were expectations which could not reasonably be indulged. Exaggerated accounts were indeed occasionally circulated of the pomp and splendour which were affected by certain high officers, of the monarchical tendencies of particular institutions, and of the dispositions which prevailed to increase the powers of the executive. That the doors of the senate were closed, and that a disposition had been manifested by that body to distinguish the President of the United States by a title,[43] gave considerable umbrage, and were represented as evincing inclinations in that branch of the legislature, unfriendly to republicanism. The exorbitance of salaries was also a subject of some declamation, and the equality of commercial privileges with which foreign bottoms entered American ports, was not free from objection. But the apprehensions of danger to liberty from the new system, which had been impressed on the minds of well meaning men, were visibly wearing off; the popularity of the administration was communicating itself to the government; and the materials with which the discontented were furnished, could not yet be efficaciously employed.

Towards the close of the session, a report on a petition which had been presented at an early period by the creditors of the public residing in the state of Pennsylvania, was taken up in the house of representatives. Though many considerations rendered a postponement of this interesting subject necessary, two resolutions were passed; the one, "declaring that the house considered an adequate provision for the support of the public credit, as a matter of high importance to the national honour and prosperity;" and the other directing, "the secretary of the treasury to prepare a plan for that purpose, and to report the same to the house at its next meeting."

Adjournment of the first session of congress.

On the 29th of September, congress adjourned to the first Monday in the succeeding January.

Throughout the whole of this laborious and important session, perfect harmony subsisted between the executive and the legislature; and no circumstance occurred which threatened to impair it. The modes of communication between the departments of government were adjusted in a satisfactory manner, and arrangements were made on some of those delicate points in which the senate participate of executive power.

The president visits the New England states.

Anxious to visit New England, to observe in person the condition of the country and the dispositions of the people towards the government and its measures, the President was disposed to avail himself of the short respite from official cares afforded by the recess of congress, to make a tour through the eastern states. His resolution being taken, and the executive business which required his immediate personal attendance being despatched,[44] he commenced his tour on the 15th of October; and, passing through Connecticut and Massachusetts, as far as Portsmouth in New Hampshire, returned by a different route to New York, where he arrived on the 13th of November.

With this visit, the President had much reason to be satisfied. To contemplate the theatre on which many interesting military scenes had been exhibited, and to review the ground on which his first campaign as Commander-in-chief of the American army had been made, were sources of rational delight. To observe the progress of society, the improvements in agriculture, commerce, and manufactures; and the temper, circumstances, and dispositions of the people, could not fail to be grateful to an intelligent mind, and an employment in all respects, worthy of the chief magistrate of the nation. The reappearance of their general, in the high station he now filled, brought back to recollection the perilous transactions of the war; and the reception universally given to him, attested the unabated love which was felt for his person and character, and indicated unequivocally the growing popularity, at least in that part of the union, of the government he administered.

His reception.

The sincerity and warmth with which he reciprocated the affection expressed for his person in the addresses presented to him, was well calculated to preserve the sentiments which were generally diffused. "I rejoice with you my fellow citizens," said he in answer to an address from the inhabitants of Boston, "in every circumstance that declares your prosperity;—and I do so most cordially because you have well deserved to be happy.

"Your love of liberty—your respect for the laws—your habits of industry—and your practice of the moral and religious obligations, are the strongest claims to national and individual happiness. And they will, I trust, be firmly and lastingly established."

But the interchange of sentiments with the companions of his military toils and glory, will excite most interest, because on both sides, the expressions were dictated by the purest and most delicious feelings of the human heart. From the Cincinnati of Massachusetts he received the following address:

"Amidst the various gratulations which your arrival in this metropolis has occasioned, permit us, the members of the society of the Cincinnati in this commonwealth, most respectfully to assure you of the ardour of esteem and affection you have so indelibly fixed in our hearts, as our glorious leader in war, and illustrious example in peace.

"After the solemn and endearing farewell on the banks of the Hudson, which our anxiety presaged as final, most peculiarly pleasing is the present unexpected meeting. On this occasion we can not avoid the recollection of the various scenes of toil and danger through which you conducted us; and while we contemplate various trying periods of the war, and the triumphs of peace, we rejoice to behold you, induced by the unanimous voice of your country, entering upon other trials, and other services alike important, and, in some points of view, equally hazardous. For the completion of the great purposes which a grateful country has assigned you, long, very long, may your invaluable life be preserved. And as the admiring world, while considering you as a soldier, have long wanted a comparison, may your virtue and talents as a statesman leave them without a parallel.

"It is not in words to express an attachment founded like ours. We can only say that when soldiers, our greatest pride was a promptitude of obedience to your orders; as citizens, our supreme ambition is to maintain the character of firm supporters of that noble fabric of federal government over which you preside.

"As members of the society of the Cincinnati, it will be our endeavour to cherish those sacred principles of charity and fraternal attachment which our institution inculcates. And while our conduct is thus regulated, we can never want the patronage of the first of patriots and the best of men."

To this address the following answer was returned:

"In reciprocating with gratitude and sincerity the multiplied and affecting gratulations of my fellow citizens of this commonwealth, they will all of them with justice allow me to say, that none can be dearer to me than the affectionate assurances which you have expressed. Dear, indeed, is the occasion which restores an intercourse with my faithful associates in prosperous and adverse fortune; and enhanced are the triumphs of peace, participated with those whose virtue and valour so largely contributed to procure them. To that virtue and valour your country has confessed her obligations. Be mine the grateful task to add the testimony of a connexion which it was my pride to own in the field, and is now my happiness to acknowledge in the enjoyments of peace and freedom.

"Regulating your conduct by those principles which have heretofore governed your actions as men, soldiers, and citizens, you will repeat the obligations conferred on your country, and you will transmit to posterity an example that must command their admiration and grateful praise. Long may you continue to enjoy the endearments of fraternal attachments, and the heartfelt happiness of reflecting that you have faithfully done your duty.

"While I am permitted to possess the consciousness of this worth, which has long bound me to you by every tie of affection and esteem, I will continue to be your sincere and faithful friend."

Soon after his return to New York, the President was informed of the ill success which had attended his first attempt to negotiate a peace with the Creek Indians. General Lincoln, Mr. Griffin, and Colonel Humphries, had been deputed on this mission, and had met M'Gillivray with several other chiefs, and about two thousand men, at Rock landing, on the Oconee, on the frontiers of Georgia. The treaty commenced with favourable appearances, but was soon abruptly broken off by M'Gillivray. Some difficulties arose on the subject of a boundary, but the principal obstacles to a peace were supposed to grow out of his personal interests, and his connexions with Spain.

North Carolina accedes to the union.

This intelligence was more than counterbalanced by the accession of North Carolina to the union. In the month of November, a second convention had met under the authority of the legislature of that state, and the constitution was adopted by a great majority.

CHAPTER VI.

Meeting of congress.... President's speech.... Report of the secretary of the treasury on public credit.... Debate thereon.... Bill for fixing the permanent seat of government.... Adjournment of congress.... Treaty with the Creek Indians.... Relations of the United States with Great Britain and Spain.... The President visits Mount Vernon.... Session of congress.... The President's speech.... Debates on the excise.... On a national bank.... The opinions of the cabinet on the law.... Progress of parties.... War with the Indians.... Defeat of Harmar.... Adjournment of congress.

1790

ON the eighth of January, 1790, the President met both houses of congress in the senate chamber.

Meeting of the second session of the first congress.

In his speech, which was delivered from the chair of the vice president, after congratulating congress on the accession of the important state of North Carolina to the union, and on the prosperous aspect of American affairs, he proceeded to recommend certain great objects of legislation to their more especial consideration.

"Among the many interesting objects," continued the speech, "which will engage your attention, that of providing for the common defence will merit your particular regard. To be prepared for war is one of the most effectual means of preserving peace.

"A free people ought not only to be armed but disciplined; to which end, a uniform and well digested plan is requisite; and their safety and interest require that they should promote such manufactories as tend to render them independent on others for essential, particularly for military supplies."

As connected with this subject, a proper establishment for the troops which they might deem indispensable, was suggested for their mature deliberation; and the indications of a hostile temper given by several tribes of Indians, were considered as admonishing them of the necessity of being prepared to afford protection to the frontiers, and to punish aggression.

The interests of the United States were declared to require that the means of keeping up their intercourse with foreign nations should be provided; and the expediency of establishing a uniform rule of naturalization was suggested.

After expressing his confidence in their attention to many improvements essential to the prosperity of the interior, the President added, "nor am I less persuaded that you will agree with me in opinion that there is nothing which can better deserve your patronage than the promotion of science and literature. Knowledge is in every country the surest basis of public happiness. In one, in which the measures of government receive their impression so immediately from the sense of the community as in ours, it is proportionably essential. To the security of a free constitution it contributes in various ways: by convincing those who are intrusted with the public administration, that every valuable end of government is best answered by the enlightened confidence of the people; and by teaching the people themselves to know and to value their own rights; to discern and provide against invasions of them; to distinguish between oppression and the necessary exercise of lawful authority; between burdens proceeding from a disregard to their convenience, and those resulting from the inevitable exigencies of society; to discriminate the spirit of liberty from that of licentiousness, cherishing the first, avoiding the last, and uniting a speedy but temperate vigilance against encroachments, with an inviolable respect to the laws.

"Whether this desirable object will be best promoted by affording aids to seminaries of learning already established, by the institution of a national university, or by any other expedients, will be well worthy of a place in the deliberations of the legislature."

Addressing himself then particularly to the representatives he said: "I saw with peculiar pleasure at the close of the last session, the resolution entered into by you, expressive of your opinion, that an adequate provision for the support of the public credit is a matter of high importance to the national honour and prosperity. In this sentiment I entirely concur; and to a perfect confidence in your best endeavours to devise such a provision as will be truly consistent with the end, I add an equal reliance on the cheerful co-operation of the other branch of the legislature. It would be superfluous to specify inducements to a measure in which the character and permanent interests of the United States are so obviously and so deeply concerned; and which has received so explicit a sanction from your declaration."

Addressing himself again to both houses, he observed, that the estimates and papers respecting the objects particularly recommended to their attention would be laid before them; and concluded with saying, "the welfare of our country is the great object to which our cares and efforts ought to be directed: and I shall derive great satisfaction from a co-operation with you in the pleasing though arduous task of insuring to our fellow citizens the blessings which they have a right to expect from a free, efficient, and equal government."

The answers of both houses were indicative of the harmony which subsisted between the executive and legislative departments.

Congress had been so occupied during its first session with those bills which were necessary to bring the new system into full operation, and to create an immediate revenue, that some measures which possessed great and pressing claims to immediate attention had been unavoidably deferred. That neglect under which the creditors of the public had been permitted to languish could not fail to cast an imputation on the American republics, which had been sincerely lamented by the wisest among those who administered the former government. The power to comply substantially with the engagements of the United States being at length conferred on those who were bound by them, it was confidently expected by the friends of the constitution that their country would retrieve its reputation, and that its fame would no longer be tarnished with the blots which stain a faithless people.

Report of the secretary of the treasury of a plan for the support of public credit.

On the 9th of January, a letter from the secretary of the treasury to the speaker of the house of representatives was read, stating that in obedience to the resolution of the 21st of September, he had prepared a plan for the support of public credit, which he was ready to report when the house should be pleased to receive it; and, after a short debate in which the personal attendance of the secretary for the purpose of making explanations was urged by some, and opposed by others, it was resolved that the report should be received in writing on the succeeding Thursday.

Availing himself of the latitude afforded by the terms of the resolution under which he acted, the secretary had introduced into his report an able and comprehensive argument elucidating and supporting the principles it contained. After displaying, with strength and perspicuity, the justice and the policy of an adequate provision for the public debt, he proceeded to discuss the principles on which it should be made.

"It was agreed," he said, "by all, that the foreign debt should be provided for according to the precise terms of the contract. It was to be regretted that, with respect to the domestic debt, the same unanimity of sentiment did not prevail."

The first point on which the public appeared to be divided, involved the question, "whether a discrimination ought not to be made between original holders of the public securities, and present possessors by purchase." After reviewing the arguments generally urged in its support, the secretary declared himself against this discrimination. He deemed it "equally unjust and impolitic; highly injurious even to the original holders of public securities, and ruinous to public credit." To the arguments with which he enforced these opinions, he added the authority of the government of the union. From the circular address of congress to the states, of the 26th of April, 1783, accompanying their revenue system of the 18th of the same month, passages were selected indicating unequivocally, that in the view of that body the original creditors, and those who had become so by assignment, had equal claims upon the nation.

After reasoning at great length against a discrimination between the different creditors of the union, the secretary proceeded to examine whether a difference ought to be permitted to remain between them and the creditors of individual states.

Both descriptions of debt were contracted for the same objects, and were in the main the same. Indeed, a great part of the particular debts of the states had arisen from assumptions by them on account of the union; and it was most equitable that there should be the same measure of retribution for all. There were many reasons, some of which were stated, for believing this would not be the case, unless the state debts should be assumed by the nation.

In addition to the injustice of favouring one class of creditors more than another which was equally meritorious, many arguments were urged in support of the policy of distributing to all with an equal hand from the same source.

After an elaborate discussion of these and some other points connected with the subject, the secretary proposed that a loan should be opened to the full amount of the debt, as well of the particular states, as of the union.

The terms to be offered were,—

First. That for every one hundred dollars subscribed payable in the debt, as well interest as principal, the subscriber should be entitled to have two-thirds funded on a yearly interest of six per cent, (the capital redeemable at the pleasure of government by the payment of the principal) and to receive the other third in lands of the western territory at their then actual value. Or,

Secondly. To have the whole sum funded at a yearly interest of four per cent., irredeemable by any payment exceeding five dollars per annum both on account of principal and interest, and to receive as a compensation for the reduction of interest, fifteen dollars and eighty cents, payable in lands as in the preceding case. Or,

Thirdly. To have sixty-six and two-thirds of a dollar funded at a yearly interest of six per cent., irredeemable also by any payment exceeding four dollars and two-thirds of a dollar per annum on account both of principal and interest, and to have at the end of ten years twenty-six dollars and eighty-eight cents funded at the like interest and rate of redemption.

In addition to these propositions the creditors were to have an option of vesting their money in annuities on different plans; and it was also recommended to open a loan at five per cent, for ten millions of dollars, payable one half in specie, and the other half in the debt, irredeemable by any payment exceeding six dollars per annum both of principal and interest.

By way of experiment, a tontine on principles stated in the report was also suggested.

The secretary was restrained from proposing to fund the whole debt immediately at the current rate of interest, by the opinion, "that although such a provision might not exceed the abilities of the country, it would require the extension of taxation to a degree, and to objects which the true interest of the creditors themselves would forbid. It was therefore to be hoped and expected, that they would cheerfully concur in such modifications of their claims, on fair and equitable principles, as would facilitate to the government an arrangement substantial, durable, and satisfactory to the community. Exigencies might ere long arise which would call for resources greatly beyond what was now deemed sufficient for the current service; and should the faculties of the country be exhausted, or even strained to provide for the public debt, there could be less reliance on the sacredness of the provision.

"But while he yielded to the force of these considerations, he did not lose sight of those fundamental principles of good faith which dictate that every practicable exertion ought to be made, scrupulously to fulfil the engagements of government; that no change in the rights of its creditors ought to be attempted without their voluntary consent; and that this consent ought to be voluntary in fact, as well as in name. Consequently, that every proposal of a change ought to be in the shape of an appeal to their reason and to their interest, not to their necessities. To this end it was requisite that a fair equivalent should be offered, for what might be asked to be given up, and unquestionable security for the remainder." This fair equivalent for the proposed reduction of interest was, he thought, offered in the relinquishment of the power to redeem the whole debt at pleasure.

That a free judgment might be exercised by the holders of public securities in accepting or rejecting the terms offered by the government, provision was made in the report for paying to non-subscribing creditors, a dividend of the surplus which should remain in the treasury after paying the interest of the proposed loans: but as the funds immediately to be provided, were calculated to produce only four per cent, on the entire debt, the dividend, for the present, was not to exceed that rate of interest.

To enable the treasury to support this increased demand upon it, an augmentation of the duties on imported wines, spirits, tea, and coffee, was proposed, and a duty on home made spirits was also recommended.

This celebrated report, which has been alike the fruitful theme of extravagant praise and bitter censure, merits the more attention, because the first regular and systematic opposition to the principles on which the affairs of the union were administered, originated in the measures which were founded on it.

On the 28th of January, this subject was taken up; and, after some animadversions on the speculations in the public debt to which the report, it was said, had already given birth, the business was postponed until the eighth of February, when it was again brought forward.

Debate thereon.

Several resolutions affirmative of the principles contained in the report, were moved by Mr. Fitzsimmons. To the first, which respected a provision for the foreign debt, the house agreed without a dissenting voice. The second, in favour of appropriating permanent funds for payment of the interest on the domestic debt, and for the gradual redemption of the principal, gave rise to a very animated debate.

Mr. Jackson declared his hostility to funding systems generally. To prove their pernicious influence, he appealed to the histories of Florence, Genoa, and Great Britain; and, contending that the subject ought to be deferred until North Carolina should be represented, moved, that the committee should rise. This question being decided in the negative, Mr. Scott declared the opinion that the United States were not bound to pay the domestic creditors the sums specified in the certificates of debts in their possession. He supported this opinion by urging, not that the public had received less value than was expressed on the face of the paper which had been issued, but that those to whom it had been delivered, by parting with it at two shillings and sixpence in the pound, had themselves fixed the value of their claims, and had manifested their willingness to add to their other sacrifices this deduction from their demand upon the nation. He therefore moved to amend the resolution before the committee so as to require a resettlement of the debt.

The amendment was opposed by Mr. Boudinot, Mr. Lawrence, Mr. Ames, Mr. Sherman, Mr. Hartley, and Mr. Goodhue. They stated at large the terms on which the debt had been contracted, and urged the confidence which the creditors had a right to place in the government for its discharge according to settlements already made, and acknowledgments already given. The idea that the legislative body could diminish an ascertained debt was reprobated with great force, as being at the same time unjust, impolitic, and subversive of every principle on which public contracts are founded. The evidences of debt possessed by the creditors of the United States were considered as public bonds, for the redemption of which the property and the labour of the people were pledged.

After the debate had been protracted to some length, the question was taken on Mr. Scott's amendment, and it passed in the negative.

Mr. Madison then rose, and, in an eloquent speech, replete with argument, proposed an amendment to the resolution, the effect of which was to discriminate between the public creditors, so as to pay the present holder of assignable paper the highest price it had borne in the market, and give the residue to the person with whom the debt was originally contracted. Where the original creditor had never parted with his claim, he was to receive the whole sum acknowledged to be due on the face of the certificate.

This motion was supported by Mr. Jackson, Mr. White, Mr. Moore, Mr. Page, Mr. Stone, Mr. Scott, and Mr. Seney.

It was opposed with great earnestness and strength of argument, by Mr. Sedgewick, Mr. Lawrence, Mr. Smith, of South Carolina, Mr. Ames, Mr. Gerry, Mr. Boudinot, Mr. Wadsworth, Mr. Goodhue, Mr. Hartley, Mr. Bland, Mr. Benson, Mr. Burke, and Mr. Livermore.

The argument was ably supported on both sides, was long, animated, and interesting. At length the question was put, and the amendment was rejected by a great majority.

This discussion deeply engaged the public attention. The proposition was new and interesting. That the debt ought to be diminished for the public advantage, was an opinion which had frequently been advanced, and was maintained by many. But a reduction from the claims of its present holders for the benefit of those who had sold their rights, was a measure which saved nothing to the public purse, and was therefore recommended only by considerations, the operation of which can never be very extensive. Against it were arranged all who had made purchases, and a great majority of those who conceived that sound policy and honest dealing require a literal observance of public contracts.

Although the decision of congress against a discrimination in favour of the original creditor produced no considerable sensation, the determination on that part of the secretary's report which was the succeeding subject of deliberation, affecting political interests and powers which are never to be approached without danger, seemed to unchain all those fierce passions which a high respect for the government and for those who administered it, had in a great measure restrained.

The manner in which the several states entered into and conducted the war of the revolution, will be recollected. Acting in some respects separately, and in others conjointly, for the attainment of a common object, their resources were exerted, sometimes under the authority of congress, sometimes under the authority of the local government, to repel the enemy wherever he appeared. The debt incurred in support of the war was therefore, in the first instance, contracted partly by the continent, and partly by the states. When the system of requisitions was adopted, the transactions of the union were carried on, almost entirely, through the agency of the states; and when the measure of compensating the army for the depreciation of their pay became necessary, this burden, under the recommendation of congress, was assumed by the respective states. Some had funded this debt, and paid the interest upon it. Others had made no provision for the interest; but all, by taxes, paper money, or purchase, had, in some measure, reduced the principal. In their exertions some degree of inequality had obtained; and they looked anxiously to a settlement of accounts, for the ascertainment of claims which each supposed itself to have upon the union. Measures to effect this object had been taken by the former government; but they were slow in their progress, and intrinsic difficulties were found in the thing itself, not easily to be overcome.

The secretary of the treasury proposed to assume these debts, and to fund them in common with that which continued to be the proper debt of the union.

The resolution which comprehended this principle of the report, was vigorously opposed.

It was contended that the general government would acquire an undue influence, and that the state governments would be annihilated by the measure. Not only would all the influence of the public creditors be thrown into the scale of the former, but it would absorb all the powers of taxation, and leave to the latter only the shadow of a government. This would probably terminate in rendering the state governments useless, and would destroy the system so recently established. The union, it was said, had been compared to a rope of sand; but gentlemen were cautioned not to push things to the opposite extreme. The attempt to strengthen it might be unsuccessful, and the cord might be strained until it should break.

The constitutional authority of the federal government to assume the debts of the states was questioned. Its powers, it was said, were specified, and this was not among them.

The policy of the measure, as it affected merely the government of the union, was controverted, and its justice was arraigned.

On the ground of policy it was objected, that the assumption would impose on the United States a burden, the weight of which was unascertained, and which would require an extension of taxation beyond the limits which prudence would prescribe. An attempt to raise the impost would be dangerous; and the excise added to it would not produce funds adequate to the object. A tax on real estate must be resorted to, objections to which had been made in every part of the union. It would be more adviseable to leave this source of revenue untouched in the hands of the state governments, who could apply to it with more facility, with a better understanding of the subject, and with less dissatisfaction to individuals, than could possibly be done by the government of the United States.

There existed no necessity for taking up this burden. The state creditors had not required it. There was no petition from them upon the subject. There was not only no application from the states, but there was reason to believe that they were seriously opposed to the measure. Many of them would certainly view it with a jealous,—a jaundiced eye. The convention of North Carolina, which adopted the constitution, had proposed, as an amendment to it, to deprive congress of the power of interfering between the respective states and their creditors: and there could be no obligation to assume more than the balances which on a final settlement would be found due to creditor states.

That the debt by being thus accumulated would be perpetuated was also an evil of real magnitude. Many of the states had already made considerable progress in extinguishing their debts, and the process might certainly be carried on more rapidly by them than by the union. A public debt seemed to be considered by some as a public blessing; but to this doctrine they were not converts. If, as they believed, a public debt was a public evil, it would be enormously increased by adding those of the states to that of the union.

The measure was unwise too as it would affect public credit. Such an augmentation of the debt must inevitably depreciate its value; since it was the character of paper, whatever denomination it might assume, to diminish in value in proportion to the quantity in circulation.

It would also increase an evil which was already sensibly felt. The state debts when assumed by the continent, would, as that of the union had already done, accumulate in large cities; and the dissatisfaction excited by the payment of taxes, would be increased by perceiving that the money raised from the people flowed into the hands of a few individuals. Still greater mischief was to be apprehended. A great part of this additional debt would go into the hands of foreigners; and the United States would be heavily burdened to pay an interest which could not be expected to remain in the country.

The measure was unjust, because it was burdening those states which had taxed themselves highly to discharge the claims of their creditors, with the debts of those which had not made the same exertions. It would delay the settlement of accounts between the individual states and the United States; and the supporters of the measure were openly charged with intending to defeat that settlement.

It was also said that, in its execution, the scheme would be found extremely embarrassing, perhaps impracticable. The case of a partial accession to the measure by the creditors, a case which would probably occur, presented a difficulty for which no provision was made, and of which no solution had been given. Should the creditors in some states come into the system, and those in others refuse to change their security, the government would be involved in perplexities from which no means of extricating itself had been shown. Nor would it be practicable to discriminate between the debts contracted for general and for local objects.

In the course of the debate, severe allusions were made to the conduct of particular states; and the opinions advanced in favour of the measure, were ascribed to local interests.

In support of the assumption, the debts of the states were traced to their origin. America, it was said, had engaged in a war, the object of which was equally interesting to every part of the union. It was not the war of a particular state, but of the United States. It was not the liberty and independence of a part, but of the whole, for which they had contended, and which they had acquired. The cause was a common cause. As brethren, the American people had consented to hazard property and life in its defence. All the sums expended in the attainment of this great object, whatever might be the authority under which they were raised or appropriated, conduced to the same end. Troops were raised, and military stores purchased, before congress assumed the command of the army, or the control of the war. The ammunition which repulsed the enemy at Bunker's Hill, was purchased by Massachusetts; and formed a part of the debt of that state.

Nothing could be more erroneous than the principle which had been assumed in argument, that the holders of securities issued by individual states were to be considered merely as state creditors;—as if the debt had been contracted on account of the particular state. It was contracted on account of the union, in that common cause in which all were equally interested.

From the complex nature of the political system which had been adopted in America, the war was, in a great measure, carried on through the agency of the state governments; and the debts were, in truth, the debts of the union, for which the states had made themselves responsible. Except the civil list, the whole state expenditure was in the prosecution of the war; and the state taxes had undeniably exceeded the provision for their civil list. The foundation for the several classes of the debt was reviewed in detail; and it was affirmed to be proved from the review, and from the books in the public offices, that, in its origin, a great part of it, even in form, and the whole, in fact, was equitably due from the continent. The states individually possessing all the resources of the nation, became responsible to certain descriptions of the public creditors. But they were the agents of the continent in contracting the debt; and its distribution among them for payment, arose from the division of political power which existed under the old confederation. A new arrangement of the system had taken place, and a power over the resources of the nation was conferred on the general government. With the funds, the debt also ought to be assumed. This investigation of its origin demonstrated that the assumption was not the creation of a new debt, but the reacknowledgment of liability for an old one, the payment of which had devolved on those members of the system, who, at the time, were alone capable of paying it. And thence was inferred, not only the justice of the measure, but a complete refutation of the arguments drawn from the constitution. If, in point of fact, the debt was in its origin continental, and had been transferred to the states for greater facility of payment, there could be no constitutional objection to restoring its original and real character.

The great powers of war, of taxation, and of borrowing money, which were vested in congress to pay the debts, and provide for the common defence and general welfare of the United States, comprised that in question. There could be no more doubt of their right to charge themselves with the payment of a debt contracted in the past war, than to borrow money for the prosecution of a future war. The impolicy of leaving the public creditors to receive payment from different sources was also strongly pressed; and the jealousy which would exist between the creditors of the union and of the states, was considered as a powerful argument in favour of giving them one common interest. This jealousy, it was feared, might be carried so far, as even to create an opposition to the laws of the union.

If the states should provide for their creditors, the same sum of money must be collected from the people, as would be required if the debt should be assumed; and it would probably be collected in a manner more burdensome, than if one uniform system should be established. If all should not make such provision, it would be unjust to leave the soldier of one state unpaid, while the services of the man who fought by his side were amply compensated; and, after having assumed the funds, it would dishonour the general government to permit a creditor for services rendered, or property advanced for the continent, to remain unsatisfied, because his claim had been transferred to the state, at a time when the state alone possessed the means of payment. By the injured and neglected creditor, such an arrangement might justly be considered as a disreputable artifice.

Instead of delaying, it was believed to be a measure which would facilitate the settlement of accounts between the states. Its advocates declared that they did not entertain, and never had entertained any wish to procrastinate a settlement. On the contrary, it was greatly desired by them. They had themselves brought forward propositions for that purpose; and they invited their adversaries to assist in improving the plan which had been introduced.

The settlement between the states, it was said, either would or would not be made. Should it ever take place, it would remedy any inequalities which might grow out of the assumption. Should it never take place, the justice of the measure became the more apparent. That the burdens in support of a common war, which from various causes had devolved unequally on the states, ought to be apportioned among them, was a truth too clear to be controverted; and this, if the settlement should never be accomplished, could be effected only by the measure now proposed. Indeed, in any event, it would be the only certain, as well as only eligible plan. For how were the debtor states to be compelled to pay the balances which should be found against them?

If the measure was recommended by considerations which rendered its ultimate adoption inevitable, the present was clearly preferable to any future time. It was desirable immediately to quiet the minds of the public creditors by assuring them that justice would be done; to simplify the forms of public debt; and to put an end to that speculation which had been so much reprobated, and which could be terminated only by giving the debt a real and permanent value.

That the assumption would impair the just influence of the states was controverted with great strength of argument. The diffusive representation in the state legislatures, the intimate connexion between the representative and his constituents, the influence of the state legislatures over the members of one branch of the national legislature, the nature of the powers exercised by the state governments which perpetually presented them to the people in a point of view calculated to lay hold of the public affections, were guarantees that the states would retain their due weight in the political system, and that a debt was not necessary to the solidity or duration of their power.

But the argument it was said proved too much. If a debt was now essential to the preservation of state authority, it would always be so. It must therefore never be extinguished, but must be perpetuated, in order to secure the existence of the state governments. If, for this purpose, it was indispensable that the expenses of the revolutionary war should be borne by the states, it would not be less indispensable that the expenses of future wars should be borne in the same manner. Either the argument was unfounded, or the constitution was wrong; and the powers of the sword and the purse ought not to have been conferred on the government of the union. Whatever speculative opinions might be entertained on this point, they were to administer the government according to the principles of the constitution as it was framed. But, it was added, if so much power follows the assumption as the objection implies, is it not time to ask—is it safe to forbear assuming? if the power is so dangerous, it will be so when exercised by the states. If assuming tends to consolidation, is the reverse, tending to disunion, a less weighty objection? if it is answered that the non-assumption will not necessarily tend to disunion; neither, it may be replied, does the assumption necessarily tend to consolidation.

It was not admitted that the assumption would tend to perpetuate the debt. It could not be presumed that the general government would be less willing than the local governments to discharge it; nor could it be presumed that the means were less attainable by the former than the latter.

It was not contended that a public debt was a public blessing. Whether a debt was to be preferred to no debt was not the question. The debt was already contracted: and the question, so far as policy might be consulted, was, whether it was more for the public advantage to give it such a form as would render it applicable to the purposes of a circulating medium, or to leave it a mere subject of speculation, incapable of being employed to any useful purpose. The debt was admitted to be an evil; but it was an evil from which, if wisely modified, some benefit might be extracted; and which, in its present state, could have only a mischievous operation.

If the debt should be placed on adequate funds, its operation on public credit could not be pernicious: in its present precarious condition, there was much more to be apprehended in that respect.

To the objection that it would accumulate in large cities, it was answered it would be a monied capital, and would be held by those who chose to place money at interest; but by funding the debt, the present possessors would be enabled to part with it at its nominal value, instead of selling it at its present current rate. If it should centre in the hands of foreigners, the sooner it was appreciated to its proper standard, the greater quantity of specie would its transfer bring into the United States.

To the injustice of charging those states which had made great exertions for the payment of their debts with the burden properly belonging to those which had not made such exertions, it was answered, that every state must be considered as having exerted itself to the utmost of its resources; and that if it could not, or would not make provision for creditors to whom the union was equitably bound, the argument in favour of an assumption was the stronger.

The arguments drawn from local interests were repelled, and retorted, and a great degree of irritation was excited on both sides.

After a very animated discussion of several days, the question was taken, and the resolution was carried by a small majority. Soon after this decision, while the subject was pending before the house, the delegates from North Carolina took their seats, and changed the strength of parties. By a majority of two voices, the resolution was recommitted; and, after a long and ardent debate, was negatived by the same majority.

This proposition continued to be supported with a degree of earnestness which its opponents termed pertinacious, but not a single opinion was changed. It was brought forward in the new and less exceptionable form of assuming specific sums from each state. Under this modification of the principle, the extraordinary contributions of particular states during the war, and their exertions since the peace, might be regarded; and the objections to the measure, drawn from the uncertainty of the sum to be assumed, would be removed. But these alterations produced no change of sentiment; and the bill was sent up to the senate with a provision for those creditors only whose certificates of debt purported to be payable by the union.

In this state of things, the measure is understood to have derived aid from another, which was of a nature strongly to interest particular parts of the union.

From the month of June, 1783, when congress was driven from Philadelphia by the mutiny of a part of the Pennsylvania line, the necessity of selecting some place for a permanent residence, in which the government of the union might exercise sufficient authority to protect itself from violence and insult, had been generally acknowledged. Scarcely any subject had occupied more time, or had more agitated the members of the former congress than this.

Bill for fixing the permanent seat of government.

In December, 1784, an ordinance was passed for appointing commissioners to purchase land on the Delaware, in the neighbourhood of its falls, and to erect thereon the necessary public buildings for the reception of congress, and the officers of government; but the southern interest had been sufficiently strong to arrest the execution of this ordinance by preventing an appropriation of funds, which required the assent of nine states. Under the existing government, this subject had received the early attention of congress; and many different situations from the Delaware to the Potomac inclusive, had been earnestly supported; but a majority of both houses had not concurred in favour of any one place. With as little success, attempts had been made to change the temporary residence of congress. Although New York was obviously too far to the east, so many conflicting interests were brought into operation whenever the subject was touched, that no motion designating a more central place, could succeed. At length, a compact respecting the temporary and permanent seat of government was entered into between the friends of Philadelphia, and the Potomac, stipulating that congress should adjourn to and hold its sessions in Philadelphia, for ten years, during which time, buildings for the accommodation of the government should be erected at some place on the Potomac, to which the government should remove at the expiration of the term. This compact having united the representatives of Pennsylvania and Delaware with the friends of the Potomac, in favour both of the temporary and permanent residence which had been agreed on between them, a majority was produced in favour of the two situations, and a bill which was brought into the senate in conformity with this previous arrangement, passed both houses by small majorities. This act was immediately followed by an amendment to the bill then pending before the senate for funding the debt of the union. The amendment was similar in principle to that which had been unsuccessfully proposed in the house of representatives. By its provisions, twenty-one millions five hundred thousand dollars of the state debts were assumed in specified proportions; and it was particularly enacted that no certificate should be received from a state creditor which could be "ascertained to have been issued for any purpose other than compensations and expenditures for services or supplies towards the prosecution of the late war, and the defence of the United States, or of some part thereof, during the same."

When the question was taken in the house of representatives on this amendment, two members representing districts on the Potomac, who, in all the previous stages of the business, had voted against the assumption, declared themselves in its favour; and thus the majority was changed.[45]

Thus was a measure carried, which was supported and opposed with a degree of zeal and earnestness not often manifested; and which furnished presages, not to be mistaken, that the spirit with which the opposite opinions had been maintained, would not yield, contentedly, to the decision of a bare majority. This measure has constituted one of the great grounds of accusation against the first administration of the general government; and it is fair to acknowledge, that though, in its progress, it derived no aid from the President, whose opinion remained in his own bosom, it received the full approbation of his judgment.

A bill, at length, passed both houses, funding the debt upon principles which lessened considerably the weight of the public burdens, and was entirely satisfactory to the public creditors. The proceeds of the sales of the lands lying in the western territory, and, by a subsequent act of the same session, the surplus product of the revenue after satisfying the appropriations which were charged upon it, with the addition of two millions, which the President was authorized to borrow at five per centum, constituted a sinking fund to be applied to the reduction of the debt.

The effect of this measure was great and rapid. The public paper suddenly rose, and was for a short time above par. The immense wealth which individuals acquired by this unexpected appreciation, could not be viewed with indifference. Those who participated in its advantages, regarded the author of a system to which they were so greatly indebted, with an enthusiasm of attachment to which scarcely any limits were assigned. To many others, this adventitious collection of wealth in particular hands, was a subject rather of chagrin than of pleasure; and the reputation which the success of his plans gave to the secretary of the treasury, was not contemplated with unconcern. As if the debt had been created by the existing government, not by a war which gave liberty and independence to the United States, its being funded was ascribed by many, not to a sense of justice, and to a liberal and enlightened policy, but to the desire of bestowing on the government an artificial strength, by the creation of a monied interest which would be subservient to its will.

The effects produced by giving the debt a permanent value, justified the predictions of those whose anticipations had been most favourable. The sudden increase of monied capital derived from it, invigorated commerce, and gave a new stimulus to agriculture.

About this time, there was a great and visible improvement in the circumstances of the people. Although the funding system was certainly not inoperative in producing this

110

improvement, it can not be justly ascribed to any single cause. Progressive industry had gradually repaired the losses sustained by the war; and the influence of the constitution on habits of thinking and acting, though silent, was considerable. In depriving the states of the power to impair the obligation of contracts, or to make any thing but gold and silver a tender in payment of debts, the conviction was impressed on that portion of society which had looked to the government for relief from embarrassment, that personal exertions alone could free them from difficulties; and an increased degree of industry and economy was the natural consequence of this opinion.

Adjournment of congress.

On the 12th of August, after an arduous session, congress adjourned, to meet in Philadelphia the first Monday in the following December.

While the discussions in the national legislature related to subjects, and were conducted in a temper, well calculated to rouse the active spirit of party, the external relations of the United States wore an aspect not perfectly serene. To the hostile temper manifested by the Indians on the western and southern frontiers, an increased degree of importance was given by the apprehension that their discontents were fomented by the intrigues of Britain and of Spain. From Canada, the Indians of the north-west were understood to be furnished with the means of prosecuting a war which they were stimulated to continue; and, to the influence of the governor of the Floridas had been partly attributed the failure of the negotiation with the Creeks. That this influence would still be exerted to prevent a friendly intercourse with that nation was firmly believed; and it was feared that Spain might take a part in the open hostilities threatened by the irritable dispositions of individuals in both countries. From the intimate connexion subsisting between the members of the house of Bourbon, this event was peculiarly deprecated; and the means of avoiding it were sought with solicitude. These considerations determined the President to make another effort at negotiation; but, to preserve the respect of these savages for the United States, it was at the same time resolved that the agent to be employed should visit the country on other pretexts, and should carry a letter of introduction to M'Gillivray, blending with other subjects a strong representation of the miseries which a war with the United States would bring upon his people; and an earnest exhortation to repair with the chiefs of his nation to the seat of the federal government, in order to effect a solid and satisfactory peace. Colonel Willett was selected for this service; and he acquitted himself so well of the duty assigned to him, as to induce the chiefs of the nation, with M'Gillivray at their head, to repair to New York, where negotiations were opened which terminated in a treaty of peace,[46] signed on the 7th day of August.[47]

Treaty with the Creek Indians.

The pacific overtures made to the Indians of the Wabash and the Miamis not having been equally successful, the western frontiers were still exposed to their destructive incursions. A long course of experience had convinced the President that, on the failure of negotiation, sound policy and true economy, not less than humanity, required the immediate employment of a force which should carry death and destruction into the heart of the hostile settlements. Either not feeling the same impressions, or disposed to indulge the wishes of the western people, who declared openly their preference for desultory military expeditions, congress did not adopt measures corresponding with the wishes of the executive, and the military establishment[48] was not equal to the exigency. The distresses of the frontier establishment, therefore, still continued; and the hostility they had originally manifested to the constitution, sustained no diminution.

United States in relations with Great Britain and Spain.

No progress had been made in adjusting the points of controversy with Spain and Britain. With the former power, the question of boundary remained unsettled; and the cabinet of Madrid discovered no disposition to relax the rigour of its pretensions respecting the navigation of the Mississippi. Its general conduct furnished no foundation for a hope that its dispositions towards the United States were friendly, or that it could view their growing power without jealousy.

The non-execution of the 4th, 5th, 6th, and 7th articles of the treaty of peace, still furnished the United States and Great Britain with matter for reciprocal crimination, which there was the more difficulty in removing, because no diplomatic intercourse was maintained between them. The cabinet of St. James having never appointed a minister to the United States, and Mr. Adams having returned from London without effecting the object of his mission, the American government felt some difficulty in repeating advances which had been treated with neglect. Yet there was much reason to desire full explanations with the English government, and to understand perfectly its views and intentions. The subjects for discussion were delicate in their nature, and could not be permitted to remain in their present state, without hazarding the most serious consequences. The detention of a part of the territory of the United States, was a circumstance of much importance to the honour, as well as to the interests of the nation, and the commercial intercourse between the two countries was so extensive, as to require amicable and permanent regulations. The early attention of the President had been directed to these subjects; and, in October, 1789, he had resolved on taking informal measures to sound the British cabinet, and to ascertain its views respecting them. This negotiation was entrusted to Mr. Gouverneur Morris, who had been carried by private business to Europe; and he conducted it with ability and address, but was unable to bring it to a happy conclusion. The result of his conferences with the Duke of Leeds, and with Mr. Pitt, was a conviction that the British government, considering the posts they occupied on the southern side of the great lakes as essential to their monopoly of the fur trade, would surrender them reluctantly, and was not desirous of entering into a commercial treaty. Those ministers expressed a wish to be on the best terms with America; but repeated the complaints which had been previously made by Lord Carmarthen, of the non-execution of the treaty of peace on the part of the United States. To the observations made by Mr. Morris, that the constitution lately adopted, and the courts established under it, amounted to a full compliance with that treaty on the part of the American government, it was answered, that losses had already been sustained in consequence of the obstructions given by the states to the fair operation of that instrument, which rendered a faithful observance of it, at present, impossible; and, in a note, the Duke of Leeds avowed the intention, if the delay on the part of the American government to fulfil its engagements made in the treaty should have rendered their final completion impracticable, to retard the fulfilment of those which depended entirely on Great Britain, until redress should be granted to the subjects of his majesty on the specific points of the treaty itself, or a fair and just compensation obtained for the non-performance of those stipulations which the United States had failed to observe. Though urged by Mr. Morris to state explicitly in what respects, and to what degree, he considered the final completion of those engagements to which the United States were bound, as having been rendered impracticable, no such statement was given; and the British government seemed inclined to avoid, for the present, those full and satisfactory explanations, which were sought on the part of the United States.

After detailing the motives which in his opinion influenced the English cabinet in wishing to suspend for a time all discussions with America, Mr. Morris observed, "perhaps there never was a moment in which this country felt herself greater; and consequently, it is the most unfavourable moment to obtain advantageous terms from her in any bargain."

Whilst these negotiations were pending, intelligence was received at London of the attack made on the British settlement at Nootka Sound; and preparations were instantly made to resent the insult alleged to have been offered to the nation. The high ground taken on this occasion by the government, and the vigour with which it armed in support of its pretensions, furnished strong reasons for the opinion that a war with Spain, and probably with France, would soon be commenced.

In America, this was considered as a favourable juncture for urging the claims of the United States to the free navigation of the Mississippi. Mr. Carmichael, their charge d'affaires at the court of Madrid, was instructed not only to press this point with earnestness, but to use his utmost endeavours to secure the unmolested use of that river in future, by obtaining a cession of the island of New Orleans, and of the Floridas. A full equivalent for this cession would be found, it was said, in the sincere friendship of the United States, and in the security it would give to the territories of Spain, west of the Mississippi.

Mr. Carmichael was also instructed to point the attention of the Spanish government to the peculiar situation of the United States. To one half of their territory, the use of the

Mississippi was indispensable. No efforts could prevent their acquiring it. That they would acquire it, either by acting separately, or in conjunction with Great Britain, was one of those inevitable events against which human wisdom could make no provision. To the serious consideration of the Spanish government, therefore, were submitted the consequences which must result to their whole empire in America, either from hostilities with the United States, or from a seizure of Louisiana by Great Britain.

The opinion, that in the event of war between Great Britain and Spain, Louisiana would be invaded from Canada, was not a mere suggestion for the purpose of aiding the negotiations at Madrid. It was seriously adopted by the American government; and the attention of the executive was turned to the measures which it would be proper to take, should application be made for permission to march a body of troops, through the unsettled territories of the United States, into the dominions of Spain; or should the attempt be made to march them, without permission.

Among the circumstances which contributed to the opinion that, in the event of war, the arms of Great Britain would be directed against the settlements of Spain in America, was the continuance of Lord Dorchester in the government of Canada. This nobleman had intimated a wish to visit New York on his return to England; but the prospect of a rupture with Spain had determined him to remain in Canada. Under the pretext of making his acknowledgments for the readiness with which his desire to pass through New York had been acceded to, his lordship despatched Major Beck with, a member of his family, to sound the American government, and if possible, to ascertain its dispositions towards the two nations. Alluding to the negotiations which had been commenced in London, this gentleman endeavoured to assign a satisfactory cause for the delays which had intervened. It was not improbable, he said, that these delays, and some other circumstances, might have impressed Mr. Morris with an idea of backwardness on the part of the British ministry. His lordship, however, had directed him to say, that an inference of this sort would not, in his opinion, be well founded, as he had reason to believe that the British cabinet was inclined not only towards a friendly intercourse, but towards an alliance with the United States.

Major Beckwith represented the particular ground of quarrel as one which ought to interest all commercial nations in favour of the views of Great Britain; and, from that circumstance, he presumed that, should a war ensue, the United States would find their interest in taking part with Britain, rather than with Spain.

After expressing the concern with which Lord Dorchester had heard of the depredations of the savages on the western frontier of the United States, he declared that his lordship, so far from countenancing these depredations, had taken every proper opportunity to impress upon the Indians a pacific disposition; and that, on his first hearing of the outrages lately committed, he had sent a messenger to endeavour to prevent them. Major Beckwith further intimated, that the perpetrators of the late murders were banditti, composed chiefly of Creeks and Cherokees, in the Spanish interest, over whom the governor of Canada possessed no influence.

These communications were laid before the President, and appeared to him to afford an explanation of the delays experienced by Mr. Morris. He was persuaded that a disposition existed in the cabinet of London to retain things in their actual situation, until the intentions of the American government should be ascertained with respect to the war supposed to be approaching. If the United States would enter into an alliance with Great Britain, and would make a common cause with her against Spain, the way would be smoothed to the attainment of all their objects: but if America should be disinclined to such a connexion, and especially, if she should manifest any partiality towards Spain, no progress would be made in the attempt to adjust the point of difference between the two nations. Taking this view of the subject, he directed that the further communications of Mr. Beckwith should be heard civilly, and that their want of official authenticity should be hinted delicately, without using any expressions which might, in the most remote degree, impair the freedom of the United States, to pursue, without reproach, in the expected war, such a line of conduct as their interests or honour might dictate.

In the opinion that it would not only be useless but dishonourable further to press a commercial treaty, or the exchange of ministers, and that the subject of the western posts ought not again to be moved on the part of the United States, until they should be in a condition to speak a decisive language, the powers given to Mr. Morris were withdrawn. Should the interest of Britain produce a disposition favourable to an amicable arrangement of differences, and to a liberal commercial intercourse secured by compact, it was believed that she would make the requisite advances; until then, or until some other change of circumstances should require a change of conduct, things were to remain in their actual situation.

About the time of adopting this resolution, the dispute between Britain and Spain was adjusted. Finding France unwilling to engage in his quarrel, his Catholic Majesty, too weak to encounter alone the force of the British empire, yielded every point in controversy; and thus were terminated for the present, both the fear of inconveniences, and the hope of advantages which might result to America from hostilities between the two powers, whose dominions were in her neighbourhood, and with each of whom she was already engaged in controversies not easily to be accommodated.

The president visits Mount Vernon.

Incessant application to public business, and the consequent change of active for sedentary habits, had greatly impaired the constitution of the President; and, during the last session of congress, he had, for the second time since entering on the duties of his present station, been attacked by a severe disease which reduced him to the brink of the grave. Exercise and a temporary relief from the cares of office being essential to the restoration of his health, he determined, for the short interval afforded by the recess of the legislature, to retire to the tranquil shades of Mount Vernon. After returning from a visit to Rhode Island,[49] which state not having then adopted the American constitution, had not been included in his late tour through New England, he took leave of New York; and hastened to that peaceful retreat, and those rural employments, his taste for which neither military glory, nor political power, could ever diminish.

After a short indulgence in these favourite scenes, it became necessary to repair to Philadelphia, in order to meet the national legislature.

The president's speech.

In the speech delivered to congress at the commencement of their third session, the President expressed much satisfaction at the favourable prospect of public affairs; and particularly noticed the progress of public credit, and the productiveness of the revenue.

Adverting to foreign nations,[50] he said, "the disturbed situation of Europe, and particularly the critical posture of the great maritime powers, whilst it ought to make us more thankful for the general peace and security enjoyed by the United States, reminds us at the same time of the circumspection with which it becomes us to preserve these blessings. It requires also, that we should not overlook the tendency of a war, and even of preparations for war among the nations most concerned in active commerce with this country, to abridge the means, and thereby at least to enhance the price, of transporting its valuable productions to their proper market." To the serious reflection of congress was recommended the prevention of embarrassments from these contingencies, by such encouragement to American navigation as would render the commerce and agriculture of the United States less dependent on foreign bottoms.

After expressing to the house of representatives his confidence arising from the sufficiency of the revenues already established, for the objects to which they were appropriated, he added, "allow me moreover to hope that it will be a favourite policy with you not merely to secure a payment of the interest of the debt funded, but as far, and as fast as the growing resources of the country will permit, to exonerate it of the principal itself." Many subjects relative to the interior government were succinctly and briefly mentioned; and the speech concluded with the following impressive and admonitory sentiment. "In pursuing the various and weighty business of the present session, I indulge the fullest persuasion that your consultations will be marked with wisdom, and animated by the love of country. In whatever belongs to my duty, you shall have all the co-operation which an undiminished zeal for its welfare can inspire. It will be happy for us both, and our best reward, if by a successful administration of our respective trusts, we can make the established government more and more instrumental in promoting the good of our fellow citizens, and more and more the object of their attachment and confidence."

The addresses of the two houses, in answer to the speech, proved that the harmony between the executive and legislative departments, with which the government had gone into operation, had sustained no essential interruption. But in the short debate which took place on the occasion, in the house of representatives, a direct disapprobation of one of the measures of the executive government was, for the first time, openly expressed.

In the treaty lately concluded with the Creeks, an extensive territory claimed by Georgia, under treaties, the validity of which was contested by the Indian chiefs, had been entirely, or in great part, relinquished. This relinquishment excited serious discontents in that state; and was censured by General Jackson with considerable warmth, as an unjustifiable abandonment of the rights and interests of Georgia. No specific motion, however, was made, and the subject was permitted to pass away for the present.

Scarcely were the debates on the address concluded, when several interesting reports were received from the secretary of the treasury, suggesting such further measures as were deemed necessary for the establishment of public credit.

It will be recollected that in his original report on this subject, the secretary had recommended the assumption of the state debts; and had proposed to enable the treasury to meet the increased demand upon it, which this measure would occasion, by an augmentation of the duties on imported wines, spirits, tea, and coffee, and by imposing duties on spirits distilled within the country. The assumption not having been adopted until late in the session, the discussion on the revenue which would be required for this portion of the public debt did not commence, until the house had become impatient for an adjournment. As much contrariety of opinion was disclosed, and the subject did not press,[51] it was deferred to the ensuing session; and an order was made, requiring the secretary of the treasury to prepare and report such further provision as might, in his opinion, be necessary for establishing the public credit. In obedience to this order, several reports had been prepared, the first of which repeated the recommendation of an additional impost on foreign distilled spirits, and of a duty on spirits distilled within the United States. The estimated revenue from these sources was eight hundred and seventy-seven thousand five hundred dollars, affording a small excess over the sum which would be required to pay the interest on the assumed debt. The policy of the measure was discussed in a well digested and able argument, detailing many motives, in addition to those assigned in his original report, for preferring the system now recommended, to accumulated burdens on commerce, or to a direct tax on lands.

A new tax is the certain rallying point for all those who are unfriendly to the administration, or to the minister by whom it is proposed. But that recommended by the secretary, contained intrinsic causes of objection which would necessarily add to the number of its enemies. All that powerful party in the United States, which attached itself to the local, rather than to the general government, would inevitably contemplate any system of internal revenue with jealous disapprobation. They considered the imposition of a tax by congress on any domestic manufacture, as the intrusion of a foreign power into their particular concerns, which excited serious apprehensions for state importance, and for liberty. In the real or supposed interests of many individuals was also found a distinct motive for hostility to the measure. A large portion of the American population, especially that which had spread itself over the extensive regions of the west, consuming imported articles to a very inconsiderable amount, was not much affected by the impost on foreign merchandize. But the duty on spirits distilled within the United States reached them, and consequently rendered them hostile to the tax.

1791

Debate on the excise law.

A bill, which was introduced in pursuance of the report, was opposed with great vehemence by a majority of the southern and western members. By some of them it was insisted that no sufficient testimony had yet been exhibited, that the taxes already imposed would not be equal to the exigencies of the public. But, admitting the propriety of additional burdens on the people, it was contended that other sources of revenue, less exceptionable and less odious than this, might be explored. The duty was branded with the hateful epithet of an excise, a species of taxation, it was said, so peculiarly oppressive as to be abhorred even in England; and which was totally incompatible with the spirit of liberty. The facility with which it might be extended to other objects, was urged against its admission into the American system; and declarations made against it by the congress of 1775, were quoted in confirmation of the justice with which inherent vices were ascribed to this mode of collecting taxes. So great was the hostility manifested against it in some of the states, that the revenue officers might be endangered from the fury of the people; and, in all, it would increase a ferment which had been already extensively manifested. Resolutions of Maryland, Virginia, and North Carolina, reprobating the assumption, were referred to as unequivocal evidences of growing dissatisfaction; and the last mentioned state had even expressed its decided hostility to any law of excise. The legislature of North Carolina had rejected with scorn, a proposal for taking an oath to support the constitution of the United States; had refused to admit persons sentenced to imprisonment under the laws of the United States into their jails; and another circumstance was alluded to, but not explained, which was said to exhibit a temper still more hostile to the general government than either of those which had been stated.

When required to produce a system in lieu of that which they so much execrated, the opponents of the bill alternately mentioned an increased duty on imported articles generally, a particular duty on molasses, a direct tax, a tax on salaries, pensions, and lawyers; a duty on newspapers, and a stamp act.

The friends of the bill contended, that the reasons for believing the existing revenue would be insufficient to meet the engagements of the United States, were as satisfactory as the nature of the case would admit, or as ought to be required. The estimates were founded on the best data which were attainable, and the funds already provided, had been calculated by the proper officer to pay the interest on that part of the debt only for which they were pledged. Those estimates were referred to as documents, from which it would be unsafe to depart. They were also in possession of official statements, showing the productiveness of the taxes from the time the revenue bill had been in operation; and arguments were drawn from these, demonstrating the danger to which the infant credit of the United States would be exposed, by relying on the existing funds for the interest on the assumed debt. It was not probable that the proposed duties would yield a sum much exceeding that which would be necessary; but should they fortunately do so, the surplus revenue might be advantageously employed in extinguishing a part of the principal. They were not, they said, of opinion, that a public debt was a public blessing, or that it ought to be perpetuated.

An augmentation of the revenue being indispensable to the solidity of the public credit, a more eligible system than that proposed in the bill, could not, it was believed, be devised. Still further to burden commerce, would be a hazardous experiment which might afford no real supplies to the treasury. Until some lights should be derived from experience, it behoved the legislature to be cautious not to lay such impositions upon trade as might probably introduce a spirit of smuggling, which, with a nominal increase, would occasion a real diminution of revenue. In the opinion of the best judges, the impost on the mass of foreign merchandise could not safely be carried further for the present. The extent of the mercantile capital of the United States would not justify the attempt. Forcible arguments were also drawn from the policy and the justice of multiplying the subjects of taxation, and diversifying them by a union of internal with external objects.

Neither would a direct tax be adviseable. The experience of the world had proved, that a tax on consumption was less oppressive, and more productive, than a tax on either property or income. Without discussing the principles on which the fact was founded, the fact itself was incontestable, that, by insensible means, much larger sums might be drawn from any class of men, than could be extracted from them by open and direct taxes. To the latter system there were still other objections. The difficulty of carrying it into operation, no census having yet been taken, would not be inconsiderable; and the expense of collection through a country thinly settled, would be enormous. Add to this, that public opinion was believed to be more decidedly and unequivocally opposed to it, than to a duty on ardent spirits. North Carolina had expressed her hostility to the one as well as to the other, and several other states were known to disapprove of direct taxes. From the real objections which existed against them, and for other reasons suggested in the report of the secretary, they ought, it was said, to remain untouched, as a resource when some great emergency should require an exertion of all the faculties of the United States.

Against the substitution of a duty on internal negotiations, it was said, that revenue to any considerable extent could be collected from them only by means of a stamp act, which was not less obnoxious to popular resentment than an excise, would be less certainly productive than the proposed duties, and was, in every respect, less eligible.

The honour, the justice, and the faith of the United States were pledged, it was said, to that class of creditors for whose claims the bill under consideration was intended to provide. No means of making the provision had been suggested, which, on examination, would be found equally eligible with a duty on ardent spirits. Much of the public prejudice which appeared in certain parts of the United States against the measure, was to be ascribed to their hostility to the term "excise," a term which had been inaccurately applied to the duty in question. When the law should be carried into operation, it would be found not to possess those odious qualities which had excited resentment against a system of excise. In those states where the collection of a duty on spirits distilled within the country had become familiar to the people, the same prejudices did not exist. On the good sense and virtue of the nation they could confidently rely for acquiescence in a measure which the public exigencies rendered necessary, which tended to equalize the public burdens, and which in its execution would not be oppressive.

A motion made by Mr. Jackson, to strike out that section which imposed a duty on domestic distilled spirits, was negatived by thirty-six to sixteen; and the bill was carried by thirty-five to twenty-one.

Some days after the passage of this bill, another question was brought forward, which was understood to involve principles of deep interest to the government.

On a national bank.

The secretary of the treasury had been the uniform advocate of a national bank. Believing that such an institution would be "of primary importance to the prosperous administration of the finances; and of the greatest utility in the operations connected with the support of public credit," he had earnestly recommended its adoption in the first general system which he presented to the view of congress; and, at the present session, had repeated that recommendation in a special report, containing a copious and perspicuous argument on the policy of the measure. A bill conforming to the plan he suggested was sent down from the senate, and was permitted to proceed, unmolested, in the house of representatives, to the third reading. On the final question, a great, and, it would seem, an unexpected opposition was made to its passage. Mr. Madison, Mr. Giles, Mr. Jackson, and Mr. Stone spoke against it. The general utility of banking systems was not admitted, and the particular bill before the house was censured on its merits; but the great strength of the argument was directed against the constitutional authority of congress to pass an act for incorporating a national bank.

The government of the United States, it was said, was limited; and the powers which it might legitimately exercise were enumerated in the constitution itself. In this enumeration, the power now contended for was not to be found. Not being expressly given, it must be implied from those which were given, or it could not be vested in the government. The clauses under which it could be claimed were then reviewed and critically examined; and it was contended that, on fair construction, no one of these could be understood to imply so important a power as that of creating a corporation.

The clause which enables congress to pass all laws necessary and proper to execute the specified powers, must, according to the natural and obvious force of the terms and the context, be limited to means *necessary* to the *end* and *incident* to the *nature* of the specified powers. The clause, it was said, was in fact merely declaratory of what would have resulted by unavoidable implication, as the appropriate, and as it were technical means of executing those powers. Some gentlemen observed, that "the true exposition of a necessary mean to produce a given end was that mean without which the end could not be produced."

The bill was supported by Mr. Ames, Mr. Sedgwick, Mr. Smith, of South Carolina, Mr. Lawrence, Mr. Boudinot, Mr. Gerry, and Mr. Vining.

The utility of banking institutions was said to be demonstrated by their effects. In all commercial countries they had been resorted to as an instrument of great efficacy in mercantile transactions; and even in the United States, their public and private advantages had been felt and acknowledged.

Respecting the policy of the measure, no well founded doubt could be entertained; but the objections to the constitutional authority of congress deserved to be seriously considered.

That the government was limited by the terms of its creation was not controverted; and that it could exercise only those powers which were conferred on it by the constitution, was admitted. If, on examination, that instrument should be found to forbid the passage of the bill, it must be rejected, though it would be with deep regret that its friends would suffer such an opportunity of serving their country to escape for the want of a constitutional power to improve it.

In asserting the authority of the legislature to pass the bill, gentlemen contended, that incidental as well as express powers must necessarily belong to every government: and that, when a power is delegated to effect particular objects, all the known and usual means of effecting them, must pass as incidental to it. To remove all doubt on this subject, the constitution of the United States had recognized the principle, by enabling congress to make all laws which may be necessary and proper for carrying into execution the powers vested in the government. They maintained the sound construction of this grant to be a recognition of an authority in the national legislature, to employ all the known and usual means for executing the powers vested in the government. They then took a comprehensive view of those powers, and contended that a bank was a known and usual instrument by which several of them were exercised.

After a debate of great length, which was supported on both sides with ability, and with that ardour which was naturally excited by the importance attached by each party to the principle in contest, the question was put, and the bill was carried in the affirmative by a majority of nineteen voices.

The opinions of the cabinet on the constitutionality of this last law.

The point which had been agitated with so much zeal in the house of representatives, was examined with equal deliberation by the executive. The cabinet was divided upon it. The secretary of state, and the attorney general, conceived that congress had clearly transcended their constitutional powers; while the secretary of the treasury, with equal clearness, maintained the opposite opinion. The advice of each minister, with his reasoning in support of it, was required in writing, and their arguments were considered by the President with all that attention which the magnitude of the question, and the interest taken in it by the opposing parties, so eminently required. This deliberate investigation of the subject terminated in a conviction, that the constitution of the United States authorized the measure;[52] and the sanction of the executive was given to the act.

Progress of parties.

The judgment is so much influenced by the wishes, the affections, and the general theories of those by whom any political proposition is decided, that a contrariety of opinion on this great constitutional question ought to excite no surprise. It must be recollected that the conflict between the powers of the general and state governments was coeval with those governments. Even during the war, the preponderance of the states was obvious; and, in a very few years after peace, the struggle ended in the utter abasement of the general government. Many causes concurred to produce a constitution which was deemed more competent to the preservation of the union, but its adoption was opposed by great numbers; and in some of the large states especially, its enemies soon felt and manifested their superiority. The old line of division was still as strongly marked as ever. Many retained the opinion that liberty could be endangered only by encroachments upon the states; and that it was the great duty of patriotism to restrain the powers of the general government within the narrowest possible limits.

In the other party, which was also respectable for its numbers, many were found who had watched the progress of American affairs, and who sincerely believed that the real danger which threatened the republic was to be looked for in the undue ascendency of the states. To them it appeared, that the substantial powers, and the extensive means of influence, which were retained by the local sovereignties, furnished them with weapons for aggression which were not easily to be resisted, and that it behoved all those who were anxious for the happiness of their country, to guard the equilibrium established in the constitution, by preserving unimpaired, all the legitimate powers of the union. These were more confirmed in their sentiments, by observing the temper already discovered in the legislatures of several states, respecting the proceedings of congress.

To this great and radical division of opinion, which would necessarily affect every question on the authority of the national legislature, other motives were added, which were believed to possess considerable influence on all measures connected with the finances.

As an inevitable effect of the state of society, the public debt had greatly accumulated in the middle and northern states, whose inhabitants had derived, from its rapid appreciation, a proportional augmentation of their wealth. This circumstance could not fail to contribute to the complacency with which the plans of the secretary were viewed by those who had felt their benefit, nor to the irritation with which they were contemplated by others who had parted with their claims on the nation. It is not impossible, that personal considerations also mingled themselves with those which were merely political.

With so many causes to bias the judgment, it would not have been wonderful if arguments less plausible than those advanced by either party had been deemed conclusive on its adversary; nor was it a matter of surprise that each should have denied to those which were urged in opposition, the weight to which they were certainly entitled. The liberal mind which can review them without prejudice, will charge neither the supporters nor the opponents of the bill with insincerity, nor with being knowingly actuated by motives which might not have been avowed.

This measure made a deep impression on many members of the legislature; and contributed, not inconsiderably, to the complete organization of those distinct and visible parties, which, in their long and dubious conflict for power, have since shaken the United States to their centre.

Among the last acts of the present congress, was an act to augment the military establishment of the United States.

War with the Indians.

The earnest endeavours of the President to give security to the north-western frontiers, by pacific arrangements, having been entirely unavailing, it became his duty to employ such other means as were placed in his hands, for the protection of the country. Confirmed by all his experience in the opinion that vigorous offensive operations alone could bring an Indian war to a happy conclusion, he had planned an expedition against the hostile tribes north-west of the Ohio, as soon as the impracticability of effecting a treaty with them had been ascertained.

General Harmar, a veteran of the revolution, who had received his appointment under the former government, was placed at the head of the federal troops. On the 30th of September, he marched from fort Washington with three hundred and twenty regulars. The whole army when joined by the militia of Pennsylvania and Kentucky amounted to fourteen hundred and fifty-three men. About the middle of October, Colonel Harden, who commanded the Kentucky militia, and who had been also a continental officer of considerable merit, was detached at the head of six hundred men, chiefly militia, to reconnoitre the ground, and to ascertain the intentions of the enemy. On his approach, the Indians set fire to their principal village, and fled with precipitation to the woods. As the object of the expedition would be only half accomplished, unless the savages could be brought to action and defeated, Colonel Harden was again detached at the head of two hundred and ten men, thirty of whom were regulars. About ten miles west of Chilicothe, where the main body of the army lay, he was attacked by a party of Indians. The Pennsylvanians, who composed his left column, had previously fallen in the rear; and the Kentuckians, disregarding the exertions of their colonel, and of a few other officers, fled on the first appearance of an enemy. The small corps of regulars commanded by Lieutenant Armstrong made a brave resistance. After twenty-three of them had fallen in the field, the surviving seven made their escape and rejoined the army.

Defeat of Harmar.

Notwithstanding this check, the remaining towns on the Scioto were reduced to ashes, and the provisions laid up for the winter were entirely destroyed. This service being accomplished, the army commenced its march towards fort Washington. Being desirous of wiping off the disgrace which his arms had sustained, General Harmar halted about eight miles from Chilicothe, and once more detached Colonel Harden with orders to find the enemy and bring on an engagement. His command consisted of three hundred and sixty men, of whom sixty were regulars commanded by Major Wyllys. Early the next morning, this detachment reached the confluence of the St. Joseph and St. Mary, where it was divided into three columns. The left division, commanded by Colonel Harden in person, crossed the St. Joseph, and proceeded up its western bank. The centre, consisting of the federal troops, was led by Major Wyllys up the eastern side of that river; and the right, under the command of Major M'Millan, marched along a range of heights which commanded the right flank of the centre division. The columns had proceeded but a short distance, when each was met by a considerable body of Indians, and a severe engagement ensued. The militia retrieved their reputation, and several of their bravest officers fell. The heights on the right having been, from some cause not mentioned, unoccupied by the American troops, the savages seized them early in the action, and attacked the right flank of the centre with great fury. Although Major Wyllys was among the first who fell, the battle was maintained by the regulars with spirit, and considerable execution was done on both sides. At length, the scanty remnant of this small band, quite overpowered by numbers, was driven off the ground, leaving fifty of their comrades, exclusive of Major Wyllys and Lieutenant Farthingham, dead upon the field. The loss sustained by the militia was also considerable. It amounted to upwards of one hundred men, among whom were nine officers. After an engagement of extreme severity, the detachment joined the main army, which continued its march to fort Washington.

General Harmar, with what propriety it is not easy to discern, claimed the victory. He conceived, not entirely without reason, that the loss of a considerable number of men, would be fatal to the Indians, although a still greater loss should be sustained by the Americans, because the savages did not possess a population from which they could replace the warriors who had fallen. The event, however, did not justify this opinion.

The information respecting this expedition was quickly followed by intelligence stating the deplorable condition of the frontiers. An address from the representatives of all the counties of Kentucky, and those of Virginia bordering on the Ohio, was presented to the President, praying that the defence of the country might be committed to militia unmixed with regulars, and that they might immediately be drawn out to oppose "the exulting foe." To this address, the President gave a conciliatory answer, but he understood too well the nature of the service, to yield to the request it contained. Such were his communications to the legislature, that a regiment was added to the permanent military establishment, and he was authorized to raise a body of two thousand men, for six months, and to appoint a major general, and a brigadier general, to continue in command so long as he should think their services necessary.

Adjournment of congress.

With the 3d of March, 1791, terminated the first congress elected under the constitution of the United States. The party denominated federal having prevailed at the elections, a majority of the members were steadfast friends of the constitution, and were sincerely desirous of supporting a system they had themselves introduced, and on the preservation of which, in full health and vigour, they firmly believed the happiness of their fellow citizens, and the respectability of the nation, greatly to depend. To organize a government, to retrieve the national character, to establish a system of revenue, and to create public credit, were among the arduous duties which were imposed upon them by the political situation of their country. With persevering labour, guided by no inconsiderable portion of virtue and intelligence, these objects were, in a great degree, accomplished. Out of the measures proposed for their attainment, questions alike intricate and interesting unavoidably arose. It is not in the nature of man to discuss such questions without strongly agitating the passions, and exciting irritations which do not readily subside. Had it even been the happy and singular lot of America to see its national legislature assemble uninfluenced by those prejudices which grew out of the previous divisions of the country, the many delicate points which they were under the necessity of deciding, could not have failed to disturb this enviable state of harmony, and to mingle some share of party spirit with their deliberations. But when the actual state of the public mind was contemplated, and due weight was given to the important consideration that, at no very distant day, a successor to the present chief magistrate must be elected, it was still less to be hoped that the first congress could pass away, without producing strong and permanent dispositions in parties, to impute to each other designs unfriendly to the public happiness. As yet, however, these imputations did not extend to the President. His character was held sacred, and the purity of his motives was admitted by all. Some divisions were understood to have found their way into the cabinet. It was insinuated that between the secretaries of state and of the treasury, very serious differences had arisen; but these high personages were believed, to be equally attached to the President, who was not suspected of undue partiality to either. If his assent to the bill for incorporating the national bank produced discontent, the opponents of that measure seemed disposed to ascribe his conduct, in that instance, to his judgment, rather than to any prepossession in favour of the party by whom it was carried. The opposition, therefore, in congress, to the measures of the government, seemed to be levelled at the secretary of the treasury, and at the northern members by whom those measures were generally supported, not at the President by whom they were approved. By taking this direction, it made its way into the public mind, without being encountered by that devoted affection which a great majority of the people felt for the chief magistrate of the union. In the mean time, the national prosperity was in a state of rapid progress; and the government was gaining, though slowly, in the public opinion. But in several of the state assemblies, especially in the southern division of the continent, serious evidences of dissatisfaction were exhibited, which demonstrated the jealousy with which the local sovereignties contemplated the powers exercised by the federal legislature.

CHAPTER VII.

General St. Clair appointed Commander-in-chief.... The President makes a tour through the southern states.... Meeting of congress.... President's speech.... Debate on the bill for apportioning representatives.... Militia law.... Defeat of St. Clair.... Opposition to the increase of the army.... Report of the Secretary of the Treasury for raising additional supplies.... Congress adjourns.... Strictures on the conduct of administration, with a view of parties.... Disagreement between the Secretaries of State and Treasury.... Letters from General Washington.... Opposition to the excise law.... President's proclamation.... Insurrection and massacre in the island of St. Domingo.... General Wayne appointed to the command of the army.... Meeting of Congress.... President's speech.... Resolutions implicating the Secretary of the Treasury rejected.... Congress adjourns.... Progress of the French revolution, and its effects on parties in the United States.

1791

MORE ample means for the protection of the frontiers having been placed in the hands of the executive, the immediate attention of the President was directed to this interesting object.

General St. Clair appointed commander-in-chief of the army.

Major General Arthur St. Clair, governor of the territory north-west of the Ohio, was appointed Commander-in-chief of the forces to be employed in the meditated expedition. This gentleman had served through the war of the revolution with reputation, though it had never been his fortune to distinguish himself. The evacuation of Ticonderoga had indeed, at one time, subjected him to much public censure; but it was found, upon inquiry, to be unmerited. Other motives, in addition to the persuasion of his fitness for the service, conduced to his appointment. With the sword, the olive branch was still to be tendered; and it was thought adviseable to place them in the same hands. The governor, having been made officially the negotiator with the tribes inhabiting the territories over which he presided, being a military man, acquainted with the country into which the war was to be carried, possessing considerable influence with the inhabitants of the frontiers, and being so placed as to superintend the preparations for the expedition advantageously, seemed to have claims to the station which were not to be overlooked. It was also a consideration of some importance, that the high rank he had held in the American army, would obviate those difficulties in filling the inferior grades with men of experience, which might certainly be expected, should a person who had acted in a less elevated station, be selected for the chief command.

Tomb of Mary, Mother of Washington
This is the original monument as it appeared before the present granite obelisk was erected over the grave of George Washington's mother in Fredericksburg, Virginia. It was in Fredericksburg that she made her home during her declining years, and it was on the Kenmore estate of her daughter, Elizabeth, and son-in-law, Fielding Lewis, that she was buried, September, 1789, having survived her husband, Augustine Washington, forty-six years.

The president makes a tour through the southern states.
After making the necessary arrangements for recruiting the army, the President prepared to make his long contemplated tour through the southern states.[53] In passing through them, he was received universally with the same marks of affectionate attachment, which he had experienced in the northern and central parts of the union. To the sensibilities which these demonstrations of the regard and esteem of good men could not fail to inspire, was added the high gratification produced by observing the rapid improvements of the country, and the advances made by the government, in acquiring the confidence of the people. The numerous letters written by him after his return to Philadelphia, attest the agreeable impressions made by these causes. "In my late tour through the southern states," said he, in a letter of the 28th of July, to Mr. Gouverneur Morris, "I experienced great satisfaction in seeing the good effects of the general government in that part of the union. The people at large have felt the security which it gives, and the equal justice which it administers to them. The farmer, the merchant, and the mechanic, have seen their several interests attended to, and from thence they unite in placing a confidence in their representatives, as well as in those in whose hands the execution of the laws is placed. Industry has there taken place of idleness, and economy of dissipation. Two or three years of good crops, and a ready market for the produce of their lands, have put every one in good humour; and, in some instances, they even impute to the government what is due only to the goodness of Providence.

"The establishment of public credit is an immense point gained in our national concerns. This, I believe, exceeds the expectation of the most sanguine among us; and a late instance, unparalleled in this country, has been given of the confidence reposed in our measures, by the rapidity with which the subscriptions to the bank of the United States were filled. In two hours after the books were opened by the commissioners, the whole number of shares was taken up, and four thousand more applied for than were allowed by the institution. This circumstance was not only pleasing as it related to the confidence in government, but also as it exhibited an unexpected proof of the resources of our citizens."

This visit had undoubtedly some tendency to produce the good disposition which the President observed with so much pleasure. The affections are perhaps more intimately connected with the judgment than we are disposed to admit; and the appearance of the chief magistrate of the union, who was the object of general love and reverence, could not be without its influence in conciliating the minds of many to the government he administered, and to its measures. But this progress towards conciliation was, perhaps, less considerable than was indicated by appearances. The hostility to the government, which was coeval with its existence, though diminished, was far from being subdued; and under this smooth exterior was concealed a mass of discontent, which, though it did not obtrude itself on the view of the man who united almost all hearts, was active in its exertions to effect its objects.

The difficulties which must impede the recruiting service in a country where coercion is not employed, and where the common wages of labour greatly exceed the pay of a soldier, protracted the completion of the regiments to a late season of the year; but the summer was not permitted to waste in total inaction.

The act passed at the last session for the defence of the frontiers, in addition to its other provisions, had given to the President an unlimited power to call mounted militia into the field. Under this authority, two expeditions had been conducted against the villages on the Wabash, in which a few of the Indian warriors were killed, some of their old men, women, and children, were made prisoners, and several of their towns and fields of corn were destroyed. The first was led by General Scott, in May, and the second by General Wilkinson, in September. These desultory incursions had not much influence on the war.

It was believed in the United States, that the hostility of the Indians was kept up by the traders living in their villages. These persons had, generally, resided in the United States; and, having been compelled to leave the country in consequence of the part they had taken during the war of the revolution, felt the resentments which banishment and confiscation seldom fail to inspire. Their enmities were ascribed by many, perhaps unjustly, to the temper of the government in Canada; but some countenance seemed to be given to this opinion by intelligence that, about the commencement of the preceding campaign, large supplies of ammunition had been delivered from the British posts on the lakes, to the Indians at war with the United States. While the President was on his southern tour, he addressed a letter to the secretary of state, to be communicated to Colonel Beckwith, who still remained in Philadelphia as the informal representative of his nation, in which he expressed his surprise and disappointment at this interference, by the servants or subjects of a foreign state, in a war prosecuted by the United States for the sole purpose of procuring peace and safety for the inhabitants of their frontiers.

On receiving this communication, Colonel Beckwith expressed his disbelief that the supplies mentioned had been delivered; but on being assured of the fact, he avowed the opinion that the transaction was without the knowledge of Lord Dorchester, to whom he said he should communicate, without delay, the ideas of the American government on the subject.

Meeting of congress.
President's speech.

On the 24th of October the second congress assembled in Philadelphia. In his speech at the opening of the session, the President expressed his great satisfaction at the prosperous situation of the country, and particularly mentioned the rapidity with which the shares in the bank of the United States were subscribed, as "among the striking and pleasing evidences which presented themselves, not only of confidence in the government, but of resources in the community."

Adverting to the measures which had been taken in execution of the laws and resolutions of the last session, "the most important of which," he observed, "respected the defence and security of the western frontiers," he had, he said, "negotiated provisional treaties, and used other proper means to attach the wavering, and to confirm in their friendship the well disposed tribes of Indians. The means which he had adopted for a pacification with those of a hostile description having proved unsuccessful, offensive operations had been directed, some of which had proved completely successful, and others were still pending. Overtures of peace were still continued to the deluded tribes; and it was sincerely to be desired that all need of coercion might cease, and that an intimate intercourse might succeed, calculated to advance the happiness of the Indians, and to attach them firmly to the United States."

In marking the line of conduct which ought to be maintained for the promotion of this object, he strongly recommended "justice to the savages, and such rational experiments for imparting to them the blessings of civilization, as might from time to time suit their condition;" and then concluded this subject with saying—"A system corresponding with the mild principles of religion and philanthropy towards an unenlightened race of men whose happiness materially depends on the conduct of the United States, would be as honourable to the national character, as conformable to the dictates of sound policy."

After stating that measures had been taken for carrying into execution the act laying duties on distilled spirits, he added—"The impressions with which this law has been received

123

by the community have been, upon the whole, such as were to have been expected among enlightened and well disposed citizens, from the propriety and necessity of the measure. The novelty, however, of the tax, in a considerable part of the United States, and a misconception of some of its provisions, have given occasion, in particular places, to some degree of discontent. But it is satisfactory to know that this disposition yields to proper explanations, and more just apprehensions of the true nature of the law. And I entertain a full confidence that it will, in all, give way to motives which arise out of a just sense of duty, and a virtuous regard to the public welfare.

"If there are any circumstances in the law, which, consistently with its main design may be so varied as to remove any well intentioned objections that may happen to exist, it will comport with a wise moderation to make the proper variations. It is desirable on all occasions, to unite with a steady and firm adherence to constitutional and necessary acts of government, the fullest evidence of a disposition, as far as may be practicable, to consult the wishes of every part of the community, and to lay the foundations of the public administration in the affections of the people."

The answers of the two houses noticed, briefly and generally, the various topics of the speech; and, though perhaps less warm than those of the preceding congress, manifested great respect for the executive magistrate, and an undiminished confidence in his patriotic exertions to promote the public interests.

Debate on the bill "for apportioning representatives among the people of the states according to the first enumeration."

Among the first subjects of importance which engaged the attention of the legislature, was a bill "for apportioning representatives among the people of the several states according to the first enumeration." The constitution, in its original form, had affixed no other limits to the power of congress over the numbers of which the house of representatives might consist, than that there should not be more than one member for every thirty thousand persons; but that each state should be entitled to at least one. Independent of the general considerations in favour of a more or less numerous representation in the popular branch of the legislature, there was one of a local nature, whose operation, though secret, was extensive, which gave to this question a peculiar interest. To whatever number of persons a representative might be allotted, there would still remain a fraction, which would be greater or less in each state, according to the ratio which congress should adopt between representation and population. The relative power of states, in one branch of the legislature, would consequently be affected by this ratio; and to questions of that description, few members can permit themselves to be inattentive.

This bill, as originally introduced into the house of representatives, gave to each state one member for every thirty thousand persons. On a motion to strike out the number thirty thousand, the debate turned chiefly on the policy and advantage of a more or less numerous house of representatives; but with the general arguments suggested by the subject, strong and pointed allusions to the measures of the preceding congress were interspersed, which indicated much more serious hostility to the administration than had hitherto been expressed. Speaking of the corruption which he supposed to exist in the British house of commons, Mr. Giles said that causes essentially different from their numbers, had produced this effect. "Among these, were the frequent mortgages of the funds, and the immense appropriations at the disposal of the executive."

"An inequality of circumstances," he observed, "produces revolutions in governments, from democracy, to aristocracy, and monarchy. Great wealth produces a desire of distinctions, rank, and titles. The revolutions of property, in this country, have created a prodigious inequality of circumstances. Government has contributed to this inequality. The bank of the United States is a most important machine in promoting the objects of this monied interest. This bank will be the most powerful engine to corrupt this house. Some of the members are directors of this institution; and it will only be by increasing the representation, that an adequate barrier can be opposed to this monied interest." He next adverted to certain ideas, which, he said, had been disseminated through the United States. "The legislature," he took occasion to observe, "ought to express some disapprobation of these opinions. The strong executive of this government," he added, "ought to be balanced by a full representation in this house."

Similar sentiments were advanced by Mr. Findley.

After a long and animated discussion, the amendment was lost, and the bill passed in its original form.

In the senate, it was amended by changing the ratio, so as to give one representative for every thirty-three thousand persons in each state; but this amendment was disagreed to by the house of representatives; and each house adhering to its opinion, the bill fell; but was again introduced into the house of representatives, under a different title, and in a new form, though without any change in its substantial provisions. After a debate in which the injustice of the fractions produced by the ratio it adopted was strongly pressed, it passed that house. In the senate, it was again amended, not by reducing, but by enlarging the number of representatives.

The constitution of the United States declares that "representatives and direct taxes shall be apportioned among the several states which may be included within this union according to their respective numbers;" and that "the number of representatives shall not exceed one for every thirty thousand, but each state shall have at least one representative." Construing the constitution to authorize a process by which the whole number of representatives should be ascertained on the whole population of the United States, and afterwards "apportioned among the several states according to their respective numbers," the senate applied the number thirty thousand as a *divisor* to the total population, and taking the *quotient*, which was one hundred and twenty, as the number of representatives given by the ratio which had been adopted in the house where the bill had originated, they apportioned that number among the several states by that ratio, until as many representatives as it would give were allotted to each. The residuary members were then distributed among the states having the highest fractions. Without professing the principle on which this apportionment was made, the amendment of the senate merely allotted to the states respectively, the number of members which the process just mentioned would give. The result was a more equitable apportionment of representatives to population, and had the rule of construing that instrument been correct, the amendment removed objections which were certainly well founded. But the rule was novel, and overturned opinions which had been generally assumed, and were supposed to be settled. In one branch of the legislature it had already been rejected; and in the other, the majority in its favour was only one.

In the house of representatives, the amendment was supported with considerable ingenuity.

After an earnest debate, however, it was disagreed to, and a conference took place without producing an accommodation among the members composing the committee. But finally, the house of representatives receded from their disagreement; and, by a majority of two voices, the bill passed as amended in the senate.

On the President, the solemn duty of deciding, whether an act of the legislature consisted with the constitution; for the bill, if constitutional, was unexceptionable.

In his cabinet, also, a difference of opinion is understood to have existed; the secretary of state and the attorney general were of opinion that the act was at variance with the constitution; the secretary of war was rather undecided; and the secretary of the treasury, thinking that, from the vagueness of expression in the clause relating to the subject, neither construction could be absolutely rejected, was in favour of acceding to the interpretation given by the legislature.

After weighing the arguments which were urged on each side of the question, the President was confirmed in the opinion that the population of each state, and not the total population of the United States, must give the numbers to which alone the process by which the number of representatives was to be ascertained could be applied. Having formed this opinion, to a correct and independent mind the course to be pursued was a plain one. Duty required the exercise of a power which a President of the United States will always find much difficulty in employing; and he returned the bill to the house in which it originated, accompanied with his objections[54] to it. In observance of the forms prescribed in the constitution, the question was then taken on its passage by ayes and noes, and it was rejected. A third bill was soon afterwards introduced, apportioning the representatives on the several states at a ratio of one for every thirty-three thousand persons in each state, which passed into a law. Thus was this interesting part of the American constitution finally settled.

Militia law.

During this session of congress, an act passed for establishing a uniform militia.

The President had manifested, from the commencement of his administration, a peculiar degree of solicitude on this subject, and had repeatedly urged it on congress.

In his speech at the opening of the present session, he again called the attention of the legislature to it; and, at length, a law was enacted which, though less efficacious than the plan reported by the secretary of war, will probably, not soon, be carried into complete execution.

Defeat of St. Clair.

In December, intelligence was received by the President, and immediately communicated to congress, that the American army had been totally defeated on the fourth of the preceding month.

Although the most prompt and judicious measures had been taken to raise the troops, and to march them to the frontiers, they could not be assembled in the neighbourhood of fort Washington until the month of September, nor was the establishment even then completed.

The immediate objects of the expedition were, to destroy the Indian villages on the Miamis, to expel the savages from that country, and to connect it with the Ohio by a chain of posts which would prevent their return during the war.

On the seventh of September, the regulars moved from their camp in the vicinity of fort Washington, and marching directly north, towards the object of their destination, established two intermediate posts[55] at the distance of rather more than forty miles from each other, as places of deposite, and of security either for convoys of provision which might follow the army, or for the army itself should any disaster befall it. The last of these works, fort Jefferson, was not completed until the 24th of October, before which time reinforcements were received of about three hundred and sixty militia. After placing garrisons in the forts, the effective number of the army, including militia, amounted to rather less than two thousand men. With this force, the general continued his march, which was rendered both slow and laborious by the necessity of opening a road. Small parties of Indians were frequently seen hovering about them, and some unimportant skirmishes took place. As the army approached the country in which they might expect to meet an enemy, about sixty of the militia deserted in a body. This diminution of force was not, in itself, an object of much concern. But there was reason to fear that the example, should those who set it be permitted to escape with impunity, would be extensively followed; and it was reported to be the intention of the deserters, to plunder convoys of provisions which were advancing at some distance in the rear. To prevent mischiefs of so serious a nature, the general detached Major Hamtranck with the first regiment in pursuit of the deserters, and directed him to secure the provisions under a strong guard.

The army, consisting of about fourteen hundred effective rank and file, continued its march; and, on the third of November, encamped about fifteen miles south of the Miamis villages. The right wing under the command of General Butler formed the first line, and lay with a creek, about twelve yards wide, immediately in its front. The left wing commanded by Lieutenant Colonel Darke, formed the second; and between the two lines, was an interval of about seventy yards.[56] The right flank was supposed to be secured by the creek, by a steep bank, and by a small body of troops; the left was covered by a party of cavalry, and by piquets. The militia crossed the creek, and advanced about a quarter of a mile in front, where they also encamped in two lines. On their approach, a few Indians who had shown themselves on the opposite side of the creek, fled with precipitation.

At this place, the general intended to throw up a slight work for the security of the baggage; and, after being joined by Major Hamtranck, to march as unincumbered, and as expeditiously as possible, to the villages he purposed to destroy.

In both these designs he was anticipated. About half an hour before sun rise the next morning, just after the troops had been dismissed from the parade, an unexpected attack was made upon the militia, who fled in the utmost confusion, and rushing into camp through the first line of continental troops, which had been formed the instant the first gun was discharged, threw them too into disorder. The exertions of the officers to restore order were not entirely successful. The Indians pressed close upon the heels of the flying militia, and engaged General Butler with great intrepidity. The action instantly became extremely warm; and the fire of the assailants, passing round both flanks of the first line, was, in a few minutes, poured with equal fury on the rear division. Its greatest weight was directed against the centre of each wing, where the artillery was posted; and the artillerists were mowed down in great numbers. Firing from the ground, and from the shelter which the woods afforded, the assailants were scarcely seen but when springing from one cover to another, in which manner they advanced close up to the American lines, and to the very mouths of the field pieces. They fought with the daring courage of men whose trade is war, and who are stimulated by all those passions which can impel the savage mind to vigorous exertions.

Under circumstances thus arduous, raw troops may be expected to exhibit that inequality which is found in human nature. While some of the American soldiers performed their duty with the utmost resolution, others seemed dismayed and terrified. Of this conduct the officers were, as usual, the victims. With a fearlessness which the occasion required, they exposed themselves to the most imminent dangers; and, in their efforts to change the face of affairs, fell in great numbers.

For several days, the Commander-in-chief had been afflicted with a severe disease, under which he still laboured, and which must have greatly affected him; but, though unable to display that activity which would have been useful in this severe conflict, neither the feebleness of his body, nor the peril of his situation, could prevent his delivering his orders with judgment and with self possession.[57]

It was soon perceived that the American fire could produce, on a concealed enemy, no considerable effect; and that the only hope of victory was placed in the bayonet. At the head of the second regiment, which formed the left of the left wing, Lieutenant Colonel Darke made an impetuous charge upon the enemy, forced them from their ground with some loss, and drove them about four hundred yards. He was followed by that whole wing; but the want of a sufficient number of riflemen to press this advantage, deprived him of the benefit which ought to have been derived from this effort; and, as soon as he gave over the pursuit, the Indians renewed their attack. In the mean time General Butler was mortally wounded, the left of the right wing was broken, the artillerists almost to a man killed, the guns seized, and the camp penetrated by the enemy. With his own regiment, and with the battalions commanded by Majors Butler[58] and Clarke, Darke was ordered again to charge with the bayonet. These orders were executed with intrepidity and momentary success. The Indians were driven out of the camp, and the artillery recovered. But while they were pressed in one point by the bravest of the American troops, their fire was kept up from every other with fatal effect. Several times particular corps charged them, always with partial success, but no universal effort could be made, and in every charge a great loss of officers was sustained, the consequences of which were severely felt. Instead of keeping their ranks, and executing the orders which were given, a great proportion of the soldiers flocked together in crowds, and were shot down without resistance. To save the remnant of his army was all that remained to be done; and, about half past nine in the morning, General St. Clair ordered Lieutenant Colonel Darke with the second regiment, to charge a body of Indians who had intercepted their retreat, and to gain the road. Major Clarke with his battalion was directed to cover the rear. These orders were executed, and a disorderly flight commenced. The pursuit was kept up about four miles, when, fortunately for the surviving Americans, that avidity for plunder which is a ruling passion among savages, called back the victorious Indians to the ramp, where the spoils of their vanquished foes were to be divided. The routed troops continued their flight to fort Jefferson, a distance of about thirty miles, throwing away their arms on the road. At this place they met Major Hamtranck with the first regiment; and a council of war was called to deliberate on the course to be pursued. As this regiment was far from restoring the strength of the morning, it was determined not to attempt to retrieve the fortune of the day: and, leaving the wounded at fort Jefferson, the army continued its retreat to fort Washington.

In this disastrous battle, the loss on the part of the Americans was very great when compared with the numbers engaged. Thirty-eight commissioned officers were killed upon the field, and five hundred and ninety-three non-commissioned officers and privates were slain and missing. Twenty-one commissioned officers, several of whom afterwards died of their wounds, and two hundred and forty-two non-commissioned officers and privates were wounded. Among the dead was the brave and much lamented General Butler. This gallant officer had served through the war of the revolution; and had, on more than one occasion, distinguished himself in a remarkable manner. In the list of those who shared his fate, were the names of many other excellent officers who had participated in all the toils, the dangers, and the glory, of that long conflict which terminated in the independence of their country. At the head of the list of wounded were Lieutenant Colonels Gibson and Darke, Major Butler, and Adjutant General Sargent, all of whom were veteran officers of great merit, who displayed their accustomed bravery on this unfortunate day. General St. Clair, in his official letter, observed: "the loss the public has sustained by the fall of so many officers, particularly of General Butler and Major Ferguson, can not be too much regretted; but it is a circumstance that will alleviate the misfortune in some measure, that all of them fell most gallantly doing their duty."

From the weight of the fire, and the circumstance of his being attacked nearly at the same time in front and rear, General St. Clair was of opinion that he was overpowered by numbers. The intelligence afterwards collected would make the Indian force to consist of from one thousand to fifteen hundred warriors. Of their loss, no estimate could be made; the probability is, that it bore no proportion to that sustained by the American army.

Nothing could be more unexpected than this severe disaster. The public had confidently anticipated a successful campaign, and could not believe, that the general who had been unfortunate, had not been culpable.

1792

The Commander-in-chief requested with earnestness that a court martial should sit on his conduct; but this request could not be granted, because the army did not furnish a sufficient number of officers of a grade to form a court for his trial on military principles. Late in the session, a committee of the house of representatives was appointed to inquire into the cause of the failure of the expedition, whose report, in explicit terms, exculpated the Commander-in-chief. This inquiry, however, was instituted rather for the purpose of investigating the conduct of civil than of military officers; and was not conducted by military men. More satisfactory testimony in favour of St. Clair is furnished by the circumstance, that he still retained the undiminished esteem and good opinion of the President.

The Indian war now assumed a still more serious aspect. There was reason to fear that the hostile tribes would derive a great accession of strength from the impression which their success would make upon their neighbours; and the reputation of the government was deeply concerned in retrieving the fortune of its arms, and affording protection to its citizens. The President, therefore, lost no time in causing the estimates for a competent force to be prepared and laid before congress. In conformity with a report made by the secretary of war, a bill was brought into the house of representatives, directing three additional regiments of infantry, and a squadron of cavalry to be raised, to serve for three years, if not sooner discharged. The whole military establishment, if completed, would amount to about five thousand men. The additional regiments, however, were to be disbanded as soon as peace should be concluded with the Indians; and the President was authorized to discharge, or to forbear to raise, any part of them, "in case events should, in his judgment, render his so doing consistent with the public safety."

Opposition to the increase of the army.

This bill met with great opposition. A motion was made to strike out the section which authorized an augmentation of force. By those who argued in favour of the motion, the justice of the war was arraigned, and the practicability of obtaining peace at a much less expense than would be incurred in its further prosecution, was urged with vehemence. An extension of the present frontier was said not to be desirable, and if the citizens of the United States were recalled within their proper boundaries, hostilities would cease. At any rate, it was an idle waste of blood and treasure, to carry the war beyond the line of forts already established. It was only exposing their arms to disgrace, betraying their own weakness, and lessening the public confidence in the government, to send forth armies to be butchered in the forests, while the British were suffered to keep possession of posts within the territory of the United States. To this cause was to be ascribed any disposition which might exist on the part of the Indians to continue hostilities, and to its removal the efforts of the government ought to be directed.

But, admitting the war to have been just in its commencement, and its continuance to be required by the honour and interest of the nation, yet as an invasion of the Indian country ought not to be attempted, this augmentation of the military establishment could not be necessary. Regular troops could only be useful as garrisons for posts to which the militia might resort for protection or supplies. Experience had proved that the sudden desultory attacks of the frontier militia and rangers were productive of more valuable consequences, than the methodical operations of a regular force. But, should it even be conceded that invasion and conquest were to be contemplated, the existing establishment, if completed, would be sufficiently great; and it was still insisted that, even for the purposes of conquest, the frontier militia were superior to any regulars whatever.

The expense of such an army as the bill contemplated was said to be an object worthy of serious attention; and members were requested to observe the progress of this business, and to say where it would stop. At first, only a single regiment had been raised, and the expense was about one hundred thousand dollars; a second was afterwards added, which swelled the expense to three hundred thousand; and now a standing force of five thousand one hundred and sixty-eight men is contemplated, at an annual expense of above a million and a quarter. They were preparing to squander away money by millions; and no one, except those who were in the secrets of the cabinet, knew why the war had been thus carried on for three years.

Against the motion for striking out, it was urged that the justice of the war could not be questioned by any man who would allow that self preservation, and indispensable necessity, could furnish sufficient motives for taking up arms. It was proved by unquestionable documents, that from the year 1783 to 1790, there had been not less than fifteen hundred persons, either the inhabitants of Kentucky, or emigrants on their way to that country, who had been massacred by the savages, or dragged into captivity; and there was reason to believe that on the frontiers of Virginia, and of Pennsylvania, the murdered and the prisoners would furnish a list almost equally numerous.

The conciliatory disposition of the government was stated, and its repeated efforts to obtain a peace were enumerated. It was particularly observed that in 1790, when a treaty was proposed at the Miamis villages, the Indians at first refused to treat;—they next required thirty days to deliberate;—this request was acceded to; and, in the interim, offensive operations were expressly prohibited by the President. Yet, notwithstanding this forbearance on the part of the whites, not less than one hundred and twenty persons were killed and captured by the savages, and several prisoners were roasted alive, during that short period; at the expiration of which, the Indians refused to give any answer to the proposition which had been made to them.

But it was now too late to inquire into the justice of the principles on which the war was originally undertaken. The nation was involved in it, and could not recede without exposing many innocent persons to be butchered by the enemy. Should the government determine to discontinue the war, would the Indians also consent to a cessation of hostilities? The government could not, without impeachment, both of its justice and humanity, abandon the inhabitants of the frontiers to the rage of their savage enemies; and although the excise might be unpopular, although money might still be wanted, what was the excise, what was money, when put in competition with the lives of their friends and brethren? A sufficient force must be raised for their defence, and the only question was what that force should be.

The calculations of the best informed men were in favour of employing an army not inferior to that proposed in the bill. When the known attachment of Indians to war and plunder was adverted to, and the excitements to that attachment which were furnished by the trophies acquired in the last two campaigns were considered, no man would venture to pronounce with confidence how extensive the combination against the United States might become, or what numbers they would have to encounter. It certainly behoved them to prepare in time for a much more vigorous effort than had hitherto been made. The objections drawn from the increased expense which such an effort would require, must entirely vanish before the eyes of any man, who looks forward to the consequences of another unsuccessful campaign. Such a disaster would eventually involve the nation in much greater expense than that which is now made the ground of opposition. Better therefore is it, to make at once a vigorous and effectual exertion to bring the contest to a close, than to continue gradually draining the treasury, by dragging on the war, and renewing hostility from year to year.

The supporters of the bill also appealed to experience for the superiority of regular troops over militia, in accomplishing all the purposes, even of Indian war; and those arguments were urged in favour of this theory, which the subject readily suggests.

The motion for striking out the section was lost; and the bill was carried for the augmentation of force required by the executive.

The treasury was not in a condition to meet the demands upon it, which the increased expenses of the war would unavoidably occasion; and sources of additional revenue were to be explored. A select committee to whom this subject was referred, brought in a resolution directing the secretary of the treasury to report his opinion to the house on the best mode of raising those additional supplies which the public service might require for the current year.

This proposition gave rise to a very animated debate.

It will be recollected that when the act for establishing the treasury department was under consideration, the clause which rendered it the duty of the secretary to digest and report plans for the improvement and management of the revenue, and for the support of public credit, was earnestly opposed. A large majority, however, was in favour of the principle; and, after being so modified, as only to admit a report if required by the house, it was retained in the bill. In complying with the various resolutions of congress, calling for reports on subjects connected with his department, the secretary had submitted plans which, having been profoundly considered, were well digested, and accompanied by arguments, the force of which it was difficult to resist. His measures were generally supported by a majority of congress; and, while the high credit of the United States was believed to attest their wisdom, the masterly manner in which his reports were drawn contributed to raise still higher, that reputation for great talents which he had long possessed. To the further admission of these reports, it was determined, on this occasion, to make a vigorous resistance.

But the opposition was not successful. On taking the question, the resolution was carried; thirty-one members voting in its favour, and twenty-seven against it.

Report of the secretary of the treasury for raising additional supplies.

The report[59] made by the secretary in pursuance of this resolution, recommended certain augmentations of the duties on imports; and was immediately referred to the consideration of a committee of the whole house. Resolutions were then passed which were to form the basis of a bill; and which adopted, not only the principles, but, with the exception of a few unimportant alterations, the minute details of the report.

Before the question was taken on the bill, a motion was made to limit its duration, the vote upon which strongly marked the progress of opinion in the house respecting those systems of finance which were believed to have established the credit of the United States.

The secretary of the treasury had deemed it indispensable to the creation of public credit, that the appropriations of funds for the payment of the interest, and the gradual redemption of the principal of the national debt, should be not only sufficient, but permanent also. A party was found in the first congress who opposed this principle; and were in favour of retaining a full power over the subject in each branch of the legislature, by making annual appropriations. The arguments which had failed in congress appear to have been more successfully employed with the people. Among the multiplied vices which were ascribed to the funding system, it was charged with introducing a permanent and extensive mortgage of funds, which was alleged to strengthen unduly the hands of the executive magistrate, and to be one of the many evidences which existed, of monarchical propensities in those who administered the government.

The report lately made by the secretary of the treasury, and the bill founded on that report, contemplated a permanent increase of the duties on certain specified articles; and a permanent appropriation of the revenue arising from them, to the purposes of the national debt. Thirty-one members were in favour of the motion for limiting the duration of the bill, and only thirty against it. By the rules of the house, the speaker has a right first to vote as a member; and, if the numbers should then be equally divided, to decide as speaker. Being opposed to the limitation, the motion was lost by his voice.

On the eighth of May, after an active and interesting session, congress adjourned to the first Monday in November.

The asperity which, on more than one occasion, discovered itself in debate, was a certain index of the growing exasperation of parties; and the strength of the opposition on those questions which brought into review the points on which the administration was to be attacked, denoted the impression which the specific charges brought against those who conducted public affairs, had made on the minds of the people, in an extensive division of the continent. It may conduce to a more perfect understanding of subsequent transactions, to present, in this place, a sketch of those charges.

Strictures on the conduct of administration, with a view of parties.

It was alleged that the public debt was too great to be paid before other causes of adding to it would occur. This accumulation of debt had been artificially produced by the assumption of what was due from the states. Its immediate effect was to deprive the government of its power over those easy sources of revenue, which, applied to its ordinary necessities and exigencies, would have answered them habitually, and thereby have avoided those burdens on the people which occasioned such murmurs against taxes, and tax gatherers. As a consequence of it, although the calls for money had not been greater than must be expected for the same or equivalent exigencies, yet congress had been already obliged, not only to strain the impost until it produced clamour, and would produce evasion, and war on their own citizens to collect it, but even to resort to an *excise* law, of odious character with the people, partial in its operation, unproductive unless enforced by arbitrary and vexatious means, and committing the authority of the government in parts where resistance was most probable, and coercion least practicable.

That the United States, if left free to act at their discretion, might borrow at two-thirds of the interest contracted to be paid to the public creditors, and thus discharge themselves from the principal in two-thirds of the time: but from this they were precluded by the irredeemable quality of the debt; a quality given for the avowed purpose of inviting its transfer to foreign countries. This transfer of the principal when completed would occasion an exportation of three millions of dollars annually for the interest, a drain of coin without example, and of the consequences of which no calculation could be made.

The banishment of coin would be completed by ten millions of paper money in the form of bank bills, which were then issuing into circulation. Nor would this be the only mischief resulting from the institution of the bank. The ten or twelve per cent, annual profit paid to the lenders of this paper medium would take out of the pockets of the people, who would have had, without interest, the coin it was banishing. That all the capital employed in paper speculation is barren and useless, producing like that on a gaming table no accession to itself, and is withdrawn from commerce and agriculture, where it would have produced addition to the common mass. The wealth therefore heaped upon individuals by the funding and banking systems, would be productive of general poverty and distress. That in addition to the encouragement these measures gave to vice and idleness, they had furnished effectual means of corrupting such a portion of the legislature as turned the balance between the honest voters. This corrupt squad, deciding the voice of the legislature, had manifested their dispositions to get rid of the limitations imposed by the constitution; limitations on the faith of which the states acceded to that instrument. They were proceeding rapidly in their plan of absorbing all power, invading the rights of the states, and converting the federal into a consolidated government.

That the ultimate object of all this was to prepare the way for a change from the present republican form of government to that of a monarchy, of which the English constitution was to be the model. So many of the friends of monarchy were in the legislature, that aided by the corrupt squad of paper dealers who were at their devotion, they made a majority in both houses. The republican party, even when united with the anti-federalists, continued a minority.

That of all the mischiefs resulting from the system of measures which was so much reprobated, none was so afflicting, so fatal to every honest hope, as the corruption of the legislature. As it was the earliest of these measures, it became the instrument for producing the rest, and would be the instrument for producing in future, a king, lords, and commons; or whatever else those who directed it might choose. Withdrawn such a distance from the eye of their constituents, they would form the most corrupt government on earth, if the means of their corruption were not prevented.

These strictures on the conduct of administration were principally directed against measures which had originated with the secretary of the treasury, and had afterwards received the sanction of the legislature. In the southern division of the continent, that officer was unknown, except to a few military friends, and to those who had engaged in the legislative or executive departments of the former or present government. His systems of revenue having been generally opposed by the southern members, and the original opposition to the constitution having been particularly great in Virginia and North Carolina, the aspersions on his views, and on the views of the eastern members by whom his plans had been generally supported, were seldom controverted. The remote tendency of particular systems, and the motives for their adoption, are so often subjects of conjecture, that the judgment, when exercised upon them, is peculiarly exposed to the influence of the passions; and where measures are in themselves burdensome, and the necessity for their adoption has not been appreciated, suspicions of their unknown advocates, can seldom be unsuccessfully urged by persons, in whom the people have placed their confidence. It is not therefore cause of astonishment, that the dark motives ascribed to the authors of tax laws, should be extensively believed.

Throughout the United States, the party opposed to the constitution had charged its supporters with a desire to establish a monarchy on the ruins of republican government; and the constitution itself was alleged to contain principles which would prove the truth of this charge. The leaders of that party had, therefore, been ready from the instant the government came into operation, to discover, in all its measures, those monarchical tendencies which they had perceived in the instrument they opposed.

The salaries allowed to public officers, though so low[60] as not to afford a decent maintenance to those who resided at the seat of government, were declared to be so enormously high, as clearly to manifest a total disregard of that simplicity and economy which were the characteristics of republics.

The levees of the President, and the evening parties of Mrs. Washington, were said to be imitations of regal institutions, designed to accustom the American people to the pomp and manners of European courts. The Vice President too was said to keep up the state and dignity of a monarch, and to illustrate, by his conduct, the principles which were inculcated in his political works.

The Indian war they alleged was misconducted, and unnecessarily prolonged for the purposes of expending the public money, and of affording a pretext for augmenting the military establishment, and increasing the revenue.

All this prodigal waste of the money of the people was designed to keep up the national debt, and the influence it gave the government, which, united with standing armies, and immense revenues, would enable their rulers to rivet the chains which they were secretly forging. Every prediction which had been uttered respecting the anti-republican principles of the government, was said to be rapidly verifying, and that which was disbelieved as prophecy, was daily becoming history. If a remedy for these ills was not found in the increased representation of the people which would take place at the ensuing elections, they would become too monstrous to be borne; and when it was recollected that the division of opinion was marked by a geographical line, there was reason to fear that the union would be broken into one or more confederacies.

These irritable symptoms had assumed appearances of increased malignity during the session of congress which had just terminated; and, to the President, who firmly believed that the union and the liberty of the states depended on the preservation of the government, they were the more unpleasant and the more alarming, because they were displayed in full force in his cabinet.

Disagreement between the secretaries of state and treasury.

Between the secretaries of the state and treasury departments, a disagreement existed, which seems to have originated in an early stage of the administration, and to have acquired a regular accession of strength from circumstances which were perpetually occurring, until it grew into open and irreconcileable hostility.

Without tracing this disagreement to those motives, which, in elective governments especially, often produce enmities between distinguished personages, neither of whom acknowledges the superiority of the other, such radical differences of opinion, on points which would essentially influence the course of the government, were supposed to exist between the secretaries, as, in a great measure, to account for this unextinguishable enmity. These differences of opinion were, perhaps, to be ascribed, in some measure, to a difference in the original structure of their minds, and, in some measure, to the difference of the situations in which they had been placed.

Until near the close of the war, Mr. Hamilton had served his country in the field; and, just before its termination, had passed from the camp into congress, where he remained for some time after peace had been established. In the former station, the danger to which the independence of his country was exposed from the imbecility of the government was perpetually before his eyes; and, in the latter, his attention was forcibly directed towards the loss of its reputation, and the sacrifice of its best interests, which were to be ascribed to the same cause. Mr. Hamilton, therefore, was the friend of a government which should possess, in itself, sufficient powers and resources to maintain the character, and defend the integrity of the nation. Having long felt and witnessed the mischiefs produced by the absolute sovereignty of the states, and by the control which they were enabled and disposed separately to exercise over every measure of general concern, he was particularly apprehensive of danger from that quarter; which he, probably, believed was to be the more dreaded, because the habits and feelings of the American people were calculated to inspire state, rather than national prepossessions. Under the influence of these impressions, he is understood to have avowed opinions in the convention favourable to a system in which the executive and senate, though elective, were to be rather more permanent, than they were rendered in that which was actually proposed. He afterwards supported the constitution, as framed, with great ability, and contributed essentially to its adoption. But he still retained, and openly avowed, the opinion, that the greatest hazards to which it was exposed arose from its weakness, and that American liberty and happiness had much more to fear from the encroachments of the great states, than from those of the general government.

Mr. Jefferson had retired from congress before the depreciation of the currency had produced an entire dependence of the general on the local governments; after which he filled the highest offices in the state of which he was a citizen. About the close of the war he was re-elected to congress; but, being soon afterwards employed on a mission to the court of Versailles, where he remained, while the people of France were taking the first steps of that immense revolution which has astonished and agitated two quarters of the world. In common with all his countrymen, he felt a strong interest in favour of the reformers; and it is not unreasonable to suppose, that while residing at that court, and associating with those who meditated some of the great events which have since taken place, his mind might be warmed with the abuses of the monarchy which were perpetually in his view, and he might be led to the opinion that liberty could sustain no danger but from the executive power. Mr. Jefferson, therefore, seems to have entertained no apprehensions from the debility of the government; no jealousy of the state sovereignties; and no suspicion of their encroachments. His fears took a different direction, and all his precautions were used to check and limit the exercise of the powers vested in the government of the United States. Neither could he perceive danger to liberty except from that government, and especially from the executive department.

He did not feel so sensibly, as those who had continued in the United States, the necessity of adopting the constitution; and had, at one time, avowed a wish that it might be rejected by such a number of states as would secure certain alterations which he thought essential. His principal objections seem to have been, the want of a bill of rights, and the re-eligibility of the President. From this opinion, however, in favour of a partial rejection, he is understood to have receded, after seeing the plan pursued by the convention of Massachusetts, and followed by other states; which was to adopt unconditionally, and to annex a recommendation of the amendments which were desired.[61]

To these causes of division, another was superadded, the influence of which was soon felt in all the political transactions of the government.

The war which was terminated in 1783, had left in the bosoms of the American people, a strong attachment to France, and enmity to Great Britain. These feelings, in a greater or less degree, were perhaps universal; and had been prevented from subsiding by circumstances to which allusions have already been made. They had evinced themselves, in the state legislatures, by commercial regulations; and were demonstrated by all those means by which the public sentiment is usually displayed. They found their way also into the national councils, where they manifested themselves in the motions respecting the favours which ought to be shown to nations having commercial treaties with the United States.

Although affection for France, and jealousy of Britain, were sentiments common to the people of America, the same unanimity did not exist respecting the influence which ought to be allowed to those sentiments, over the political conduct of the nation. While many favoured such discriminations as might eventually turn the commerce of the United States into new channels, others maintained that, on this subject, equality ought to be observed; that trade ought to be guided by the judgment of individuals, and that no sufficient motives existed for that sacrifice of general and particular interests, which was involved in the discriminations proposed;—discriminations which, in their view, amounted to a tax on American agriculture, and a bounty on the navigation and manufactures of a favoured foreign nation.

The former opinion was taken up with warmth by the secretary of state; and the latter was adopted with equal sincerity by the secretary of the treasury. This contrariety of sentiment respecting commercial regulations was only a part of a general system. It extended itself to all the relations which might subsist between America and those two great powers.

In all popular governments, the press is the most ready channel by which the opinions and the passions of the few are communicated to the many; and of the press, the two great parties forming in the United States, sought to avail themselves. The Gazette of the United States supported the systems of the treasury department, while other papers enlisted themselves under the banners of the opposition. Conspicuous among these, was the National Gazette, a paper edited by a clerk in the department of state. The avowed purpose for which the secretary patronized this paper, was to present to the eye of the American people, European intelligence derived from the Leyden gazette, instead of English papers; but it soon became the vehicle of calumny against the funding and banking systems, against the duty on home-made spirits, which was denominated an excise, and against the men who had proposed and supported those measures. With perhaps equal asperity, the papers attached to the party which had defended these systems, assailed the motives of the leaders of the opposition.

Letters from Washington on this subject.

This schism in his cabinet was a subject of extreme mortification to the President. Entertaining a high respect for the talents, and a real esteem for the characters, of both gentlemen, he was unwilling to part with either; and exerted all the influence he possessed to effect a reconciliation between them. In a letter of the 23d of August, addressed to the secretary of state, after reviewing the critical situation of the United States with respect to its external relations, he thus expressed himself on this delicate subject. "How unfortunate and how much is it to be regretted then, that, while we are encompassed on all sides with avowed enemies, and insidious friends, internal dissensions should be harassing and tearing our vitals. The last, to me, is the most serious, the most alarming, and the most afflicting of the two; and, without more charity for the opinions of one another in governmental matters, or some more infallible criterion by which the truth of speculative opinions, before they have undergone the test of experience, are to be forejudged, than has yet fallen to the lot of fallibility, I believe it will be difficult, if not impracticable, to manage the reins of government, or to keep the parts of it together: for if, instead of laying our shoulders to the machine, after measures are decided on, one pulls this way, and another that, before the utility of the thing is fairly tried, it must inevitably be torn asunder; and, in my opinion, the fairest prospect of happiness and prosperity that ever was presented to man will be lost, perhaps, for ever.

"My earnest wish and my fondest hope therefore is, that instead of wounding suspicions, and irritating charges, there may be liberal allowances, mutual forbearances, and temporizing yielding on all sides. Under the exercise of these, matters will go on smoothly; and if possible, more prosperously. Without them, every thing must rub; the wheels of government will clog; our enemies will triumph; and, by throwing their weight into the disaffected scale, may accomplish the ruin of the goodly fabric we have been erecting."

"I do not mean to apply this advice, or these observations, to any particular person or character. I have given them in the same general terms to other officers[62] of the government, because the disagreements which have arisen from difference of opinions, and the attacks which have been made upon almost all the measures of government, and most of its executive officers, have for a long time past filled me with painful sensations, and can not fail, I think, of producing unhappy consequences, at home and abroad."

In a subsequent letter to the same gentleman, in answer to one which enclosed some documents designed to prove that, though desirous of amending the constitution, he had favoured its adoption, the President said—"I did not require the evidence of the extracts which you enclosed me, to convince me of your attachment to the constitution of the United States, or of your disposition to promote the general welfare of this country; but I regret, deeply regret, the difference of opinion which has arisen, and divided you and another principal officer of the government—and wish devoutly there could be an accommodation of them by mutual yieldings.

"A measure of this sort would produce harmony and consequent good in our public councils; and the contrary will inevitably produce confusion and serious mischiefs—and for what? because mankind can not think alike, but would adopt different means to attain the same end. For I will frankly and solemnly declare that I believe the views of both to be pure and well meant, and that experience only will decide with respect to the salubrity of the measures which are the subjects of this dispute.

"Why then, when some of the best citizens of the United States—men of discernment—uniform and tried patriots—who have no sinister views to promote, but are chaste in their ways of thinking and acting, are to be found some on one side, and some on the other of the questions which have caused these agitations—why should either of you be so tenacious of your opinions as to make no allowance for those of the other?

"I could, and indeed was about to add more on this interesting subject, but will forbear, at least for the present, after expressing a wish that the cup which has been presented to us may not be snatched from our lips by a discordance of action, when I am persuaded there is no discordance in your views. I have a great, a sincere esteem and regard for you both; and ardently wish that some line could be marked out by which both of you could walk."

These earnest endeavours to sooth the angry passions, and to conciliate the jarring discords of the cabinet, were unsuccessful. The hostility which was so much and so sincerely lamented sustained no diminution, and its consequences became every day more diffusive.

Among the immediate effects of these internal dissensions, was the encouragement they afforded to a daring and criminal resistance which was made to the execution of the laws imposing a duty on spirits distilled within the United States.

To the inhabitants of that part of Pennsylvania which lies west of the Alleghany mountains, this duty was, from local considerations, peculiarly odious; nor was their hostility to the measure diminished by any affection for the source in which it originated. The constitution itself had encountered the most decided opposition from that part of the state; and that early enmity to the government which exerted every faculty to prevent its adoption, had sustained no abatement. Its measures generally, and the whole system of finance particularly, had been reprobated with peculiar bitterness by many of the most popular men of that district. With these dispositions, a tax law, the operation of which was extended to them, could not be favourably received, however generally it might be supported in other parts of the union. But when, to this pre-existing temper, were superadded the motives which arose from perceiving that the measure was censured on the floor of congress as unnecessary and tyrannical; that resistance to its execution was treated as probable; that a powerful and active party, pervading the union, arraigned with extreme acrimony the whole system of finance as being hostile to liberty; and, with all the passionate vehemence of conviction, charged its advocates with designing to subvert the republican institutions of America; we ought not to be surprised that the awful impressions, which usually restrain combinations to resist the laws, were lessened; and that the malcontents were emboldened to hope that those combinations might be successful.

Opposition to the excise law.

Some discontents had been manifested in several parts of the union on the first introduction of the act; but the prudence and firmness of the government and its officers had dissipated them; and the law had been carried into general operation. But in the western district of Pennsylvania, the resistance wore the appearance of system, and was regularly progressive. In its commencement, it manifested itself by the circulation of opinions calculated to increase the odium in which the duty was held, and by endeavours to defeat its collection by directing the public resentments against those who were inclined either to comply with the law, or to accept the offices through which it was to be executed. These indications of ill temper were succeeded by neighbourhood meetings, in which resolutions of extreme violence were adopted, and by acts of outrage against the persons of revenue officers. At length, in September, 1791, a meeting of delegates from the malcontent counties was held at Pittsburg, in which resolutions were adopted breathing the same spirit with those which had previously been agreed to in county assemblies. Unfortunately, the deputy marshal, who was entrusted with the process against those who had committed acts of violence on the persons of revenue officers, was so intimidated by the turbulent spirit which was generally displayed, that he returned without performing his duty; and thus added to the confidence felt by the disaffected in their strength. Appearances were such as to justify apprehensions, that the judiciary would be found unable to punish the violators of the laws; and the means of obtaining aid from the executive had not been furnished by the legislature. This state of things was the more embarrassing, because the prejudices which had been widely disseminated, and the misconceptions of the act which had been extensively diffused, authorized some fears respecting the support which the law, while yet in the infancy of its operation, would receive from the people. These considerations, added to that repugnance which was felt by the government to the employment of harsh means, induced a forbearance to notice further these riotous proceedings, until the measure, by being carried into full effect in other parts of the union, should be better understood; and until congress should assemble, and modify the system in such a manner as to remove any real objections to it, the existence of which might be suggested by experience. Accordingly, in the legislature which convened in October, 1791, this subject was taken up in pursuance of the recommendation of the President, and an amendatory act was passed in May, 1792, in which the whole system was revised, and great pains were taken to alter such parts of it as could be deemed exceptionable.

This conciliatory measure did not produce the desired effect. No abatement took place in the violence and outrage with which the resistance to the law was conducted. To carry it into execution, officers of inspection were necessary in every county. The malcontents, for a considerable time, deterred every person from consenting to permit an office to be held at his house; and when at length this difficulty was supposed to be overcome, those who had been prevailed on to accede to the propositions of the supervisor in this respect, were compelled, by personal violence, and by threats of the destruction of property, and even of death, to retract the consent they had given.

A meeting was again convened at Pittsburg, in which, among other very exceptionable resolutions, committees were established to correspond with any committees of a similar nature that might be appointed in other parts of the United States. By this meeting it was declared, that they would persist in every legal measure to obstruct the execution of the law, and would consider those who held offices for the collection of the duty as unworthy of their friendship; that they would have no intercourse or dealings with them; would withdraw from them every assistance, and withhold all the comforts of life which depend upon those duties which, as men and fellow citizens, they owed to each other; and would, upon all occasions, treat them with contempt. It was at the same time earnestly recommended to the people at large to adopt the same line of conduct.

President's proclamation.

No man could be more sensible than the President of the dangerous tendency of these measures, nor more indignant at the outrage thus offered to the government of the United States. But his prudence, and his high respect for the laws restrained him within the narrow limits which the legislature had prescribed. A proclamation[63] was issued exhorting and admonishing all persons to desist from any combinations or proceedings whatsoever, tending to obstruct the execution of the laws, and requiring the interference of the civil magistrate; and prosecutions against the offenders were directed to be instituted in every case in which they could be supported.

This proclamation produced no salutary effect. Many of the civil magistrates were themselves concerned in stimulating the excesses they were required to suppress; and those who had not embarked in the criminal enterprise, found themselves totally unable to maintain the sovereignty of the laws.

With a laudable solicitude to avoid extremities, the government still sought for means to recall these misguided people to a sense of duty, without the employment of a military force. To obtain this desirable object, the following system was digested and pursued:

Prosecutions were instituted against delinquents in those cases in which it was believed that they could be maintained. The spirits distilled in the non-complying counties were intercepted on their way to market, and seized by the officers of the revenue; and the agents for the army were directed to purchase only those spirits on which the duty had been paid. By thus acting on the interests of the distillers, the hope was indulged that they might be induced to comply with the law. Could they have obeyed their wishes, these measures would have produced the desired effect; but they were no longer masters of their own conduct. Impelled by a furious multitude, they found it much more dangerous to obey the laws than to resist them. The efficacy of this system too was diminished by a circumstance, which induced the necessity of a second application to the legislature. The act had not been extended to the territory north-west of the Ohio, in which great part of the army lay; and the distillers eluded the vigilance of the government by introducing their spirits into that territory.

While from causes which were incessant and active in their operation, some of which seem too strongly fixed in the human mind ever to be removed, a broad foundation was thus laid for those party struggles whose fury is generally proportioned to the magnitude of the objects to be attained, and to the means which may be employed in attaining them, the external affairs of the United States sustained no material change.

Of the good understanding which was preserved with France, a fresh proof had been recently given by the employment of Mr. Ternan, a person peculiarly acceptable to the American government, to succeed the Count de Moustiers, as minister plenipotentiary of his Most Christian Majesty; and in turn, Mr. Gouverneur Morris, who was understood to have rendered himself agreeable to the French government, was appointed to represent the United States at the court of Versailles.

In addition to these interchanges of civility, a melancholy occasion had presented itself for giving much more substantial evidence of the alacrity with which the American administration would embrace any proper opportunity of manifesting its disposition to promote the interests of France.

Insurrection and massacre in the island of St. Domingo.

Early and bitter fruits of that malignant philosophy, which, disregarding the actual state of the world, and estimating at nothing the miseries of a vast portion of the human race, can coolly and deliberately pursue, through oceans of blood, abstract systems for the attainment of some fancied untried good, were gathered in the French West Indies. Instead of proceeding in the correction of any abuses which might exist, by those slow and cautious steps which gradually introduce reform without ruin, which may prepare and fit society for that better state of things designed for it; and which, by not attempting impossibilities, may enlarge the circle of happiness, the revolutionists of France formed the mad and wicked project of spreading their doctrines of equality among persons, between whom distinctions and prejudices exist to be subdued only by the grave. The rage excited by the pursuit of this visionary and baneful theory, after many threatening symptoms, burst forth on the 23d day of August 1791, with a fury alike destructive and general. In one night, a preconcerted insurrection of the blacks took place throughout the colony of St. Domingo; and the white inhabitants of the country, while sleeping in their beds, were involved in one indiscriminate massacre, from which neither age nor sex could afford an exemption. Only a few females, reserved for a fate more cruel than death, were intentionally spared; and not many were fortunate enough to escape into the fortified cities. The insurgents then assembled in vast numbers, and a bloody war commenced between them and the whites inhabiting the towns. The whole French part of the island was in imminent danger of being totally lost to the mother country. The minister of his Most Christian Majesty applied to the executive of the United States for a sum of money which would enable him to preserve this valuable colony, to be deducted out of the debt to his sovereign; and the request was granted in a manner evincing the interest taken by the administration in whatever might concern France.

On the part of Spain, a desire had been expressed to adjust the subjects in controversy between the two nations by negotiations to be carried on at Madrid; and Mr. Carmichael, and Mr. Short, had been appointed commissioners, with powers equal to the object. In the mean time, the officers of that nation persisted in measures which were calculated to embroil the United States with the southern Indians. By their intrigues with the Creeks, the treaty formed in 1790 with M'Gillivray, was prevented from being ratified, and the boundary line then agreed upon was not permitted to be run. The indefinite claim of territory set up by Spain was alleged to constitute a sufficient objection to any new line of demarcation, until that claim should be settled; and her previous treaties and relations with the Creeks were declared to be infringed by their stipulation, acknowledging themselves to be under the protection of the United States.

An official diplomatic intercourse had at length been opened with Great Britain also. Mr. Hammond, the minister plenipotentiary of that nation to the United States, arrived at Philadelphia in the autumn of 1791; upon which, Mr. Thomas Pinckney, a gentleman of South Carolina, who was highly and justly respected, had been charged with the interests of his country at the court of London.[64]Soon after the arrival of Mr. Hammond, the non-execution of the treaty of peace became the subject of a correspondence between him and the secretary of state, in which the complaints of their respective nations were urged in terms manifesting clearly the sense entertained by each of the justice of those complaints, without furnishing solid ground for the hope that they would be immediately removed on either side.

Mr. Hammond's powers on the subject of a commercial treaty were far from being satisfactory. To the inquiries of Mr. Jefferson on this point, he replied, that he was authorized to enter into a negotiation respecting the commercial intercourse between the two countries, and to discuss those principles which might serve as a basis for a treaty, but not to *conclude* any definitive arrangements. In fact, there was much reason to believe that the obstacles to a commercial treaty between the two countries would not be soon or easily surmounted. In America, such an alteration in the law of nations as would permit the goods of an enemy to pass freely in the bottom of a neutral, was a favourite project; and a full participation of the colonial trade was also most earnestly desired. That the latter of these objects would not be readily conceded by Great Britain did not admit of a doubt; but many intelligent men, possessing great political influence, had embraced the opinion that she could be forced out of that colonial system which every European power having settlements in America had adopted, by regulations restricting her navigation and commerce with the

United States. To those who entertained this opinion, no commercial treaty could be acceptable, which did not contain the concessions they required.

In addition to a general knowledge of the sentiments of the British cabinet on these points, particular evidence had lately been received of its positive decision respecting them. A comprehensive report on American affairs had been made to the privy council by a committee of that body, which was laid before the king. A few copies of it had been printed for the members of the cabinet, which were soon called in by a sudden order of council; but one of these copies was obtained, and transmitted to the secretary of state of the United States. This report manifested a willingness to form a commercial treaty with the American government on principles of perfect equality, both with respect to navigation and commerce, so far as regarded the dominions of his Britannic Majesty in Europe; but it also discovered a determination, to adhere inflexibly to the existing regulations for the colonies; and to reject the principle that free bottoms make free goods.

In this state paper the opinion was advanced, that several important articles of exportation from the United States, especially tobacco, had been peculiarly favoured in Great Britain; but that these friendly regulations were not reciprocated by America. The means of retaliating injuries which might be inflicted on British commerce were stated, but those means, it was said, ought not hastily to be adopted, the more especially, as the existing government of the United States had discovered dispositions more favourable to a liberal and fair intercourse between the two countries, than had been manifested by the respective states. For several reasons it was deemed adviseable not suddenly to disturb the existing state of things, but to regulate the trade of the two nations by a treaty, the stipulations of which should be equal, and mutually beneficial, provided such a treaty could be formed without a departure from those principles which were considered as fundamental.

General Wayne appointed to the command of the army.

No abatement of hostility having taken place among the north-western Indians, the preparations for terminating the war by the sword were earnestly pressed. Major General Wayne was appointed to succeed General St. Clair, who resigned the command of the army; and the utmost exertions were made to complete it to the establishment; but the laws furnished such small inducements to engage in the service, that the highest military grades, next to that of Commander-in-chief, were declined by many to whom they were offered; and the recruiting business advanced too slowly to authorize a hope that the decisive expedition which was meditated, could be prudently undertaken in the course of the present year. Meanwhile, the public clamour against the war continued to be loud and violent. It was vehemently asserted, that if the intentions of the government respecting the savages were just and humane, those intentions were unknown to them, and that their resentments were kept up by the aggressions of whites, and by the opinion that their expulsion from the country they occupied was the object of the hostilities carried on against them. However satisfied the President might be of the fallacy of these opinions, they were too extensively maintained not to be respected, as far as was compatible with a due regard to the real interests of the nation. While, therefore, the preparations for offensive operations were hastened by a vigorous exertion of the means at the disposal of the executive, it was thought adviseable to make another effort to terminate the war by a direct communication of the pacific views of the United States.—The failure of these attempts was still less to be lamented than the fate of those who were employed in them. Colonel Harden and Major Trueman, two brave officers and valuable men, were severally despatched with propositions of peace, and each was murdered by the savages.

Meeting of congress.
President's speech.

On the 5th of November congress again convened. In the speech delivered at the commencement of the session, Indian affairs were treated at considerable length, and the continuance of the war was mentioned as a subject of much regret. "The reiterated endeavours," it was said, "which had been made to effect a pacification, had hitherto issued in new and outrageous proofs of persevering hostility on the part of the tribes with whom the United States were in contest.

"A detail of the measures that had been pursued, and of their consequences, which would be laid before congress, while it would confirm the want of success thus far, would evince that means as proper and as efficacious as could have been devised, had been employed. The issue of some of them was still pending; but a favourable one, though not to be despaired of, was not promised by any thing that had yet happened."

That a sanction, commonly respected even among savages, had been found insufficient to protect from massacre the emissaries of peace, was particularly noticed; and the families of those valuable citizens who had thus fallen victims to their zeal for the public service, were recommended to the attention of the legislature.

That unprovoked aggression had been made by the southern Indians, and that there was just cause for apprehension that the war would extend to them also, was mentioned as a subject of additional concern.

"Every practicable exertion had been made to be prepared for the alternative of prosecuting the war, in the event of a failure of pacific overtures. A large proportion of the troops authorized to be raised, had been recruited, though the numbers were yet incomplete; and pains had been taken to discipline them, and put them in a condition for the particular kind of service to be performed. But a delay of operations, besides being dictated by the measures that were pursuing towards a pacific termination of the war, had been in itself deemed preferable to immature efforts."

The humane system which has since been successfully pursued, of gradually civilizing the savages by improving their condition, of diverting them in some degree from hunting to domestic and agricultural occupations by imparting to them some of the most simple and useful acquisitions of society, and of conciliating them to the United States by a beneficial and well regulated commerce, had ever been a favourite object with the President, and the detailed view which was now taken of Indian affairs, was concluded with a repetition of his recommendations of these measures.

The subject next adverted to in the speech, was the impediments which in some places continued to embarrass the collection of the duties on spirits distilled within the United States. After observing that these impediments were lessening in local extent, but that symptoms of such increased opposition had lately manifested themselves in certain places as, in his judgment, to render his special interposition adviseable, the President added,— "Congress may be assured that nothing within constitutional and legal limits which may depend on me, shall be wanting to assert and maintain the just authority of the laws. In fulfilling this trust, I shall count entirely on the full co-operation of the other departments of government, and upon the zealous support of all good citizens."

After noticing various objects which would require the attention of the legislature, the President addressed himself particularly to the house of representatives, and said, "I entertain a strong hope that the state of the national finances is now sufficiently matured to enable you to enter upon a systematic and effectual arrangement for the regular redemption and discharge of the public debt, according to the right which has been reserved to the government. No measure can be more desirable, whether viewed with an eye to its intrinsic importance, or to the general sentiments and wish of the nation."

The addresses of the two houses in answer to the speech, were, as usual, respectful and affectionate. The several subjects recommended to the attention of congress were noticed either in general terms, or in a manner to indicate a coincidence of sentiment between the legislative and executive departments. The turbulent spirit which had manifested itself in certain parts of the union was mentioned by both houses with a just degree of censure, and the measures adopted by the President, as well as the resolution he expressed to compel obedience to the laws, were approved; and the house of representatives, in the most unqualified terms, declared opinions in favour of systematic and effectual arrangements for discharging the public debt. But the subsequent proceedings of the legislature did not fulfil the expectations excited by this auspicious commencement of the session.

At an early day, in a committee of the whole house on the President's speech, Mr. Fitzsimmons moved "that measures for the reduction of so much of the public debt as the

United States have a right to redeem, ought to be adopted: and that the secretary of the treasury be directed to report a plan for that purpose."

This motion was objected to by Mr. Madison as being premature. The state of the finances, he thought, was not sufficiently understood to authorize the adoption of the measure it contemplated. The debate however soon took a different direction. That part of the resolution which proposed a reference to the secretary of the treasury was particularly opposed; and an ardent discussion ensued, in which, without much essential variation, the arguments which had before been urged on the same subject were again employed. After a vehement contest, the motion to amend the resolution by striking out the proposed reference was overruled, and it was carried in its original form.

1793

In obedience to this order, the secretary made a report, in which he proposed a plan for the annual redemption of that portion of the debt, the payment of which was warranted by the contract between the United States and their creditors. But the expenses of the Indian war rendering it, in his opinion, unsafe to rest absolutely on the existing revenue, he proposed to extend the internal taxes to pleasure horses, or pleasure carriages, as the legislature might deem most eligible. The consideration of this report was deferred on various pretexts; and a motion was made to reduce the military establishment. The debate on this subject was peculiarly earnest; and, in its progress, the mode of conducting the Indian war, the relative merits and expensiveness of militia and of regular troops, and the danger to liberty from standing armies, were elaborately discussed. It was not until the fourth of January that the motion was rejected. While that question remained undecided, the report of the secretary was unavoidably postponed, because, on its determination would depend, in the opinion of many, the necessity of additional taxes. It would seem not improbable that the opponents of the American system of finances, who constituted rather a minority of the present congress, but who indulged sanguine hopes of becoming the majority in the next, were desirous of referring every question relating to the treasury department to the succeeding legislature, in which there would be a more full representation of the people. Whatever might be the operating motives for delay, neither the extension of the law imposing a duty on spirits distilled within the United States to the territory north-west of the river Ohio, nor the plan for redeeming the public debt, which was earnestly pressed by the administration, could be carried through the present congress. Those who claimed the favour and confidence of the people as a just reward for their general attachment to liberty, and especially for their watchfulness to prevent every augmentation of debt, were found in opposition to a system for its diminution, which was urged by men who were incessantly charged with entertaining designs for its excessive accumulation, in order to render it the corrupt instrument of executive influence. It might be expected that the public attention would be attracted to such a circumstance. But when party passions are highly inflamed, reason itself submits to their control, and becomes the instrument of their will. The assertion that the existing revenues, if not prodigally or corruptly wasted, were sufficient for the objects contemplated by the President in his speech, would constitute an ample apology for the impediments thrown in the way of a system which could not be directly disapproved, and would justify a continuance of the charge that the supporters of the fiscal system were friends to the augmentation of the public debt.

Soon after the motion for the reduction of the military establishment was disposed of, another subject was introduced, which effectually postponed, for the present session, every measure connected with the finances of the nation.

An act of congress, which passed on the fourth of August, 1790, authorized the President to cause to be borrowed any sum not exceeding twelve millions of dollars, to be applied in payment of the foreign debt of the United States.

A subsequent act, which passed on the 12th of the same month, authorized another loan not exceeding two millions, to be applied, in aid of the sinking fund, towards the extinguishment of the domestic debt.

A power to make these loans was delegated by the President to the secretary of the treasury by a general commission referring to the acts. This commission was accompanied by written instructions, directing the payment of such parts of the foreign debt as should become due at the end of the year 1791; but leaving the secretary, with respect to the residue, to be regulated by the interests of the United States.

Under this commission two loans were negotiated in 1790, and others at subsequent periods.

As many considerations of convenience opposed such an arrangement as would appropriate all the monies arising from either of these loans to one object, to the total exclusion of the other; and no motive was perceived for thus unnecessarily fettering the operations of the treasury; each loan was negotiated under both laws; and consequently the monies produced by each were applicable to both objects, in such proportions as the President might direct. It has been already observed that his written instructions had ordered the payment of those instalments of the foreign debt which should become due before the first of January, 1792; but no further sums on that account were to be borrowed until supplemental orders to that effect should be given, unless a loan could be made on such terms as would render it advantageous to the United States to anticipate the payments to their foreign creditors. It being the opinion of both the President and secretary that the official powers of the latter authorized him to draw the monies borrowed for domestic purposes into the treasury, where they would form a part of the sinking fund, and be applicable to the objects of that fund in conformity with the laws of appropriation, no written instructions were given respecting that part of the subject; but in the progress of the business, every material step which was taken was communicated to the President, and his directions obtained upon it. While the chief magistrate remained at the seat of government, these communications were verbal; when absent, they were made by letter.

At this period, the domestic debt bore a low price in the market, and foreign capital was pouring into the United States for its purchase. The immediate application of the sinking fund to this object would consequently acquire a large portion of the debt, and would also accelerate its appreciation. The best interests of the United States, and his own fame, thus impelling the secretary to give the operations of the sinking fund the utmost activity of which it was susceptible, he had, with the approbation of the President, directed a part of the first loan to be paid in discharge of the instalments of the foreign debt which were actually due, and had drawn a part of it into the public treasury in aid of the sinking fund.

In May, 1791, instructions were given to the agent of the United States in Europe, to apply the proceeds of future loans, as they should accrue, in payments to France, except such sums as should be previously and specially reserved. In the execution of these instructions, some delay intervened, which was to be ascribed, among other causes, to representations made by the French minister of marine that a plan would be adopted, to which a decree of the national assembly was requisite, for converting a large sum into supplies for St. Domingo: and to a desire on the part of the agent to settle, previously to further payments, a definitive rule by which the monies paid should be liquidated, and credited to the United States. The disordered state of French affairs protracted both the one and the other of these causes of delay, to a later period than had been expected; and, in the mean time, the secretary continued to draw into the United States such portions of these loans, as were destined to be brought in aid of the sinking fund. Such was the state of this transaction, when the commencement of those calamities, which have finally overwhelmed St. Domingo, induced the American government, on the urgent application of the French minister, to furnish supplies to that ill fated colony, in payment of the debt to France. This being a mode of payment which, to a certain extent, was desired by the creditor, and was advantageous to the debtor, a consequent disposition prevailed to use it so far as might comport with the wish of the French government; and a part of the money designed for foreign purposes, was drawn into the United States. In the course of these operations, a portion of the instalments actually due to France, had been permitted to remain unsatisfied.

A part of the money borrowed in Europe being thus applicable to the extinguishment of the domestic debt, and a part of the domestic revenue being applicable to the payment of interest due on the loans made in Europe, the secretary of the treasury had appropriated a part of the money arising from foreign loans to the payment of interest due abroad, which had been replaced by the application of money in the treasury arising from domestic resources, to the purchase of the domestic debt.

The secretary had not deemed it necessary to communicate these operations in detail to the legislature: but some hints respecting them having been derived either from certain papers which accompanied a report made to the house of representatives early in the session, or from some other source, Mr. Giles, on the 23d of January, moved several resolutions, requiring information, among other things, on the various points growing out of these loans, and the application of the monies arising from them, and respecting the unapplied revenues of the United States, and the places in which the sums so unapplied were deposited. In the speech introducing these resolutions, observations were made which very intelligibly implied charges of a much more serious nature than inattention to the exact letter of an appropriation law. Estimates were made to support the position that a large balance of public money was unaccounted for.

The resolutions were agreed to without debate; and, in a few days, the secretary transmitted a report containing the information that was required.

This report comprehended a full exposition of the views and motives which had regulated the conduct of the department, and a very able justification of the measures which had been adopted; but omitted to state explicitly that part of the money borrowed in Europe had been drawn into the United States with the sanction of the President.—It is also chargeable with some expressions which can not be pronounced unexceptionable, but which may find their apology in the feelings of a mind conscious of its own uprightness, and wounded by the belief that the proceedings against him had originated in a spirit hostile to fair inquiry.

These resolutions, the observations which accompanied them, and the first number of the report, were the signals for a combined attack on the secretary of the treasury, through the medium of the press. Many anonymous writers appeared, who assailed the head of that department with a degree of bitterness indicative of the spirit in which the inquiry was to be conducted.

Resolutions implicating the secretary of the treasury rejected.

On the 27th of February, not many days after the last number of the report was received, Mr. Giles moved sundry resolutions which were founded on the information before the house. The idea of a balance unaccounted for was necessarily relinquished; but the secretary of the treasury was charged with neglect of duty in failing to give congress official information of the monies drawn by him from Europe into the United States; with violating the law of the 4th of August, 1790, by applying a portion of the principal borrowed under it to the payment of interest, and by drawing a part of the same monies into the United States, without instructions from the President; with deviating from the instructions of the President in other respects; with negotiating a loan at the bank, contrary to the public interest, while public monies to a greater amount than were required, lay unemployed in the bank; and with an indecorum to the house, in undertaking to judge of its motives in calling for information which was demandable of him from the constitution of his office; and in failing to give all the necessary information within his knowledge relative to subjects on which certain specified references had been previously made to him.

These resolutions were followed by one, directing that a copy of them should be transmitted to the President of the United States.

The debate on this subject, which commenced on the 28th of February, was continued to the 1st of March, and was conducted with a spirit of acrimony towards the secretary, demonstrating the soreness of the wounds that had been given and received in the political and party wars which had been previously waged.[65] It terminated in a rejection of all the resolutions. The highest number voting in favour of any one of them was sixteen.

Congress adjourns.

On the 3d of March, a constitutional period was put to the existence of the present congress. The members separated with obvious symptoms of extreme irritation. Various causes, the most prominent of which have already been noticed, had combined to organize two distinct parties in the United States, which were rapidly taking the form of a ministerial and an opposition party. By that in opposition, the President was not yet openly renounced. His personal influence was too great to be encountered by a direct avowal that he was at the head of their adversaries; and his public conduct did not admit of a suspicion that he could allow himself to rank as the chief of a party. Nor could public opinion be seduced to implicate him in the ambitious plans and dark schemes for the subversion of liberty, which were ascribed to a part of the administration, and to the leading members who had supported the measures of finance adopted by the legislature.

Yet it was becoming apparent that things were taking a course which must inevitably involve him in the political conflicts which were about to take place. It was apparent that the charges against the secretary of the treasury would not be relinquished, and that they were of a nature to affect the chief magistrate materially, should his countenance not be withdrawn from that officer. It was equally apparent that the fervour of democracy, which was perpetually manifesting itself in the papers, in invectives against levees, against the trappings of royalty, and against the marks of peculiar respect[66] which were paid to the President, must soon include him more pointedly in its strictures.

These divisions, which are inherent in the nature of popular governments, by which the chief magistrate, however unexceptionable his conduct, and however exalted his character, must, sooner or later, be more or less affected, were beginning to be essentially influenced by the great events of Europe.

Progress of the French revolution and its effects on parties in the United States.

That revolution which has been the admiration, the wonder, and the terror of the civilized world, had, from its commencement, been viewed in America with the deepest interest. In its first stage, but one sentiment respecting it prevailed; and that was a belief, accompanied with an ardent wish, that it would improve the condition of France, extend the blessings of liberty, and promote the happiness of the human race. When the labours of the convention had terminated in a written constitution, this unanimity of opinion was in some degree impaired. By a few who had thought deeply on the science of government, and who, if not more intelligent, certainly judged more dispassionately than their fellow citizens, that instrument was believed to contain the principles of self destruction. It was feared that a system so ill balanced could not be permanent. A deep impression was made on the same persons by the influence of the galleries over the legislature, and of mobs over the executive; by the tumultuous assemblages of the people, and their licentious excesses during the short and sickly existence of the regal authority. These did not appear to be the symptoms of a healthy constitution, or of genuine freedom. Persuaded that the present state of things could not last, they doubted, and they feared for the future.

In total opposition to this sentiment was that of the public. There seems to be something infectious in the example of a powerful and enlightened nation verging towards democracy, which imposes on the human mind, and leads human reason in fetters. Novelties, introduced by such a nation, are stripped of the objections which had been preconceived against them; and long settled opinions yield to the overwhelming weight of such dazzling authority. It wears the semblance of being the sense of mankind, breaking loose from the shackles which had been imposed by artifice, and asserting the freedom, and the dignity, of his nature.

The constitution of France, therefore, was generally received with unqualified plaudits. The establishment of a legislature consisting of a single body, was defended not only as being adapted to the particular situation of that country, but as being right in itself. Certain anonymous writers, who supported the theory of a balanced government, were branded as the advocates of royalty, and of aristocracy. To question the duration of the present order of things was thought to evidence an attachment to unlimited monarchy, or a blind prejudice in favour of British institutions; and the partiality of America in favour of a senate was visibly declining.

In this stage of the revolution, however, the division of sentiment was not marked with sufficient distinctness, nor the passions of the people agitated with sufficient violence, for any powerful effect to be produced on the two parties in America. But when the monarchy was completely overthrown, and a republic decreed,[67]the people of the United States seemed electrified by the measure, and its influence was felt by the whole society. The war in which the several potentates of Europe were engaged against France, although in almost every instance declared by that power, was pronounced to be a war for the extirpation of human liberty, and for the banishment of free government from the face of the earth. The preservation of the constitution of the United States was supposed to depend on its issue; and the coalition against France was treated as a coalition against America also.

A cordial wish for the success of the French arms, or rather that the war might terminate without any diminution of French power, and in such a manner as to leave the people of that country free to choose their own form of government, was, perhaps, universal; but, respecting the probable issue of their internal conflicts, perfect unanimity of opinion did not prevail. By some few individuals, the practicability of governing by a system formed on the republican model, an immense, populous, and military nation, whose institutions, habits, and morals, were adapted to monarchy, and which was surrounded by armed neighbours, was deemed a problem which time alone could solve. The circumstances under which the abolition of royalty was declared, the massacres which preceded it, the scenes of turbulence and violence which were acted in every part of the nation, appeared to them, to present an awful and doubtful state of things, respecting which no certain calculations could be made; and the idea that a republic was to be introduced and supported by force, was, to them, a paradox in politics. Under the influence of these appearances, the apprehension was entertained that, if the ancient monarchy should not be restored, a military despotism would be established. By the many, these unpopular doubts were deemed unpardonable heresies; and the few to whom they were imputed, were pronounced hostile to liberty. A suspicion that the unsettled state of things in France had contributed to suspend the payment of the debt to that nation, had added to the asperity with which the resolutions on that subject were supported; and the French revolution will be found to have had great influence on the strength of parties, and on the subsequent political transactions of the United States.

<h2 style="text-align:center">NOTES.</h2>

NOTE—No. I. *See* <u>*Page 98*</u>.

THE following is an extract from the orders of the preceding day. "The Commander-in-chief orders the cessation of hostilities between the United States of America and the king of Great Britain to be publicly proclaimed to-morrow at twelve at the new building; and that the proclamation which will be communicated herewith, be read to-morrow evening at the head of every regiment, and corps of the army; after which the chaplains with the several brigades will render thanks to Almighty God for all his mercies, particularly for his overruling the wrath of man to his own glory, and causing the rage of war to cease among the nations.

"Although the proclamation before alluded to, extends only to the prohibition of hostilities and not to the annunciation of a general peace, yet it must afford the most rational and sincere satisfaction to every benevolent mind, as it puts a period to a long and doubtful contest, stops the effusion of human blood, opens the prospect to a more splendid scene, and like another morning star, promises the approach of a brighter day than hath hitherto illuminated the western hemisphere. On such a happy day, which is the harbinger of peace, a day which completes the eighth year of the war, it would be ingratitude not to rejoice; it would be insensibility not to participate in the general felicity.

"The Commander-in-chief, far from endeavouring to stifle the feelings of joy in his own bosom, offers his most cordial congratulations on the occasion to all the officers of every denomination, to all the troops of the United States in general, and in particular to those gallant and persevering men, who had resolved to defend the rights of their invaded country, so long as the war should continue. For these are the men who ought to be considered as the pride and boast of the American Army; and who, crowned with well-earned laurels, may soon withdraw from the field of glory, to the more tranquil walks of civil life.

"While the general recollects the almost infinite variety of scenes through which we have passed with a mixture of pleasure, astonishment and gratitude; while he contemplates the prospect before us with rapture, he can not help wishing that all the brave men (of whatever condition they may be,) who have shared in the toils and dangers of effecting this · glorious revolution, of rescuing millions from the hand of oppression, and of laying the

145

foundation of a great empire, might be impressed with a proper idea of the dignified part they have been called to act (under the smiles of Providence) on the stage of human affairs. For happy, thrice happy shall they be pronounced hereafter, who have contributed any thing; who have performed the meanest office in erecting this stupendous *fabric of freedom* and empire on the broad basis of independency; who have assisted in protecting the rights of human nature, and establishing an asylum for the poor and oppressed of all nations and religions. The glorious task for which we first flew to arms being thus accomplished, the liberties of our country being fully acknowledged and firmly secured by the smiles of heaven, on the purity of our cause, and on the honest exertions of a feeble people determined to be free, against a powerful nation disposed to oppress them, and the character of those who have persevered through every extremity of hardship, suffering, and danger, being immortalized by the illustrious appellation of the *patriot army*, nothing now remains but for the actors of this mighty scene to preserve a perfect unvarying consistency of character through the very last act; to close the drama with applause, and to retire from the military theatre with the same approbation of angels and men which has crowned all their former virtuous actions. For this purpose, no disorder or licentiousness must be tolerated: every considerate and well disposed soldier must remember, it will be absolutely necessary to wait with patience until peace shall be declared, or congress shall be enabled to take proper measures for the security of the public stores, &c. As soon as these arrangements shall be made, the general is confident there will be no delay in discharging with every mark of distinction and honour all the men enlisted for the war who will then have faithfully performed their engagements with the public. The general has already interested himself in their behalf, and he thinks he need not repeat the assurances of his disposition to be useful to them on the present and every other proper occasion. In the mean time, he is determined that no military neglects or excesses shall go unpunished while he retains the command of the army."

NOTE—No. II. *See Page 106*.

On his way, he stopped a few days at Philadelphia, for the purpose of settling his accounts with the comptroller. The following account of this part of his duty is extracted from Mr. Gordon; "while in the city he delivered in his accounts to the comptroller, down to December the 13th, all in his own hand writing, and every entry made in the most particular manner, stating the occasion of each charge, so as to give the least trouble in examining and comparing them with the vouchers with which they were attended.

"The heads as follows, copied from the folio manuscript paper book in the file of the treasury office, number 3700, being a black box of tin containing, under lock and key, both that and the vouchers."

Total of expenditures from 1775 to 1783, exclusive of provisions from commissaries and contractors, and of liquors, &c. from them and others,	3 ,387	4	
Secret intelligence and service,	1 ,982	0	
Spent in reconnoitring and travelling,	1 ,874		
Miscellaneous charges,	2 ,952	0	
Expended besides, dollars according to the scale of depreciation,	6 ,114	4	

	L	16,311	17	1

"Two hundred guineas advanced to General M'Dougal are not included in the *L* 1982 10 0 not being yet settled, but included in some of the other charges, and so reckoned in the general sum.

"Note; 104,364, of the dollars were received after March, 1780, and although credited at forty for one, many did not fetch at the rate of a hundred for one; while 27,775 of them are returned without deducting any thing from the above account (and, therefore, actually made a present of to the public)."

General Washington's account from June, 1778 to the end of June, 1783,		16,311	7	
Expenditure from July 1, 1783, to December 13,		1,717		
Added afterward from thence to December 28,		213		
Mrs. Washington's travelling expenses in coming to the general and returning,		1,064		
	L	19,306	11	9
Lawful money of Virginia, the same as Massachusetts, or sterling,	.	14,479	8	-4

The general entered in his book—"I find upon the final adjustment of these accounts, that I am a considerable loser, my disbursements falling a good deal short of my receipts, and the money I had upon hand of my own: for besides the sums I carried with me to Cambridge in 1775, I received monies afterwards on private account in 1777, and since, which (except small sums, that I had occasion now and then to apply to private uses) were all expended in the public service: through hurry, I suppose, and the perplexity of business, (for I know not how else to account for the deficiency) I have omitted to charge the same, whilst every debit against me is here credited."

July 1st, 1783.

NOTE—No. III. *See* *Page 179*.

The year 1784 had nearly passed away before the determination of the British cabinet not to evacuate the western posts was known to the government of the United States. In the spring of that year, General Knox, who commanded the troops still retained in the service of the United States, was directed to "open a correspondence with the Commander-in-chief of his Britannic majesty's forces in Canada, in order to ascertain the precise time when each of the posts within the territories of the United States then occupied by the British troops should be delivered up." The measures produced by this resolution exhibit a curious specimen of the political opinions on the subject of federal powers, which then prevailed in congress.

It being at that time believed that the British garrisons would certainly be withdrawn, it became necessary to provide for occupying the posts when surrendered, with troops belonging to the United States. A number deemed sufficient for the purpose not having been retained in service, a motion was made for raising seven hundred men, by requisitions on the states for that and other objects specified in the resolution. The power of congress to make these requisitions was seriously contested, and it was gravely urged that such a power, connected with the rights to borrow money, and to emit bills of credit, would be dangerous to liberty, and alarming to the states. The motion for raising this small number of regulars did not prevail; and an order was made that except twenty-five privates to guard the stores at fort Pitt, and fifty-five to guard those at West Point and other magazines, with a proportionable number of officers, no one to exceed the rank of captain, the troops already in service should be discharged, unless congress, before its recess, should dispose of them in some other manner. For the purpose of garrisoning the posts, seven hundred militia were required from Connecticut, New York, New Jersey and Pennsylvania, who should serve twelve months. While the discussions on this subject were pending, instructions from the legislature of New York to their delegates were laid before congress, requesting that body in terms of great strength, in pursuance of the confederation, to declare the number of troops of which the garrisons of those posts which were within the limits of that state should consist. The resolutions asserted a constitutional right to demand from congress a declaration upon this point, and avowed a determination to raise the troops should such declaration be withheld. After the determination of the British government not to surrender the posts was known, the militia ordered to be raised to garrison them, who were not in actual service, were discharged.

NOTE—No. IV. *See* *Page 370*.

In the formation of this treaty, a question came on to be considered and decided which involved a principle that on an after occasion, and in a different case, excited a ferment never to be forgotten by those who took an active part in the politics of the day.

The whole commerce of the Creek nation was in the hands of M'Gillivray, who received his supplies from a company of British merchants, free from duty, through the territories belonging to Spain. This circumstance constituted no inconsiderable impediment to the progress of the negotiation. M'Gillivray derived emoluments from the arrangement which he would not consent to relinquish; and was not without apprehensions, that Spain, disgusted by his new connexions with the United States, might throw embarrassments in the way of this profitable traffic. In addition to this consideration, it was, on the part of the United States, desirable to alter the channel through which the Indians should receive their supplies, and thereby to render them more dependent on the American government. But it would be necessary to exempt the goods designed for the Indian nation from the duties imposed by law on imported articles, and the propriety of such an exemption might well be questioned.

With that cautious circumspection which marked his political course, the president took this point into early consideration, and required the opinion of his constitutional advisers respecting it. The secretary of state was of opinion that the stipulation for importing his goods through the United States, duty free, might safely be made. "A treaty made by the president with the concurrence of two-thirds of the senate, was," he said, "a law of the land," and a law of superior order, because it not only repeals past laws, but can not itself be repealed by future ones. The treaty then will legally control the duty act, and the act for licensing traders in this particular instance. From this opinion there is no reason to suppose that any member of the cabinet dissented. A secret article providing for the case was submitted to the senate, and it has never been understood that in advising and consenting to it, that body was divided.

NOTE—No. V. *See* *Page 394*.

This question was investigated with great labour, and being one involving principles of the utmost importance to the United States, on which the parties were divided, the subject was presented in all the views of which it was susceptible. A perusal of the arguments used on the occasion would certainly afford much gratification to the curious, and their insertion at full length would perhaps be excused by those who recollect the interest which at the time was taken in the measure to which they related, and the use which was made of it by the opponents of the then administration; but the limits prescribed for this work will not permit the introduction of such voluminous papers. It may, however, be expected that the outline of that train of reasoning with which each opinion was supported, and on which the judgment of the president was most probably formed, should be briefly stated.

To prove that the measure was not sanctioned by the constitution, the general principle was asserted, that the foundation of that instrument was laid on this ground, "that all powers not delegated to the United States by the constitution, nor prohibited by it to the states, are reserved to the states or to the people." To take a single step beyond the boundaries thus specially drawn around the powers of congress, is to take possession of a boundless field of power, no longer susceptible of definition.

The power in question was said not to be among those which were specially enumerated, nor to be included within either of the general phrases which are to be found in the constitution.

The article which contains this enumeration was reviewed; each specified power was analyzed; and the creation of a corporate body was declared to be distinct from either of them.

The general phrases are,

1st. To lay taxes to provide for the general welfare of the United States. The power here conveyed, it was observed, was "to lay taxes," the purpose was "the general welfare." Congress could not lay taxes *ad libitum*, but could only lay them for the general welfare; nor did this clause authorize that body to provide for the general welfare otherwise than by laying taxes for that purpose.

2dly. To make all laws which shall be necessary and proper for carrying into execution the enumerated powers.

But they can all be carried into execution without a bank. A bank, therefore, is not necessary, and consequently not authorized by this phrase.

It had been much urged that a bank would give great facility or convenience in the collection of taxes. Suppose this were true; yet the constitution allows only the means which are necessary, not those which are convenient. If such a latitude of construction be allowed this phrase, as to give any non-enumerated power, it will go to every one; for there is no one which ingenuity may not torture into a *convenience, in some way or other, to some one* of so long a list of enumerated powers. It would swallow up all the list of enumerated powers, and reduce the whole to one phrase. Therefore it was that the constitution restrained them to *necessary* means, that is to say, to those means without which the grant of the power must be nugatory.

The convenience was then examined. This had been stated in the report of the secretary of the treasury to congress, to consist in the augmentation of the circulation medium, and in preventing the transportation and retransportation of money between the states and the treasury.

The first was considered as a demerit. The second, it was said, might be effected by other means. Bills of exchange and treasury drafts would supply the place of bank notes. Perhaps indeed bank bills would be a more convenient vehicle than treasury orders; but a little difference in the degree of convenience can not constitute the*necessity* which the constitution makes the ground for assuming any non-enumerated power.

Besides, the existing state banks would, without doubt, enter into arrangements for lending their agency. This expedient alone suffices to prevent the existence of that *necessity* which may justify the assumption of a non-enumerated power as a means for carrying into effect an enumerated one.

It may be said that a bank whose bills would have a currency all over the states, would be more convenient than one whose currency is limited to a single state. So it would be still more convenient that there should be a bank whose bills should have a currency all over the world; but it does not follow from this superior conveniency, that there exists any where a power to establish such a bank, or that the world may not go on very well without it.

For a shade or two of convenience, more or less, it can not be imagined that the constitution intended to invest congress with a power so important as that of erecting a corporation.

In supporting the constitutionality of the act, it was laid down as a general proposition, "that every power vested in a government is in its nature *sovereign*," and includes by *force* of the *term*, a right to employ all the *means* requisite and *fairly applicable to* the attainment of the *ends* of such power; and which are not precluded by restrictions and exceptions specified in the constitution, are not immoral, are not contrary to the essential ends of political society.

This principle, in its application to government in general, would be admitted as an axiom; and it would be incumbent on those who might refuse to acknowledge its influence in American affairs to *prove* a distinction; and to show that a rule which, in the general system of things, is essential to the preservation of the social order, is inapplicable to the United States.

The circumstance that the powers of sovereignty are divided between the national and state governments, does not afford the distinction required. It does not follow from this, that each of the portions of power delegated to the one or to the other, is not sovereign with regard to its *proper objects*. It will only follow from it, that each has sovereign power as to certain things, and not as to other things. If the government of the United States does not possess sovereign power as to its declared purposes and trusts, because its power does not extend to all cases, neither would the several states possess sovereign power in any case; for their powers do not extend to every case. According to the opinion intended to be combated, the United States would furnish the singular spectacle of *a political society* without *sovereignty*, or a people *governed* without a *government*.

If it could be necessary to bring proof of a proposition so clear as that which affirms that the powers of the federal government, *as to its objects*, were sovereign, there is a clause in the constitution which is decisive. It is that which declares the constitution of the United States, the laws made in pursuance of it, and the treaties made under its authority to be the supreme law of the land. The power which can create the supreme law in any case, is doubtless sovereign as to such case.

This general and indisputable principle puts an end to the abstract question, whether the United States have power to erect a corporation: for it is unquestionably incident to sovereign power to erect corporations, and consequently to that of the United States, in relation to the objects intrusted to the management of the government. The difference is this: where the authority of the government is general, it can create corporations *in all cases;* where it is confined to certain branches of legislation, it can create corporations only *in those cases.*

That the government of the United States can exercise only those powers which are delegated by the constitution, is a proposition not to be controverted; neither is it to be denied on the other hand, that there are implied as well as express powers, and that the former are as effectually delegated as the latter. For the sake of accuracy it may be observed, that there are also *resulting* powers. It will not be doubted that if the United States should make a conquest of any of the territories of its neighbours, they would possess sovereign jurisdiction over the conquered territory. This would rather be a result of the whole mass of the powers of the government, and from the nature of political society, than a consequence of either of the powers specially enumerated. This is an extensive case in which the power of erecting corporations is either implied in, or would result from some or all of the powers vested in the national government.

Since it must be conceded that implied powers are as completely delegated as those which are expressed, it follows that, as a power of erecting a corporation may as well be implied as any other thing, it may as well be employed as an *instrument* or *mean* of carrying into execution any of the specified powers as any other *instrument* or *mean* whatever. The question in this as in every other case must be, whether the mean to be employed has a natural relation to any of the acknowledged objects or lawful ends of the government. Thus a corporation may not be created by congress for superintending the police of the city of Philadelphia, because they are not authorized to regulate the police of that city; but one may be created in relation to the collection of the taxes, or to the trade with foreign countries, or between the states, or with the Indian tribes, because it is in the province of the federal government to regulate those objects; and because it is incident to a general sovereign or legislative power to regulate a thing, to employ all the means which relate to its regulation, to the best and greatest advantage.

A strange fallacy seems to have crept into the manner of thinking and reasoning upon this subject. The imagination has presented an incorporation as some great, *independent, substantive* thing—as a political end of peculiar magnitude and moment; whereas it is truly to be considered as a quality, capacity, or mean to an end. Thus a mercantile company is formed with a certain capital for the purpose of carrying on a particular branch of business. The business to be prosecuted is the *end*. The association in order to form the requisite capital is the primary *mean*. Let an incorporation be added, and you only add a new quality to that association which enables it to prosecute the business with more safety and convenience. The association when incorporated still remains the *mean*, and can not become the *end*.

To this reasoning respecting the inherent right of government to employ all the means requisite to the execution of its specified powers, it is objected, that none but *necessary* and *proper* means can be employed; and none can be *necessary*, but those without which the grant of the power would be nugatory. So far has this restrictive interpretation been pressed as to make the case of *necessity* which shall warrant the constitutional exercise of a power, to depend on casual and temporary circumstances; an idea, which alone confutes the construction. The expedience of exercising a particular power, at a particular time, must indeed depend on circumstances, but the constitutional right of exercising it must be uniform and invariable. All the arguments, therefore, drawn from the accidental existence of certain state banks which happen to exist to-day, and for aught that concerns the government of the United States may disappear to-morrow, must not only be rejected as fallacious, but must be viewed as demonstrative that there is a radical source of error in the reasoning.

But it is essential to the being of the government that so erroneous a conception of the meaning of the word *necessary* should be exploded.

It is certain that neither the grammatical nor popular sense of the term requires that construction. According to both, *necessary* often means no more than *needful, requisite, incidental, useful,* or *conducive to.* It is a common mode of expression to say that it is necessary for a government or a person to do this or that thing, where nothing more is intended or understood than that the interests of the government or person require, or will be promoted by doing this or that thing.

This is the true sense in which the word is used in the constitution. The whole turn of the clause containing it indicates an intent to give by it a liberal latitude to the exercise of the specified powers. The expressions have peculiar comprehensiveness. They are "to make *all laws* necessary and proper for carrying into execution the foregoing powers, and *all other* powers vested by the constitution in the government of the United States, or in any *department* or *office* thereof." To give the word "necessary" the restrictive operation contended for, would not only depart from its obvious and popular sense, but would give it the same force as if the word *absolutely* or *indispensably* had been prefixed to it.

Such a construction would beget endless uncertainty and embarrassment. The cases must be palpable and extreme in which it could be pronounced with certainty that a measure was absolutely necessary, or one without which a given power would be nugatory. There are few measures of any government which would stand so severe a test. To insist upon it would be to make the criterion of the exercise of an implied power *a case of extreme necessity*; which is rather a rule to justify the overleaping the bounds of constitutional authority than to govern the ordinary exercise of it.

The degree in which a measure is necessary can never be a test of the legal right to adopt it. The relation between the *measure* and the *end*; between the nature of the *mean* employed towards the execution of a power, and the object of that power must be the criterion of constitutionality, not the more or less *necessity* or *utility*.

The means by which national exigencies are to be provided for, national inconveniences obviated, and national prosperity promoted, are of such infinite variety, extent, and complexity, that here must of necessity be great latitude of discretion in the selection and application of those means. Hence the necessity and propriety of exercising the authority intrusted to a government on principles of liberal construction.

While on the one hand, the restrictive interpretation of the word *necessary* is deemed inadmissible, it will not be contended on the other, that the clause in question gives any new and independent power. But it gives an explicit sanction to the doctrine of implied powers, and is equivalent to an admission of the proposition that the government, *as to its specified powers and objects*, has plenary and sovereign authority.

It is true that the power to create corporations is not granted in terms. Neither is the power to pass any particular law, nor to employ any of the means by which the ends of the government are to be attained. It is not expressly given in cases in which its existence is not controverted. For by the grant of a power to exercise exclusive legislation in the territory which may be ceded by the states to the United States, it is admitted to pass; and in the power "to make all needful rules and regulations respecting the territory or other property of the United States," it is acknowledged to be implied. In virtue of this clause, has been implied the right to create a government; that is, to create a body politic or corporation of the highest nature; one that, in its maturity, will be able itself to create other corporations. Thus has the constitution itself refuted the argument which contends that, had it been designed to grant so important a power as that of erecting corporations, it would have been mentioned. But this argument is founded on an exaggerated and erroneous conception of the nature of the power. It is not of so transcendent a kind as the reasoning supposes. Viewed in a just light, it is a *mean* which ought to have been left to implication, rather than an *end* which ought to have been expressly granted.

The power of the government then to create corporations in certain cases being shown, it remained to inquire into the right to incorporate a banking company, in order to enable it the more effectually to accomplish *ends* which were in themselves lawful.

To establish such a right it would be necessary to show the relation of such an institution to one or more of the specified powers of government.

It was then affirmed to have a relation more or less direct to the power of collecting taxes, to that of borrowing money, to that of regulating trade between the states, to those of raising, supporting, and maintaining fleets and armies; and in the last place to that which authorizes the making of all needful rules and regulations concerning the property of the United States, as the same had been practised upon by the government.

The secretary of the treasury next proceeded, by a great variety of arguments and illustrations, to prove the position that the measure in question was a proper mean for the execution of the several powers which were enumerated, and also contended that the right to employ it resulted from the whole of them taken together. To detail those arguments would occupy too much space, and is the less necessary, because their correctness obviously depends on the correctness of the principles which have been already stated.

NOTE—No. VI. *See Page 434.*

The officer to whom the management of the finances was confided was so repeatedly charged with a desire to increase the public debt and to render it perpetual, and this charge had such important influence in the formation of parties, that an extract from this report can not be improperly introduced.

After stating the sum to be raised, the secretary says, "three expedients occur to the option of the government for providing this:

"One, to dispose of the interest to which the United States are entitled in the bank of the United States. This at the present market price of bank stock would yield a clear gain to the government much more than adequate to the sum required.

"Another, to borrow the money upon an establishment of funds either merely commensurate with the interest to be paid, or affording a surplus which will discharge the principal by instalments within a short term.

"The third is to raise the amount by taxes."

After stating his objections to the first and second expedients, the report proceeds thus, "but the result of mature reflection is, in the mind of the secretary, a strong conviction that the last of the three expedients which have been mentioned, is to be preferred to either of the other two.

"Nothing can more interest the national credit and prosperity than a constant and systematic attention to husband all the means previously possessed for extinguishing the present debt, and to avoid, as much as possible, the incurring of any new debt.

"Necessity alone, therefore, can justify the application of any of the public property, other than the annual revenues, to the current service, or the temporary and casual exigencies; or the contracting of an additional debt by loans, to provide for those exigencies.

"Great emergencies indeed might exist, in which loans would be indispensable. But the occasions which will justify them must be truly of that description.

"The present is not of such a nature. The sum to be provided is not of magnitude enough to furnish the plea of necessity.

"Taxes are never welcome to a community. They seldom fail to excite uneasy sensations more or less extensive. Hence a too strong propensity in the governments of nations, to anticipate and mortgage the resources of posterity, rather than to encounter the inconveniencies of a present increase of taxes.

"But this policy, when not dictated by very peculiar circumstances, is of the worst kind. Its obvious tendency is, by enhancing the permanent burdens of the people, to produce lasting distress, and its natural issue is in national bankruptcy."

It will be happy if the councils of this country, sanctioned by the voice of an enlightened community, shall be able to pursue a different course.

NOTE—No. VII. *See <u>Page 450</u>.*

About the same time a letter was addressed to the attorney general on the same subject. The following extract is taken from one of the twenty-sixth of August to the secretary of the treasury.

"Differences in political opinions are as unavoidable as, to a certain point, they may be necessary; but it is exceedingly to be regretted that subjects can not be discussed with temper, on the one hand, or decisions submitted to on the other, without improperly implicating the motives which led to them; and this regret borders on chagrin when we find that men of abilities, zealous patriots, having the same *general* objects in view, and the same upright intentions to prosecute them, will not exercise more charity in deciding on the opinions and actions of each other. When matters get to such lengths, the natural inference is that both sides have strained the cords beyond their bearing, that a middle course would be found the best until experience shall have decided on the right way; or, which is not to be expected, because it is denied to mortals, until there shall be some infallible rule by which to forejudge events.

"Having premised these things, I would fain hope that liberal allowances will be made for the political opinions of each other; and instead of those wounding suspicions, and irritating charges with which some of our gazettes are so strongly impregnated, and which can not fail, if persevered in, of pushing matters to extremity, and thereby tearing the machine asunder, that there might be mutual forbearance and temporising yieldings on *all sides*. Without these, I do not see how the reins of government are to be managed, or how the union of the states can be much longer preserved.

"How unfortunate would it be if a fabric so goodly, erected under so many providential circumstances, after acquiring in its first stages, so much respectability, should, from diversity of sentiment, or internal obstructions to some of the acts of government (for I can not prevail on myself to believe that these measures are as yet the acts of a determined party) be brought to the verge of dissolution. Melancholy thought! But while it shows the consequences of diversified opinions, where pushed with too much tenacity, it exhibits evidence also of the necessity of accommodation, and of the propriety of adopting such healing measures as may restore harmony to the discordant members of the union, and the governing powers of it.

"I do not mean to apply this advice to any measures which are passed, or to any particular character. I have given it, in the same *general* terms, to other officers of the government. My earnest wish is that balm may be poured into *all* the wounds which have been given, to prevent them from gangrening, and to avoid those fatal consequences which the community may sustain if it is withheld. The friends of the union must wish this: those who are not, but who wish to see it rended, will be disappointed; and all things I hope will go well."

<h2 style="text-align:center">NOTE—No. VIII. See Page 479.</h2>

The gazettes of the day contain ample proofs on this subject. All the bitterness of party spirit had poured itself out in the most severe invectives against the heads of the state and treasury departments.

The secretary of the treasury was represented as the advocate of "aristocracy, monarchy, hereditary succession, a titled order of nobility, and all the other mock pageantry of kingly government." He was arraigned at the bar of the public for holding principles unfavourable to the sovereignty of the people, and with inculcating doctrines insinuating their inability to rule themselves. The theory of the British monarchy was said to have furnished his model for a perfect constitution; and all his systems of finance, which were represented as servile imitations of those previously adopted by England, were held up to public execration as being intended to promote the favourite project of assimilating the government of the United States to that of Great Britain. With this view, he had entailed upon the nation a heavy debt, and perpetual taxes; had created an artificial monied interest which had corrupted, and would continue to corrupt the legislature; and was endeavouring to prostrate the local authorities as a necessary step towards erecting that great consolidated monarchy which he contemplated.

To support some of these charges, sentences and parts of sentences were selected from his reports, which expressed the valuable purposes to which a funded debt might be applied, and were alleged to affirm, as an abstract principle, "that a public debt was a public blessing." He was, it was added, the inveterate enemy of Mr. Jefferson, because, in the republican principles of that gentleman, he perceived an invincible obstacle to his views.

If the counter charges exhibited against the secretary of state were less capable of alarming the fears of the public for liberty, and of directing the resentments of the people against that officer as the enemy of their rights, they were not less calculated to irritate his personal friends, and to wound his own feelings.

The adversaries of this gentleman said, that he had been originally hostile to the constitution of the United States, and adverse to its adoption; and "that his avowed opinions tended to national disunion, national insignificance, public disorder, and discredit." Under the garb of democratic simplicity, and modest retiring philosophy, he covered an inordinate ambition which grasped unceasingly at power, and sought to gratify itself, by professions of excessive attachment to liberty, and by traducing and lessening in the public esteem, every man in whom he could discern a rival. To this aspiring temper they ascribed, not only "those pestilent whispers which, clandestinely circulating through the country, had, as far as was practicable, contaminated some of its fairest and worthiest characters," but also certain publications affecting the reputation of prominent individuals whom he might consider as competitors with himself for the highest office in the state. A letter written by Mr. Jefferson to a printer, transmitting for publication the first part of "the rights of man," which letter was prefixed to the American edition of that pamphlet, contained allusions to certain "political heresies" of the day, which were understood to imply a serious censure on the opinions of the vice president: and the great object of the national gazette, a paper known to be edited by a clerk in the department of state, was "to calumniate and blacken public characters, and, particularly, to destroy the public confidence in the secretary of the treasury, who was to be hunted down for the unpardonable sin of having been the steady and invariable friend of broad principles of national government." It was also said that his connexions with this paper, and the patronage he afforded it, authorized the opinion that it might fairly be considered "the mirror of his views," and thence was adduced an accusation not less serious in its nature than that which has been already stated.

The national gazette was replete with continual and malignant strictures on the leading measures of the administration, especially those which were connected with the finances. "If Mr. Jefferson's opposition to these measures had ceased when they had received the sanction of law, nothing more could have been said than that he had transgressed the rules of official decorum in entering the lists with the head of another department, and had been culpable in pursuing a line of conduct which was calculated to sow the seeds of discord in the executive branch of the government in the infancy of its existence. But when his opposition extended beyond that point, when it was apparent that he wished to *render odious*, and of course to *subvert* (for in a popular government these are convertible terms) all those deliberate and solemn acts of the legislature which had become the pillars of the public credit, his conduct deserved to be regarded with a still severer eye." It was also said to be peculiarly unfit for a person remaining at the head of one of the great executive departments, openly to employ all his influence in exciting the public rage against the laws and the legislature of the union, and in giving circulation to calumnies against his colleagues in office, from the contamination of which the chief magistrate himself could not hope entirely to escape.

END OF VOLUME IV.

FOOTNOTES

[1]Higher up, this river is called the Catawba.

[2]This account of the battle of Hobkirk's Hill varies in several particulars from that contained in the first edition. In making the alteration the author has followed the letter of General Davie, published in Mr. Johnson's biography of General Greene. General Davie was known to the author to be a gentleman in whose representations great confidence is to be placed on every account, and his situation in the army enabled him to obtain the best information.

[3]There is some variance between this statement and that which has been made by Mr. Ramsay and Mr. Gordon, although their estimates are supposed to have been formed on the same document—the field return made by the adjutant general of the southern army, dated the 26th of April. This return contains a column of the present fit for duty, and also exhibits the killed, wounded, and missing, but contains no column of total numbers. Mr. Ramsay and Mr. Gordon are supposed to have taken the column of present fit for duty as exhibiting the strength of the army on the day of the battle; but as this return was made the day after the action, the author has supposed that the killed, wounded, and missing, must be added to the numbers fit for duty on the day of the return, to give the actual strength of the army at the time of the engagement.

[4]Mr. Johnson states that Captain M'Cauley, of South Carolina, had joined Armstrong and Carrington. Some of the troopers were killed on the bridge.

[5]The execution of Colonel Hayne has been generally ascribed to Lord Rawdon, and that gallant nobleman has been censured throughout America for an act which has been universally execrated. A letter addressed by him to the late General Lee, on receiving the memoirs of the southern war, written by that gentleman, which has been published in the "View of the Campaign of 1781, in the Carolinas, by H. Lee," gives the British view of that transaction, and exonerates Lord Rawdon from all blame. Lieutenant Colonel Balfour commanded, and Lord Rawdon sought to save Colonel Hayne.

[6]The British accounts acknowledge only two hundred and fifty-seven missing; but General Greene, in his letter of the ninth of September, says, that including seventy wounded who were left at Eutaw, he made five hundred prisoners.

[7]During this campaign a very effective expedition against the Cherokees was conducted by General Pickens. When the struggle for South Carolina recommenced, those savages were stimulated to renew their incursions into the settlements of the whites. At the head of about four hundred mounted militia, Pickens penetrated into their country, burned thirteen of their villages, killed upwards of forty Indians, and took a number of prisoners, without the loss of a single man. On this occasion a new and formidable mode of attack was introduced. The militia horse rushed upon the Indians, and charged them sword in hand. Terrified at the rapidity of the pursuit, the Cherokees humbly sued for peace, which was granted on terms calculated to restrain depredations in future.

[8]In the judicious orders given to Wayne, Greene endeavoured to impress on that officer the importance of a course of conduct, always observed by himself, which might tend to conciliate parties. "Try," says he, "by every means in your power, to soften the malignity and dreadful resentments subsisting between the Whig and Tory; and put a stop as much as possible to that cruel custom of putting men to death after they surrender themselves prisoners. The practice of plundering you will endeavour to check as much as possible; and point out to the militia the ruinous consequences of the policy. Let your discipline be as regular and as rigid as the nature and constitution of your troops will admit."—2 *Johnson*, 277.

[9]The distresses of the southern army were such that, if plainly described, truth would wear the appearance of fiction. They were almost naked and barefooted, frequently without food, and always without pay. That he might relieve them when in the last extremity, without diminishing the exertions of their general to derive support from other sources, by creating an opinion that supplies could be drawn from him, Mr. Morris, as was stated by himself in conversation with the author, employed an agent to attend the southern army as a volunteer, whose powers were unknown to General Greene. This agent was instructed to watch its situation; and, whenever it appeared impossible for the general to extricate himself from his embarrassments, to furnish him, on his pledging the public faith for repayment, with a draught on the financier for such a sum as would relieve the urgency of the moment. Thus was Greene occasionally rescued from impending ruin by aids which appeared providential, and for which he could not account.

[10]Secret Journals of Congress, vol. 2, pp. 305, 399, 400, 452.

[11]Secret Journals of Congress, v. 2, pp. 412, 418, 454.

[12]Secret Journals of Congress, v. 3, p. 249.

[13]In addition to the public documents and accounts, the author received a statement of this action in a letter from his friend Captain Parker.

[14]By a resolution of the preceding year, the inquiry into his conduct had been dispensed with, and he had been restored to his command in the army.

[15]See note, No. I. at the end of the volume.

[16]Gordon.

[17]See note, No. II. at the end of the volume.

[18]General Mifflin.

[19]"Resolved that the statue be of bronze: the general to be represented in a Roman dress, holding a truncheon in his right hand, and his head encircled with a laurel wreath. The statue to be supported by a marble pedestal on which are to be represented, in basso relievo, the following principal events of the war, in which General Washington commanded in person: the evacuation of Boston:—the capture of the Hessians at Trenton:—the battle of Princeton:—the action of Monmouth:—and the surrender of York.—On the upper part of the front of the pedestal to be engraved as follows: the United States in congress assembled, ordered this statue to be erected in the year of our Lord 1783, in honour of George Washington, the illustrious Commander-in-chief of the armies of the United States of America, during the war which vindicated and secured their liberty, sovereignty and independence."

[20]This resolution has been carried into execution. The statue it ordained now stands in the capitol of Virginia, in a spacious area in the centre of the building. A bust of the Marquis de Lafayette, which was also directed by the legislature, is placed in a niche of the wall in the same part of the building.

[21]About one hundred and fifty miles.

[22]Mr. Jefferson.

[23]General Gates was associated with him in the mission.

[24]It is in these words; "whereas it is the desire of the representatives of this commonwealth to embrace every suitable occasion of testifying their sense of the unexampled merits of George Washington, esquire, towards his country, and it is their wish in particular that those great works for its improvement, which both as springing from the liberty which he has been so instrumental in establishing, and as encouraged by his patronage, will be durable monuments of his glory, may be made monuments also of the

gratitude of his country. Be it enacted, &c." This bill is understood to have been drawn by Mr. Madison.

[25]Mr. Madison.

[26]Mr. Fitzsimmons, and Mr. Rutledge.

[27]On a subsequent occasion, an attempt was made to obtain a resolution of congress, recommending as an additional amendment to the eighth article of the confederation, that the taxes for the use of the continent should be laid and levied separate from any other tax, and should be paid directly into the national treasury; and that the collectors respectively should be liable to an execution to be issued by the treasurer, or his deputy, under the direction of congress, for any arrears of taxes by him to be collected, which should not be paid into the treasury in conformity with the requisitions of congress.

Such was the prevalence of state policy, even in the government of the union, or such the conviction of the inutility of recommending such an amendment, that a vote of congress could not be obtained for asking this salutary regulation as a security for the revenue only for eight years.

[28]See note, No. III. at the end of the volume.

[29]The facts relative to this negotiation were stated in the correspondence of General Washington. The statement is supported by the Secret Journals of Congress, vol. 4, p. 329, and those which follow.

[30]Edmund Randolph, James Madison, Walter Jones, St. George Tucker, and Meriwether Smith.

[31]Mr. Jay.

[32]New York, New Jersey, Pennsylvania, Delaware, Maryland, and Virginia.

[33]Mr. Madison.

[34]Mr. Randolph.

[35]General Knox.

[36]This sentiment was far from being avowed by any correspondent of General Washington, but is stated in the private letters to him, to have been taken up by some.

[37]In a subsequent part of the same letter, this gentleman draws the outlines of a constitution such as he would wish. It is essentially the same with that which was recommended by the convention.

[38]This valuable officer died in Georgia in the year 1786.

[39]Colonel Hamilton, Mr. Madison, and Mr. Jay.

[40]North Carolina and Rhode Island did not at first accept the constitution, and New York was apparently dragged into it by a repugnance to being excluded from the confederacy. By the convention of that state a circular letter was addressed to the several states in the union inviting them to unite in calling a general convention to revise the constitution. Its friends seem to have been persuaded that this measure, if successful, would effectually destroy the edifice they had erected with so much labour, before an experience of its advantages could dissipate the prejudices which had been excited against it. "You will have seen," said one of its most effective advocates, "the circular letter from the convention of this state. It has a most pernicious tendency. If an early general convention can not be parried, it is seriously to be feared that the system which has resisted so many direct attacks, may be at length successfully undermined by its enemies. It is now perhaps to be wished that Rhode Island may not accede until this new crisis of danger be over; some think it would be better if even New York had held out until the operation of the government could have dissipated the fears which artifice had created, and the attempts resulting from those fears and artifices."

[41]The reluctance with which General Washington assumed his new dignity, and that genuine modesty which was a distinguished feature of his character, are further illustrated by the following extract from a letter to General Knox. "I feel for those members of the new congress, who, hitherto, have given an unavailing attendance at the theatre of action. For myself, the delay may be compared to a reprieve; for in confidence, I tell *you* (with the *world* it would obtain *little credit*,) that my movements to the chair of government will be accompanied by feelings not unlike those of a culprit who is going to the place of his execution; so unwilling am I in the evening of life, nearly consumed in public cares, to quit a

peaceful abode for an ocean of difficulties, without that competency of political skill, abilities, and inclination, which are necessary to manage the helm. I am sensible that I am embarking the voice of the people, and a good name of my own on this voyage; but what returns will be made for them heaven alone can foretell.—Integrity and firmness are all I can promise; these, be the voyage long or short, shall never forsake me, although I may be deserted by all men; for of the consolations which are to be derived from these, under any circumstances, the world can not deprive me."

[42]This has since been denominated the department of state.

[43]The following extract from a letter written July 1789, to Doctor Stuart, who had communicated to him this among other private insinuations, shows the ideas entertained by the President on this subject. "It is to be lamented that a question has been stirred which has given rise to so much animadversion, and which I confess has given me much uneasiness, lest it should be supposed by some unacquainted with facts that the object in view was not displeasing to me. The truth is, the question was moved before I arrived, without any privity or knowledge of it on my part, and urged after I was apprised of it contrary to my opinion;—for I foresaw and predicted the reception it has met with, and the use that would be made of it by the enemies of the government. Happily the matter is now done with, I hope never to be revived."

[44]Just before his departure from New York the President received from the Count de Moustiers, the minister of France, official notice that he was permitted by his court to return to Europe. By the orders of his sovereign he added, "that His Majesty was pleased at the alteration which had taken place in the government, and congratulated America on the choice they had made of a President." As from himself, he observed that the government of this country had been hitherto of so fluctuating a nature, that no dependence could be placed on its proceedings; in consequence of which foreign nations had been cautious of entering into treaties, or engagements of any kind with the United States: but that in the present government there was a head to look up to, and power being placed in the hands of its officers, stability in its measures might be expected. The disposition of his Christian Majesty to cultivate the good will of the new government was also manifested by his conduct in the choice of a minister to replace the Count de Moustiers. Colonel Ternan was named as a person who would be particularly acceptable to America, and his appointment was preceded by the compliment of ascertaining the sense of the President respecting him.

[45]It has ever been understood that these members were, on principle, in favour of the assumption as modified in the amendment made by the senate; but they withheld their assent from it when originally proposed in the house of representatives, in the opinion that the increase of the national debt, added to the necessity of giving to the departments of the national government a more central residence. It is understood that a greater number would have changed had it been necessary.

[46]On the first information at St. Augustine that M'Gillivray was about to repair to New York, the intelligence was communicated to the governor at the Havanna, and the secretary of East Florida came to New York, with a large sum of money to purchase flour, as it was said; but to embarrass the negotiations with the Creeks was believed to be his real design. He was closely watched, and measures were taken to render any attempts he might make abortive.

[47]See note, No. IV. at the end of the volume.

[48]On giving his assent to the bill "regulating the military establishment of the United States," the President subjoined to the entry in his diary the remark, that although he gave it his sanction, "he did not conceive that the military establishment was adequate to the exigencies of the government, and to the protection it was intended to afford." It consisted of one regiment of infantry, and one battalion of artillery, amounting in the total, exclusive of commissioned officers, to twelve hundred and sixteen men.

[49]Rhode Island had adopted the constitution in the preceding May, and had thus completed the union.

[50]In a more confidential message to the senate, all the objects of the negotiation in which Mr. Morris had been employed were detailed, and the letters of that gentleman, with the full opinion of the President were communicated.

[51]The interest on the assumed debt was to commence with the year 1792.

[52]See note, No. V. at the end of the volume.

[53]He stopped several days on the Potomac, where he executed finally the powers vested in him by the legislature for fixing on a place which should become the residence of congress, and the metropolis of the United States.

[54]The following is the message which he delivered on this occasion.

Gentlemen of the house of representatives—

I have maturely considered the act passed by the two houses, entitled "an act for the apportionment of representatives among the several states according to the first enumeration," and I return it to your house, wherein it originated, with the following objections.

First. The constitution has prescribed that representatives shall be apportioned among the several states according to their respective numbers, and there is no proportion or divisor which, applied to the respective numbers of the states, will yield the number and allotment of representatives proposed by the bill.

Secondly. The constitution has also provided, that the number of representatives shall not exceed one for thirty thousand, which restriction is by the context, and by fair and obvious construction, to be applied to the separate and respective numbers of the states, and the bill has allotted to eight of the states more than one for thirty thousand.

[55]Forts Hamilton and Jefferson.

[56]In his official letter, General St. Clair says that the ground would not admit a larger interval.

[57]The following extract from the official letter of the Commander-in-chief is inserted, as showing both his own situation and his opinion of the behaviour of his troops. "I have nothing, sir, to lay to the charge of the troops but their want of discipline, which, from the short time they had been in service, it was impossible they should have acquired; and which rendered it very difficult when they were thrown into confusion, to reduce them again to order; and is one reason why the loss has fallen so heavily upon the officers who did every thing in their power to effect it. Neither were my own exertions wanting; but worn down with illness, and suffering under a painful disease, unable either to mount, or dismount a horse without assistance, they were not so great as they otherwise would, or perhaps ought to have been."

[58]Although his leg had been broken by a ball, Major Butler, mounted on horseback, led his battalion to the charge.

[59]See note, No. VI. at the end of the volume.

[60]The salary of the secretary of state, which was the highest, was three thousand five hundred dollars.

[61]See Mr. Jefferson's correspondence.

[62]See note, No. VII. at the end of the volume.

[63]In his letter enclosing the proclamation to the secretary of the treasury, the President observed, "I have no doubt but that the proclamation will undergo many strictures; and, as the effect proposed may not be answered by it, it will be necessary to look forward in time to ulterior arrangements. And here, not only the constitution and laws must strictly govern, but the employment of the regular troops avoided, if it be possible to effect order without their aid; yet if no other means will effectually answer, and the constitution and laws will authorize these, they must be used as the dernier ressort."

[64]In consequence of these nominations of foreign ministers, a motion was made in the senate on a point which is of some importance in settling the principles of the American government. It was contended that the power of that body over the appointment of a foreign minister gave the right to inquire into the policy of making any appointment whatever; and that in exercising this power, they were not to confine themselves to a consideration of the fitness of the person nominated, but were to judge of the propriety of the mission; and were consequently to be informed of the motives which had decided the President to adopt the measure. This opinion was overruled by a small majority.

[65]See note, No. VIII. at the end of the volume.

[66]On the 22d of February, the birthday of the President, a motion was made to adjourn for half an hour. It was perfectly understood that this motion was made to give the members an opportunity of waiting on the chief magistrate to make the compliments adapted to the occasion.

This was seriously opposed, and the ayes and noes called upon the question. The adjournment was carried by forty-one to eighteen. The day was celebrated by several companies, and some toasts were published manifesting the deep sense which was entertained of the exalted services of this illustrious citizen. These circumstances gave great umbrage to some of those who could perceive monarchical tendencies in every act of respect, and the offenders were rebuked in the National Gazette for setting up an idol who might become dangerous to liberty, and for the injustice of neglecting all his compatriots of the revolution, and ascribing to him the praise which was due to others.

[67]This event was announced to the President by the minister plenipotentiary of France at Philadelphia, in February, 1793. Through the secretary of state, an answer was returned, of which the following is an extract, "the President receives with great satisfaction this attention of the executive council, and the desire they have manifested of making known to us the resolution entered into by the national convention even before a definitive regulation of their new establishment could take place. Be assured, sir, that the government and the citizens of the United States, view with the most sincere pleasure, every advance of your nation towards its happiness, an object essentially connected with its liberty, and they consider the union of principles and pursuits between our two countries as a link which binds still closer their interests and affections.

"We earnestly wish, on our part, that these our mutual dispositions may be improved to mutual good, by establishing our commercial intercourse on principles as friendly to natural right and freedom as are those of our governments."

Made in the USA
Monee, IL
07 December 2023

48496096R00095